DATA
MANAGEMENT

DATA
MANAGEMENT

in

A Guide for Social Scientists

MARTIN ELFF

Los Angeles | London | New Delhi
Singapore | Washington DC | Melbourne

Los Angeles | London | New Delhi
Singapore | Washington DC | Melbourne

SAGE Publications Ltd
1 Oliver's Yard
55 City Road
London EC1Y 1SP

SAGE Publications Inc.
2455 Teller Road
Thousand Oaks, California 91320

SAGE Publications India Pvt Ltd
B 1/I 1 Mohan Cooperative Industrial Area
Mathura Road
New Delhi 110 044

SAGE Publications Asia-Pacific Pte Ltd
3 Church Street
#10-04 Samsung Hub
Singapore 049483

Editor: Natalie Aguilera
Production editor: Ian Antcliff
Copyeditor: QuADS Prepress Pvt Ltd
Proofreader: Neville Hankins
Marketing manager: George Kimble
Cover design: Lisa Harper-Wells
Typeset by: C&M Digitals (P) Ltd, Chennai, India
Printed in the UK

Library of Congress Control Number: 2020938317

British Library Cataloguing in Publication data

A catalogue record for this book is available from the British Library

ISBN 978-1-5264-5996-1
ISBN 978-1-5264-5997-8 (pbk)

CONTENTS

ABOUT THE AUTHOR

Martin Elff is Professor of Political Sociology at Zeppelin University in Friedrichshafen, Germany. He is a political scientist with research interests in the fields of political behaviour, party competition, and political methodology. He has published research articles in journals such as the *British Journal of Political Science, Electoral Studies*, the *European Journal of Political Research, Perspectives on Politics*, and *Political Analysis*. He is the author of several R packages, of which the *memisc, mclogit*, and *munfold* packages have been published on the *Comprehensive R Archive Network* (http://cran.r-project.org). Since 2006 he has been teaching courses on R at the *Essex Summer School of Social Science Data Analysis* at the University of Essex as well as at various other institutions.

PREFACE

This book is the fruit of not only a resolved misunderstanding but also a long unacknowledged desire. In 2017, I had the privilege to chair a panel on 'big data' at the annual conference of the European Political Science Association in Milan, Italy, even though I do not consider myself a 'big data' expert. SAGE Publications at that time were looking for potential authors of textbooks about 'big data' and related matters, but they were also open to suggestions from academics about different promising topics. Therefore, we agreed that I would submit a book proposal to find out whether there is a demand for a book about data management with R.

What motivated me to write a book about data management is my own experience that data management usually takes up as much time of a research project as does the actual statistical analysis of data but there is relatively little literature about it. The reason for this might be that it is possible to build an academic career by writing about research findings and data analysis but the chances of earning academic laurels with work on data management appear to be rather low. Of course, in recent years, 'data science' is on the verge of establishing itself as an academic field if not an academic discipline. But what literature exists on data science seems to be better suited to the needs of business analytics than to the needs of social science research.

What also motivated me to write this book is that I have been enthusiastic about free and open source software for decades and that R is the best available free and open source software for data analysis. While I have worked with commercial software for social science data analysis and management in the earlier stages of my academic career and was able to gain experience in data management and data analysis with SPSS (IBM, 2017), SAS (SAS Institute, 2013), and Stata (StataCorp, 2019), I nevertheless developed the ambition to do all of this in R.

Many of my colleagues are swayed by the high-quality graphics that can be produced with R and by the fact that the most advanced techniques of data analysis are first implemented, and usually very quickly so, in R. Nevertheless, many of them also stick to commercial software like SPSS or Stata for data management. Part of the reason for this is that these colleagues work with data from social science surveys and SPSS and Stata provide functionality that makes it relatively easy to manage such data. Besides, R offers little out-of-the-box support for the management of the kind of data that come from social science surveys, or rather, it offers little support apart from hitherto not so well-known packages such as *memisc* (Elff, 2019). It is therefore an aim of this book to enable social scientists to conduct not only their data analysis but also their data management with R.

Due to the fact that R allows the user to produce high-quality graphics and to use the most advanced techniques of data analysis, and also (and perhaps even more so) that it can be used without the obligation to pay any licence fees, R finds expanding use in social science education at the graduate and postgraduate levels and is also gaining ground at the undergraduate level. From my own experience as a teacher and instructor, I know that many students who are using R struggle at least as much with preparing their data for data analysis as they do with conducting data analysis and understanding the complex concepts involved. I hope that this book is also helpful for these students.

To make sure that the book is useful for as wide an audience as possible, writing it moved me to the margins of and beyond my own intellectual comfort zone of managing and analysing survey data. Writing this book was at times challenging but always stimulating. I hope that readers find the material presented in the book fun and stimulating as well. I dedicate this book to my parents, my friends, and my colleagues and also to the brilliant minds that created and contributed to the wonderful open source software project that is R.

1

Introduction

The free and open source software package R (R Core Team, 2020) is perhaps mainly known for the quality of graphics that one can create with it and for the availability of many of the most advanced techniques of data analysis. But in order to create high-quality graphics or to conduct state-of-the-art statistical analyses, one first needs to prepare the data for this. Yet data preparation can be a challenge because data are not always 'ready for use'. The first challenge one may face here is to actually 'get the data into' R – that is, to make the software understand the format in which the data are arranged in a computer file and to load the data from the file. The second challenge is to rearrange the data once loaded into R memory in such a way that graphics can be produced and data analyses can be conducted. There are two sources for this challenge: the first is that the implementation of many data-analytical techniques is based on a very specific assumption about how the data are structured, and the second is that the data one wants to analyse are only a subset of the available data or, conversely, are distributed in several data objects and data files. Dealing with these challenges is the content of data management and the topic of this book.

This book gives an overview of the main kinds of data that social scientists may encounter in their research and how they can work with these different kinds using R. The present chapter reviews the basic data concepts relevant for working with R, such as objects, variables, and workspaces, as well as packages, data files, and scripts. The second chapter discusses the building blocks and concepts from which almost all other data structures in this book are built: vectors, lists, attributes, and classes. The third chapter discusses the management of data frames, the kind of data object that corresponds to what many researchers who have worked with other software have the most experience with: data arranged in rows and columns, where rows correspond to – depending on the terminology of the discipline and the software being used – observations, cases, objects, units, or individuals, and columns correspond to variables that contain measurements. It also discusses how such data can be imported into R. For those readers who have already worked with R and merely want to expand their knowledge about how to tackle data management issues or how to work with some unusual types of data, much, if not all, of what is discussed in the first three chapters will seem quite familiar. Nevertheless, a book on data management would be incomplete without a discussion of these topics, while a discussion of these concepts may be a useful point of reference in later chapters. Further, introductory texts on data analysis with R do not give much room to these topics, so reviewing them in this book may be worth the while.

The fourth chapter discusses extensions to data frames that are provided by the extension package *data.table* and the 'Tidyverse' collection of extension packages. They provide a re-implementation of the data management functions discussed in Chapter 3, with the aim of increasing their efficiency. These packages appear to be highly popular among people engaged in data science, but they are not indispensable for the kind of data management that social scientists are usually concerned with. The focus of this chapter is therefore a comparison of the approaches of these packages with what is already available from a standard installation of R.[1]

Chapter 5 discusses how a serious limitation of the standard installation of R can be addressed, the limited support for what researchers who work with social science surveys and with

---

[1]There are already more thorough introductions available, at least to the Tidyverse (e.g. Wickham and Grolemund, 2016).

commercial packages such as SPSS (IBM, 2017) and Stata (StataCorp, 2019) can take for granted – that is, variable labels, value labels, and missing value declarations. These limitations can be overcome with the help of the extension package *memisc*, which has been created and is maintained by the author of this book (Elff, 2019). The discussion of the topics of this chapter is based on the author's own experience with the management and analysis of survey data.

Most data sets that survey researchers work with are based on complex samples. Nevertheless, the adequate handling of such data for the purposes of inferential statistics is not very often included in research methods curricula for social scientists. Support for these methods in commercial software is limited: while Stata provides an infrastructure for dealing with complex samples, SPSS (at least in its standard edition) does not. It can be regarded as one of the strengths of the R package ecosystem that support for complex samples is provided by the publicly available extension package *survey* (Lumley, 2019), which is the focus of Chapter 6.

Time series data play an important role in econometrics and political economy. It is fortunate that R provides special data structures that allow the user to deal with temporal and time-dependent data. These are the topics of Chapter 7. On the one hand, the special challenges that are posed by times and dates are discussed – for example, that there are leap years and that not all months in a year have the same length. It also discusses infrastructures for defining and managing time series data.

Chapter 8 discusses the infrastructure that R provides for the handling of spatial data – that is, geographical locations, routes, and areas. This infrastructure demonstrates the strength that lies in the flexible data model of R and its capability to go beyond the conventional tabular arrangement of data. It makes it possible to record not only the location of events, such as those related to intra-state conflicts, but also the description of spatial relations, such as neighbourhood or spatial coverage.

The final chapter is concerned with textual data, that is kinds of data that do not easily fit with the tabular data paradigm. On the one hand, it shows how one can work with character strings – for example, finding and replacing patterns within them. On the other, it discusses the management of corpora of text documents and how they can be prepared for quantitative text analysis based on document–term matrices or document–feature matrices.

The concepts and functions with which this book is concerned are mostly explained with the help of actual R code and the output it produces. Runnable R is shown in monotype font in framed boxes with a light grey background. Output created by the code is shown by framed boxes with a white background. The book is accompanied by a website that makes this code (as well as the required data)[2] available for download and makes it possible for readers to reproduce the result shown in the book. Observant readers will realize that the word *we* is often used in the context of code examples. This is, of course, not an auctorial or presidential *we*, but is meant to indicate that both the author of the book and the reader can run the code in question and see the output shown by R.

It should be noted that the examples cannot be exhaustive in the sense of demonstrating all the possibilities provided by the functions used in the code. Very often, they have several options, and only one of them is applied in an example. So it is advisable for users to consult

---

[2]There are exceptions: for some data sets, redistribution is prohibited. In those cases, information is provided on how to obtain the data sets. The website address is http://www.elff.eu/Data-Management-in-R

the documentation that accompanies R after they have, hopefully with the help of the examples in this book, figured out the basic usage of those functions.

While it is unlikely that this book will be read by users who do not have any prior exposure to R, it tries to assume as little as possible, except that readers have downloaded R – for example, from http://cran.r-project.org – and installed it on their computer and that they are able to run some code with their installation. It also does not rely on any particular graphical user interface, and none of the user interfaces, be they as popular as RStudio (RStudio, Inc, 2020), are discussed. Instead, the book relies on the reader's ability to run R code, because only with code collected into R scripts is it possible to make one's data management and data analysis replicable.

Finally, it should be noted that of the many extension packages available for R, this book can discuss only a small fraction. This makes it likely that some readers feel that their favourite package has not received enough attention. The reason for this may be my ignorance but also the fact that, at the time of writing, there are no less than 16,133 packages available for download from the official Comprehensive R Archive Network.

Objects, variables, and workspaces

One thing that sets R apart from most other statistical packages is its immensely flexible data model. In this regard, it differs from most statistical software packages common in the social sciences, such as SPSS (IBM, 2017), SAS (SAS Institute, 2013), and Stata (StataCorp, 2019), which are built on the assumption that the data one works with are organized in a regular row-by-column structure. In these data sets, rows represent individuals, cases, observations, or units, while columns represent properties, such as height, income, or vote intentions, in terms of which these individuals or things can be described. In the terminology of the widely used commercial software SPSS, the rows are usually referred to as 'cases', while in the terminology of Stata, another widely used commercial software for data analysis, the rows are referred to as 'observations'. In most, if not all, commercial software packages, the columns are referred to as 'variables'.

In contrast to these software packages, data in R can have all kinds of types and shapes, and the chunks of data one works with are referred to as 'objects' in the terminology of R.[3] Variables in R, on the other hand, are names that are associated with such objects by an operation called 'assigning a value to a variable'.[4] A very simple example of an assignment of a value to a variable is

```
a <- 1
```

---

[3]There is also the narrower sense in which objects can be used in the terminology of R - that is, objects in the sense of the various frameworks for object-oriented programming available in R or any of its extension packages. However, such distinctions are of interest only for users interested in the advanced programming aspects of R.

[4]In that regard, R seems more similar to programming languages that computer scientists and data scientists work with - such as C, Fortran, Java, or Python. To be more precise, R is less strict than C, Fortran, or Java in how it associates variables with data of particular types and more similar to Python.

Here, the value **1** (the number one) is assigned to a variable with the name **a**. If the variable does not already exist, it is newly created; otherwise, the existing value of the variable is overwritten.

The most basic types of objects are sequences of numbers, but there are many other types available in R. They range from objects with only a little less simple structure, such as character strings, to very complicated structures that represent estimated statistical models. Of course, R also supports data in the rectangular shape familiar from SAS, SPSS, or Stata. These objects are usually called 'data frames' in the terminology of R. These data frames are discussed in the next chapter. In the present chapter, we discuss the 'building blocks' of such more complex data structures.

Another concept on which everything else in R builds is that of 'functions'. A function is a special kind of object to which input values can be given and which usually creates (or computes) output values from them. The input values are called 'arguments', and the output values are called 'function values' or 'return values'. It is common to say and write that a function is 'called with' certain arguments and 'returns' certain values. In the syntax of the R language, the call of a function is written or coded by writing the name of the function together with the arguments between parentheses. For example, **mean** is the name of a function that returns the arithmetic mean of a sample of numbers. If **x** is a variable that represents a sample that consists of the four numbers 0, 3, 5, and 7, then **mean(x)** gives the arithmetic mean of these four numbers, namely 3.75. (In the following, to make it easier to distinguish between 'ordinary' variables and names that refer to functions, the latter are always written with parentheses affixed – as in **mean()**.)

Almost everything one does when working in R is having the software evaluate some functions. Even the simple assignment **a <- 1** is, in fact, behind the scenes so to speak, a call to the function **assign()**, namely **assign("a",1)**. Also, if the name of a variable is entered at the R command line, it is equivalent to calling either the function **print()** or the function **show()** with this variable as argument. For example, after the assignment **a <- 1**, typing **a**, **print(a)**, or **show(a)** on the command line will lead the contents of the variable **a** – that is, the object that **a** refers to – to be displayed in the R console window.

Assignments like **a <- 1** create associations between variable names and objects, and such associations are collected into structures called 'environments'. In general, there are several such environments in existence during an R session or while R is running an R script. However, most users normally need only to be concerned with one particular environment, the *global* environment or 'workspace', where all the user-defined variables exist. Other environments are created when a function defined in the R language is called (in which case, the existence of the environment is temporary) or when an extension package is activated for the session by a call to the function **library()**. The contents of the workspace or any particular environment can be listed using the function **ls()** or its synonym, **objects()**. The result of **ls()** is a sequence that contains the names of all the variables in the relevant environment. To check whether certain individual variables are present in the environment, one can use the function **exists()**.

Variables can also be removed from an environment with the function **rm()** or its synonym, **remove()**. If **rm()** is called with certain variables as arguments, they are removed from the workspace or designated environment. Another way of removing variables from an environment is putting their names in a character vector and calling **rm()** with this character vector as argument.

The creation and removal of variables are demonstrated in the following example. First, we define two variables **a** and **b** by assigning them the values **1** and **2**:

```
a <- 1
b <- 2
```

If we enter the name of a variable on the command line, it is equivalent to calling `print(a)`; that is, the content of the variable appears as a response in the console output.

```
a
```

```
[1] 1
```

The function call `ls()` returns the names of the variables defined in the current environment. In the present case, this is the global environment, and the result should at least contain `"a"` and `"b"`.

```
ls()
```

```
[1] "a" "b"
```

We now remove both variables using the `rm()` function:

```
rm(a,b)
```

Now the two variables no longer exist,

```
exists("a")
```

```
[1] FALSE
```

and they are no longer listed by `ls()`:

```
ls()
```

```
character(0)
```

`character(0)` here means, 'There could be character strings with variable names, but there aren't any.' (If you try running the above code starting with a non-empty workspace, your results may look different.)

To remove *all* variables from the workspace, use `rm(list=ls(all=TRUE))`, as in the following example:

```
a <- 1
b <- 2
x <- 3
y <- 4
```

```
z <- 42
.zzyx <- 1412
rm(list=ls(all=TRUE))
ls()
```

```
character(0)
```

Note that **rm(list=ls())** without **all=TRUE** would leave the variable **.zzyx** in the work-space, because with a name starting with a dot, it is a 'hidden' one.

━━━━━ **Overview Box 1.1** ━━━━━

Objects, variables, workspaces: key concepts

Object: any 'piece of data' that exists in the main memory of R and is not part of another 'piece of data'.

Variable: a named entity in the main memory of R that has an object as value or content. A variable name can consist of any set of printable characters. Unless the variable name starts with a period (.) or a letter and consists only of letters, digits, underscores (_), and periods, it has to be enclosed in 'backticks' (`) when used in R expressions (e.g. `12e` <- 1).

Function: a specific kind of object to which objects can be passed as input (the 'arguments' of the function) and that returns a result (the '(return) value' of the function).

Environment: a specific kind of data structure that describes the association between variables (or, rather, variable names) and objects in the memory of R.

Package: a set of predefined functions and variables available to the user. Functions or variables not defined by the user are normally contained in a package.

Workspace: the environment that contains all variables defined by the user.

━━━━━ **Overview Box 1.2** ━━━━━

Some important functions related to the housekeeping of the workspace and the activation of packages

print() This function causes its argument to be displayed in the console output of R (unless the output stream is redirected into a file). In an interactive R session, typing just a variable name on the command line is equivalent to calling the function **print()** with this variable as argument. The **print()** function has several options with which the user controls aspects of the output created by the function.

(Continued)

`library()` A call to this function 'activates' a package by making the variables and functions contained in it available for use in R expressions.

`install.packages()` A call to this function installs packages so that they are available later for activation using `library()`. The argument in a call to this function is either one or several package names, or the name of a file that contains the package.

`ls(), objects()` With this function, one can check for the variables defined in the user's workspace or in an environment. When called, it returns the names of the variables currently defined.

`rm(), remove()` This function can be used to remove a variable from a workspace or an environment.

1.2 Working with external files: data files, scripts, file paths, and working directories

1.2.1 Saving variables and objects in data files and restoring them from files

It is usually a good idea to save variables that contain the results of data preparation or data analysis into a file on the computer's hard drive, in particular if running the code that leads to these results takes a long time, because otherwise these variables will disappear if the R session is ended and/or the computer is switched off. There are several options to do this. The most basic way of saving data is by calling the function **save()** in the form **save(a,b,file="somefile.RData")**, where **a** and **b** are variables, while the argument tagged with **file=** specifies the name of the file into which the variables are saved. The contents of the file thus specified can be loaded into the workspace by using the function **load()**. It is also possible to save the complete workspace by calling the function **save.image()**. It should be noted (and many readers will already have noticed this) that when an R session is ended, the user will be asked by the software whether the current workspace should be saved, unless the software is explicitly configured not to do so (e.g. by starting the R program with the command line option **--save** or **--no-save**). If the user answers this question in the affirmative or if R was called with the command line option **--save**, then the workspace will be saved in a file named **".RData"** in the current working directory. Conversely, unless R is called with the command line option **--no-restore**, the contents of the file **".RData"** will be loaded into the current workspace on start-up, and R will show the message [**Previously saved workspace restored**] or any translation of it according to the language settings of the operating system of the computer. The functions **save()** and **load()** are demonstrated by the following example. In this example, we create the two variables **a** and **b**:

```
a <- 1
b <- 1
```

We save them in the data file **"ab.RData"**:

```
save(a,b,file="ab.RData")
```

We then remove the two variables:

```
rm(a,b)
```

We then load the data file:

```
load("ab.RData")
```

and verify that the two variables are restored:

```
a
```

```
[1] 1
```

```
b
```

```
[1] 1
```

1.2.2 R scripts

Computers are much better than human beings at conducting routine tasks repeatedly in prescribed ways. Also, few things are more boring to human beings than doing things repeatedly, and this also includes repeatedly typing the same R code into the R command line interface. Also, while graphical user interfaces may seem visually attractive, their apparent user-friendliness becomes elusive once users try to do the same kind of data management or data analysis repeatedly, in which case they are challenged with either searching through the drop-down menus again and again or remembering and recalling lengthy traversals through the menu system of the software. For these reasons, R users are well advised to collect the code they use into R scripts instead of typing the code directly into the command line interface or relying too much on a series of mouse-click actions.

An R script is merely a text file containing expressions in the R language. Such text files can be easily created by text editor software, such as emacs, vim, atom, Sublime Text, or Notepad++. By convention, the filenames containing R scripts end with '.r' or '.R'. This usually allows the software to identify a text file as an R script. One can tell R to run a script – that is, to evaluate all the expressions contained in it – using the function `source()`, as in `source("object-examples.R")`, where `"object-examples.R"` is the name of a script file. Without further arguments other than a filename, `source()` will make R run the code in the script file 'silently' – that is, without creating any console output other than that caused by calls to functions such as `print()`, `show()`, or `cat()`. If `source()` is called with the additional argument `echo=TRUE`, as in `source("object-examples.R",echo=TRUE)`, then running the script will make R run the code in a more 'verbose' way; that is, every expression evaluated will be 'echoed' in the R output window, and every result of an expression will also appear in the R output window. For example, if the script file `"source-echo-demo.R"` contains the following code

```
cat("Hello world!\n")
a <- 1
b <- 2
a
print(a)
b
show(b)
```

then

```
source("source-echo-demo.R")
```

leads to this output

```
Hello world!
[1] 1
[1] 2
```

while

```
source("source-echo-demo.R",echo=TRUE)
```

leads to a more extensive output:

```
> cat("Hello world!\n")
Hello world!
> a <- 1
> b <- 2
> a
[1] 1
> print(a)
[1] 1
> b
[1] 2
> show(b)
[1] 2
```

Graphical user interfaces for R, such as RStudio, or the graphical user interface that comes with the implementations of R for Microsoft Windows or for macOS, often allow one to create such text files in their editing windows and to send individual lines or several lines at once to the R command line and have these lines run by R. Running individual lines of code from an R script may be useful for experimenting with code, for checking whether code works as intended or causes R to signal any substantial or syntax errors. However, in order to make them most useful, R scripts should be composed in such a way that they can be run in their entirety, without any intermittent user intervention. To succeed in this, one needs to keep the following simple rules in mind:

1   The order in which expressions are supposed to be evaluated by R is reflected in the order in which they occur in the script. The first expression in the script (when going down through the text file from the top) is evaluated first, the next expression is evaluated second, and so on.

2   Variables that are used later in a script should be defined earlier by assigning some value to them. Otherwise, R may throw out an error message complaining about an unknown object.

3   Expressions in the script should be syntactically correct; for example, every open parenthesis should be followed by a closing parenthesis somewhere later in the script, function arguments should be separated by commas, and so on. If an R script contains a syntax error, calling **source()** on the script will cause R to send an error message.

Apart from these three basic rules, there are two recommendations one should heed when working with script files, in particular long ones or scripts that one wants to reuse after a long period of time:

- Code should be provided with comments that explain what it is supposed to do, unless the relevant expressions are short and self-explanatory. (A short expression like **a <- 1** does not really need an explanation.)
- It is not necessary for each expression to appear in a single line. More complex expressions can and should be broken into several lines. Unlike Stata or earlier dialects of Fortran, R is a free-format language that allows a relatively liberal use of spaces and line breaks.

The code shown throughout this book follows these recommendations. A simple example is the one-line expression

```
v <- c(1.0001,2.0001,3.0001,4.0001,5.0001,6.0001,7.0001,8.0001)
```

which can be rearranged in a free-format manner as

```
v <- c(1.0001,
       2.0001,
       3.0001,
       4.0001,
       5.0001,
       6.0001,
       7.0001,
       8.0001)
```

1.2.3 Files, paths, and working directories

The functions **load()**, **save()**, and **source()** take filenames or paths to files as their most important argument. Since filenames can be given as arguments to any of these functions, the question arises of how R finds the appropriate files on the computer hard disk. The second question is how a file path has to be composed in order to ensure that a file can be found.

The file systems on the hard disks of contemporary computers are organized in a hierarchical way. In Unix-derived or Unix-like operating systems, such as Linux, macOS, or Solaris, the files and directories form a single hierarchy with a single 'root' directory that contains all other files or directories: every file the operating system knows of is contained in the root directory, in a subdirectory of the root directory, in a subdirectory of a subdirectory of the root directory, and so on. Even if files and directories are distributed over several storage devices, they are all integrated by 'mounting' these devices into the file system hierarchy. The exact location of any file can thus be described by its path, starting with the root directory and connecting the names of directories or subdirectories with forward slashes (/). A path of a file would, for example, look like this: `"/home/tyrion/research/analysis-1.R"`. This path refers to the file `"analysis-1.R"` located in the directory named 'research', which in turn is located in 'tyrion', which is in the subdirectory 'home' of the root directory of the file system. On a typical Linux system, `"/home/tyrion"` would be the home directory of the user 'tyrion'; that is, the directory is also the working directory when this user logs into the computer.

In variants of Microsoft Windows operating systems, file systems have a slightly different structure. They have several parallel file hierarchies, each starting with a letter that corresponds to a physical or virtual storage device, but still file paths are built from directory names and a filename. Further, the notation of paths in Windows is slightly different, in so far as a *backward* slash (\) is used instead of a forward slash. Because in R syntax the backward slash is used to represent special characters (e.g. \n for the character that starts a new line), the backward slash has to be duplicated to obtain valid file paths. Thus, a path analogous to the one in the previous paragraph would look like `"C:\\Users\\tyrion\\research\\analysis-1.R"` if `"C:\\Users\\tyrion"` is the home directory of the user 'tyrion' on a typical Windows system. Newer versions of R make it possible to write file paths in a simpler way by using the forward slash, as in Unix-like systems. This facilitates the porting of scripts between Windows and Unix-based systems.

Newer versions of R also allow for the so-called tilde expansion of file paths. This means that in scripts the users' home directory is represented by the tilde character (~) on both Unix-like and Windows systems. Thus, if our example user has his or her files organized in the same way on a desktop computer running Windows and on his or her account on a supercomputer running Linux, he or she can use the same call `source("~/research/analysis-1.R")` to run an analysis.

Even though the use of the tilde expansion may make it easier to port R scripts between computer systems, it is better to use relative paths instead of absolute paths in one's code. A path is absolute if it starts with the root directory of the file system (on Unix-like systems) or a storage device (on Windows systems). Paths with a tilde character (~) are also absolute because the tilde is an abbreviation of the path of the user's home directory. A relative path is any path that is not absolute and is interpreted relative to the current working directory. For example, if the user 'tyrion' has an R session running with `"~/research"` as working directory, then the call `source("analysis-1.R")` is equivalent to `source("~/research/analysis-1.R")` and the call `load("datasets/sample1.RData")` is equivalent to the call `load("~/research/datasets/sample1.RData")`.

There are several ways to set the working directory of an R session. If R is started from a command line shell – for example, from *bash* on a Linux or macOS system – or from *PowerShell* on a Windows system, then the current working directory of the command line shell becomes the working directory of the R session. If R is started from a graphical user interface, then the initial working directory is usually the user's home directory.

The widely popular R user interface RStudio also allows one to organize one's work in various projects, each of which consists of a set of R script files, a working directory, and an R session started in this working directory. Whatever the initial working directory at the beginning of an R session, the working directory can be changed using the function `setwd()` and enquired using the function `getwd()`. For example, if the working directory of the example user 'tyrion' is `"~/research"` then the result of the function call

```
getwd()
```

may be the character vector printed as

```
[1] "/home/tyrion/research"
```

After the function call

```
setwd("datasets")
```

the new working directory will be `"~/research/datasets"` printed as

```
[1] "/home/tyrion/research/datasets"
```

It is also possible to move up in the file system hierarchy; for example, after

```
setwd("..")
getwd()
```

the output will be

```
[1] "/home/tyrion/research"
```

━━━━━ Overview Box 1.3 ━━━━━

Working with files: key concepts

Script: a text file that contains R code. Script files make it possible to collect function definitions for later use or to make data preparations and data analyses replicable. Instead of typing individual lines of code on the R command line, users are strongly advised to use scripts.

Path: a character string that describes where a file is located in the file system of a computer operating system. File paths are either *absolute*, if they start at the root of the file system hierarchy, or *relative*, if they do not – in which case they are interpreted as starting at the current working directory of the program.

━━━━━━━━━━ **Overview Box 1.4** ━━━━━━━━━━

Some important functions for working with code and data stored in files

save() With this function, variables can be saved into a file (in a format that is specific for the R software). Unnamed arguments are the variables to be saved, and the argument tagged **file=** is the file where the variable and its value are stored. The variant **save.image()** stores *all* variables defined in the user's workspace.

load() A call to this function reads the contents of the file given as argument and recreates the variables stored in the file.

saveRDS() A call to this function stores the *value* of the variable given as first argument in the file specified with the argument tagged **file=**.

readRDS() With this function, the data saved with **saveRDS()** can be restored from the file specified by its argument. Note that **readRDS()** is incompatible with data saved with the function **save()**.

source() With this function, the contents of a script given as first argument are read in, and the contained R expressions are evaluated. The function can be run in a relatively silent mode (which is the default setting) or a more 'verbose' mode. The most silent way of using **source()** is

```
source("filename.R")
```

to show the results of evaluations,

```
source("filename.R",print.eval=TRUE)
```

to also show the expressions that are evaluated,

```
source("filename.R",echo=TRUE)
```

2

Building Blocks of Data

R supports a wide variety of different data structures suitable for a wide variety of applications and analytical purposes. Most of these data structures can be built up from a set of fundamental data types. This chapter introduces these fundamentals on which almost everything else is built. It starts with discussing the three fundamental data types of numeric, logical, and character vectors, as well as the important data type of ordered and unordered factors. Another topic is the basic manipulation of these vector data types – that is, extracting and replacing (subsets of) their elements and reordering them. Before the chapter closes, it discusses the main structures used to build the more complicated data structures discussed in the later chapters. The final section of the chapter discusses working with external files: with script files that contain R code and with data files that contain objects and variables created in R.

2.1 Basic data types

2.1.1 Numeric vectors

From the outset, R is conceived as software for doing statistics. Statistics in turn is all about summarizing data and drawing inferences from such summaries. For this reason, the most basic numeric data type that R supports is not that of single numbers but of *numeric vectors*. One should not be misled by the term *vector*, however. Numeric vectors in R are just sequences of numbers, whereas the mathematical interpretation in terms of linear algebra or analytical geometry is optional.[1]

A numeric vector can be constructed, for example, as follows:

```
c(1.2,3.5,5.0,6.7,1.09e-3)
```

where c(…) stands for 'concatenate', in this case concatenate the numbers 1.2, 3.5, 5.0, 6.7, 1.09×10^{-3} (which equals 0.00109). The result of this expression looks like this

```
[1] 1.20000 3.50000 5.00000 6.70000 0.00109
```

where the '[1]' before '1.20000' means that it is the first element of the sequence.

Any vector, whether it is a numeric vector or belongs to some other data type described further below, has a length, which can be enquired by the function **length()**, as in the following example:

```
x <- c(1.2,3.5,5.0,6.7,1.09e-3)
length(x)
```

```
[1] 5
```

---

[1]Indeed, R provides functions and operators from linear algebra, but these are beyond the scope of this book on data management.

The vector assigned to variable **x** has five elements, therefore the result of the function call **length(x)** is a vector with a single element with a value of 5. In principle, vectors can have any length, except for the limits set by the operating system of the computer on which R is running.

Another common way of creating a numeric vector is the sequence operator ':'. For example, to create a numeric vector that equals the sequence of all integer numbers from 1 to 100, one can use the code

```
1:100
```

which leads to

```
 [1]   1   2   3   4   5   6   7   8   9  10  11  12  13  14
[15]  15  16  17  18  19  20  21  22  23  24  25  26  27  28
[29]  29  30  31  32  33  34  35  36  37  38  39  40  41  42
[43]  43  44  45  46  47  48  49  50  51  52  53  54  55  56
[57]  57  58  59  60  61  62  63  64  65  66  67  68  69  70
[71]  71  72  73  74  75  76  77  78  79  80  81  82  83  84
[85]  85  86  87  88  89  90  91  92  93  94  95  96  97  98
[99]  99 100
```

where each of the bracketed numbers indicates which element of the sequence appears at the start of each line.

What sets numeric data apart from the other data types discussed in this section is that one can do computations on them – that is, apply arithmetic operators and functions. Arithmetic operators include addition (represented by '+' in R code), multiplication (represented by '*'), subtraction ('−'), and division ('/'). These operators work in an element-wise fashion: if **x** and **y** are two numeric vectors of the same length, then after

```
z <- x + y
```

each element of **z** equals the sum of an element of **x** and an element of **y**. For example, the code

```
x <- c(1,2,3,4,5)
y <- c(3,2,3,2,3)
z <- x + y
print(z)
```

leads to the output

```
[1] 4 4 6 6 8
```

because $1 + 3 = 4$, $2 + 2 = 4$, $3 + 3 = 6$, $4 + 2 = 6$, $5 + 3 = 8$.

The vectors being added, subtracted, or multiplied do not need to have the same length. In general, the result of such an operation has the length of the longest operand. This comes in handy if one wants to add the same number to all the elements of a vector, for example. In case of a five-element vector **x**, one can use the code

```
x <- c(3,2,4,8,7)
y <- x + 1
print(y)
```

to get the same result as

```
x <- c(3,2,4,8,7)
y <- x + c(1,1,1,1,1)
print(y)
```

which is

```
[1] 4 3 5 9 8
```

The 'reuse' of the elements of a shorter operand in an addition or other operation is called *recycling* in the terminology of R.

In research, one often has to deal with the fact that the information one intends to measure is not available. Certain countries' statistical offices do not collect statistics about, say, youth unemployment, or have not have collected such data for certain years. Certain respondents in a social survey decline to state their vote intention, income, or year of birth, or they refuse to continue the interview before the entire questionnaire is completed. In R, such missing information is represented by the special value **NA** (which means 'not available' or 'not applicable'). Any arithmetic operation that involves such a missing value results in a missing value – for example,

```
1 + NA
```

```
[1] NA
```

In contrast to some other statistics packages (e.g. Stata or SPSS), there are special values representing the results of arithmetic operations that are undefined for mathematical reasons. For example, dividing a number by 0 does not lead (as in Stata or SPSS) to a generic missing value but to the value **Inf**, meaning [positive] *infinity*, ' ∞' in mathematical notation. Further, if it is clear for mathematical reasons that the result of an operation is not finite but unclear whether it is positive or negative, the result is **NaN**, meaning 'not a (finite) number'. This is illustrated in the following short piece of code:

```
x <- c(-2,-1,0,1,2)
1/x
```

```
[1] -0.5 -1.0 Inf 1.0 0.5
```

```
x/0
```

```
[1] -Inf -Inf NaN Inf Inf
```

Here, 1.0 and 0.5 divided by 0 result in +∞ ('positive infinity'), −1.0 and −0.5 divided by 0 result in −∞ ('negative infinity'), and 0 divided by 0 is not a finite number but is neither positive nor negative infinity.

2.1.2 Logical vectors

Sometimes one is interested not so much in the numeric summaries of a bunch of data but in whether the data points are equal to a particular value or whether two sequences of measure are all equal or equal in some of their elements or which elements are larger than a particular value. For example, one may be interested in knowing which of a set of voters who turn out in a current election are old enough to have been eligible to vote in the previous election. The results of such comparisons are in general either *true* or *false*; that is, they have a so-called logical value.

In R, such comparisons are made by the application of comparison operators, such as == (equal), != (not equal), > (greater than), >= (greater than or equal), < (less than), or <= (less than or equal), and the results of the application of such comparison operators are *logical vectors* – that is, vectors that are either **TRUE** or **FALSE**.

Like the arithmetic operators we discussed earlier, comparison vectors recycle their operands. It is thus relatively easy to compare a sequence of numbers – a numeric vector – with a single number and to obtain a logical vector that contains the result of a comparison of each element of the vector with that number. But, of course, it is also possible to compare two vectors element by element. For an illustration, we compare a vector that contains a sequence of numbers with the single number 0. This example vector (which again we call **x**) contains the integer numbers from −3 to 3 and thus is a vector of length 7:

```
x <- -3:3
x
```

```
[1] -3 -2 -1  0  1  2  3
```

When we compare this vector (or, rather, its elements) with 0, we get a logical vector with length 7:

```
x == 0
```

```
[1] FALSE FALSE FALSE TRUE FALSE FALSE FALSE
```

This is so, because the single number 0 is recycled to the length of **x**.

If we compare two vectors of the same length, again say 7, the result is ('of course', one may say) a vector of length 7:

```
x <- -3:3
y <- c(1:3,0,1:3)
x == y
```

```
[1] FALSE FALSE FALSE TRUE TRUE TRUE TRUE
```

Sometimes one is interested in whether several conditions (which can be checked by comparisons) or one of several conditions or none of them applies. For example, one may be interested in whether a set of citizens under study is eligible to vote and has voted or whether one set of possible reasons for a person's unemployment applies. The results of a combination of such comparisons are obtained by *logical operators*. While arithmetic operators work on numbers (or numeric vectors) and result in numbers (or numeric vectors), logical operators work on logical values (or logical vectors) and result in logical values (or logical vectors). There are three elementary logical operators available in R: (1) the 'and' operator, in R syntax represented by an ampersand (&); (2) the 'or' operator, in R syntax represented by a vertical bar (|); and (3) the 'not' operator, in R syntax represented by the exclamation mark (!). If two logical values are combined by the 'and' operator, the result is TRUE only if they are both TRUE – that is, TRUE & TRUE is TRUE, but TRUE & FALSE is FALSE. If two logical values are combined with the 'or' operator, the result is TRUE if at least one of them is TRUE, so that TRUE | FALSE and FALSE | TRUE are TRUE, but only FALSE | FALSE is FALSE. Notably TRUE | TRUE ('true or true') is TRUE; that is, it is an 'inclusive or' and not, as is common in ordinary language, an 'exclusive or' (or 'either/or' combination).[2] Finally, the 'not' operator, in R syntax '!', results in TRUE if and only if the operand has the value FALSE and results in FALSE if and only if the operand has the value TRUE. For illustration, we create two vectors that provide an overview of all possible combinations of logical values with a logical operator:

```
a <- c(TRUE,FALSE,TRUE,FALSE)
b <- c(TRUE,TRUE,FALSE,FALSE)
```

We now look at the results of applying the various logical operators. First, look at the result of applying the logical 'and' operator:

```
a & b
```

```
[1]   TRUE FALSE FALSE FALSE
```

second, the logical 'or' operator:

```
a | b
```

```
[1]   TRUE  TRUE  TRUE FALSE
```

and, third, the logical 'not' operator:

```
!a
```

---

[2]This gives rise to the (perhaps silly) joke that if a robber tells you that he or she will take your money or your life, you better hope he or she is not a logician or a programmer!

```
[1] FALSE   TRUE FALSE   TRUE
```

Like arithmetic operators, logical operators can be combined, as in the following line

```
a & !b
```

```
[1] FALSE FALSE   TRUE FALSE
```

or

```
!(a | b)
```

```
[1] FALSE FALSE FALSE TRUE
```

Since logical vectors are usually the result of comparisons, we take a look at how logical operators work in combination with comparisons. For this purpose, we look again at the sequence of numbers from –3 to 3. If we combine the results of x > 1 and x < 1 with the 'and' operator, the result is FALSE for all elements, because there is no number that is both less than –1 and greater than +1:

```
x <- -3:3
x > 1 & x < -1
```

```
[1] FALSE FALSE FALSE FALSE FALSE FALSE FALSE
```

The result of the combination of the two comparisons with the 'or' operator is different because there are several numbers that are less than –1 or greater than +1 in x – namely, the numbers –3, –2, +2, and +3:

```
x > 1 | x < -1
```

```
[1]   TRUE   TRUE FALSE FALSE FALSE   TRUE   TRUE
```

Like numeric vectors, logical vectors also can have missing values. However, the way missing values in logical vectors are handled by logical operators differs a little from how missing values in numeric vectors are handled by arithmetic operators. When applied to a missing logical value (which also appears as an NA in R code as well as in output), the result of a logical operator is not always missing. Rather, the result is a sensible one given that the missing value stands in for a value that can be either TRUE or FALSE but is unknown. Therefore, while NA & TRUE is NA (because the result is different depending on whether we substitute TRUE or FALSE for the missing value), NA & FALSE is FALSE because it suffices that one of the operands is FALSE to make the result to be FALSE. For similar reasons, NA | TRUE results in TRUE, while NA | FALSE results in NA. The following two vectors contain all possible combinations of logical values, *including* missing values, in the application of a logical operator:

```
a <- c(TRUE,FALSE,NA,TRUE,FALSE,NA,TRUE,FALSE,NA)
b <- c(TRUE,TRUE,TRUE,FALSE,FALSE,FALSE,NA,NA,NA)
```

Appling the 'and' operator to **a** and **b** gives

```
a & b
```

```
[1]   TRUE FALSE    NA FALSE FALSE FALSE    NA FALSE    NA
```

while applying the 'or' operator gives

```
a | b
```

```
[1]   TRUE   TRUE   TRUE   TRUE FALSE    NA   TRUE    NA    NA
```

2.1.3 Character vectors

Sometimes it is impossible or inconvenient to encode measurements or other data into numbers. Take, for example, the names of countries in an internationally comparative study. Even if it is possible to let predetermined country codes represent the countries in such an application, it would be convenient to have a data type in R that helps document the meaning of such codes. In fact, R provides such a data type: *character vectors*. The R terminology is a bit misleading in this case, in so far as the elements of a character vector are not single characters – for example, letters and digits – but character *strings*, that is sequences that are composed of characters. In R code as well as in output generated by the function `print()`, character strings, the elements of character vectors, usually appear as sequences of printable characters (i.e. letters, digits, and symbols) enclosed in quotation marks, where the quotation marks are not part of the strings themselves but syntactical markers for the start and end of each string. The following code defines a variable containing a character vector of length 4:

```
Beatles <- c("John", "Paul", "George", "Ringo")
Beatles
```

```
[1] "John"    "Paul"    "George" "Ringo"
```

Of course, the application of arithmetic or logical operators is not sensible for a character vector. Yet there are some operations that are sensible when applied to character vectors. One can paste them together:

```
paste("one","and","only")
```

```
[1] "one and only"
```

```
Beatles <- c("John", "Paul", "George", "Ringo")
paste(Beatles, collapse=" & ")
```

```
[1] "John & Paul & George & Ringo"
```

Here, the optional argument `collapse=` tells the function `paste()` to collapse all the elements of the character vector given as first argument into a single character string. Without the `collapse=` argument, the result of `paste()` is not a single character string but a character vector with as many elements as the longest character vector argument. We apply `paste()` to two four-element character vectors, so that the result is also a four-element character vector:

```
First <- c("Mick","Keith","Ronnie","Charlie")
Last <- c("Jagger","Richards","Wood","Watts")
paste(First,Last)
```

```
[1] "Mick Jagger"    "Keith Richards" "Ronnie Wood"
[4] "Charlie Watts"
```

The result contains each element of the first argument pasted onto the corresponding element of the second argument, with a whitespace as separator. This separator can, in turn, be changed with the optional `sep=` argument of the `paste()` function:

```
paste(First,Last,sep="_")
```

```
[1] "Mick_Jagger"    "Keith_Richards" "Ronnie_Wood"
[4] "Charlie_Watts"
```

One can also extract substrings using the function `substr()`. For example, to get the first two characters of the given names of the Fab Four, the function `substr` is used as follows:

```
Beatles <- c("John", "Paul", "George", "Ringo")
substr(Beatles,1,2)
```

```
[1] "Jo" "Pa" "Ge" "Ri"
```

The first argument here is the vector of character strings from which the substrings are extracted; the first argument is the starting position, and the second argument is the end position of the substring. Of course, one can also have sequences of start and end positions:

```
Beatles <- c("John", "Paul", "George", "Ringo")
substr(Beatles,1:4,2:5)
```

```
[1] "Jo" "au" "or" "go"
```

Finally, one can also get a modified copy of a character vector where substring substitutions are applied to its elements:

```
Led.Zeppelin.song <- "Whole Lotta Love"
ACDC.song <- sub("Love","Rosie",Led.Zeppelin.song)
print(ACDC.song)
```

```
[1] "Whole Lotta Rosie"
```

Character vectors are useful because they make it possible to assign names to the elements of a vector. This allows one, for example, to attach the names of independent variables to a coefficient vector that results from a linear regression. There is a dedicated function, `names()`, to access the names attached to the elements of a vector. If **x** is a vector, then the names attached to its elements can be enquired by `names(x)`. However, it is possible to assign names to the elements of a vector with an expression like `names(x) <- nn`, which could be interpreted as the declaration 'The result of the call `names(x)` henceforth shall be what the value of the variable **nn** is' or 'The value of **nn** shall become the names of the elements of **x**'. In the following example, we assign names to the elements of a vector, enquire these names, and print a numeric vector with the names:

```
onetofour <- 1:4
names(onetofour) <- c("first","second","third","fourth")
names(onetofour)
```

```
[1] "first" "second" "third" "fourth"
```

```
onetofour
```

```
first second third fourth
    1      2     3      4
```

R does not prepend `[1]` to the output here because the names attached to the elements of the vector should suffice to identify them. Also, the names of the vectors are not enclosed within quotation marks, in order to distinguish them from a 'bare' character vector.

Since it is quite common to have vectors with named elements, there is a special syntax for constructing a vector from individual elements and the names associated with these elements:

```
onetofour <- c(first=1,second=2,third=3,fourth=4)
print(onetofour)
```

```
first second third fourth
    1      2     3      4
```

2.1.4 Factors

Much of social science research is centred on categorical data: the political party people prefer, the religion they adhere to, the social class they are members of, the region in which they live, to give just a few examples. Such data could be represented by character vectors, but in R, such data are usually represented by *factors*. More precisely, R allows one to distinguish between ordered categorical data (representing measurements at the ordinal level), in the form of ordered factors, and unordered categorical data (representing measurements at the nominal level), in the form of unordered factors.

A factor is characterized by a finite (usually small) number of 'levels' that describe the different values it can assume. These levels are internally encoded as integer numbers and usually provided with labels to facilitate their interpretation. The internal codes of factor levels are always integer numbers, starting from 1. The labels of the factor levels can be any character strings. Factors and unordered factors do not differ much in their internal construction but mainly in how they are handled in the construction of regression models (a topic beyond the scope of a book on data management). The following example illustrates the construction of factors and the enquiry of their aspects.

The first factor that we create is constructed from numbers. Its (fictitious) role is to represent the level of life satisfaction of 20 survey respondents. We therefore draw a sample of size 20 from the numbers from 1 to 4. (Sampling has to be with replacement, otherwise it would be impossible to get a sample with a size larger than 4.)

```
satisfaction <- sample(1:4,size=20,replace=TRUE)
satisfaction
```

```
[1] 1 1 1 1 2 4 2 2 1 4 3 4 3 4 1 1 2 4 2 2
```

In order to get an *ordered* factor, we call the function `ordered()`. The `levels=` argument specifies the values of its argument (the numeric vector `satisfaction`) that are to be interpreted as levels of the factor that is constructed by the function. The `labels=` argument specifies the labels of the factor levels.

```
satisfaction <- ordered(satisfaction,
                        levels=1:4,
                        labels=c(
                            "not at all",
                            "low",
                            "medium",
                            "high"))
satisfaction
```

```
 [1] not at all not at all not at all not at all low
 [6] high        low            low            not at all high
[11] medium      high           medium         high           not at all
[16] not at all low            high           low            low
Levels: not at all < low < medium < high
```

If a factor is written to the console, the factor levels appear without quotation marks. This is how a factor can be distinguished in the output from a character vector.

It should be noted that the `levels=` argument is not really necessary in this case, because by default all unique numbers are interpreted as factor levels.

Usually, it makes sense to look at a table of frequencies when one works with factors. The factor levels appear in the table according to their predefined order:

```
table(satisfaction)
```

```
satisfaction
not at all          low          medium          high
         7            6               2             5
```

We can inspect the levels of the factor using the function `levels()`, which shows the factor levels in their predefined order:

```
levels(satisfaction)
```

```
[1] "not at all" "low"        "medium"      "high"
```

For an example of an unordered factor, we draw a 'representative' sample of 50 persons of the four constituent countries of the UK, where the persons' origins are represented by character strings. Here, the sampling occurs with unequal probabilities, proportional to the population size of the constituent countries in 2015.[3]

```
country.orig <- sample(
    c("England","Northern Ireland","Scotland","Wales"),
    size=50,
    prob=c(54786300,5373000,3099100,1851600)/65110000,
    replace=TRUE
)
```

To create an unordered factor from the character vector, we can use the function `factor()`:

```
country <- factor(country.orig)
```

Even though in the present case no 'inherent' order of the factor levels is assumed, they have to be presented in some order simply because they form a sequence. By default, if a factor is constructed from a character vector, the factor levels are ordered alphabetically. If we want to change the order of the factor levels, we have to explicitly specify with the `levels=` argument:

```
country <- factor(country.orig,
                 levels=c("England","Wales","Scotland",
                          "Northern Ireland"))
table(country)
```

```
country
        England              Wales           Scotland
             39                  3                  3
Northern Ireland
              5
```

Irrespective of whether a factor is constructed from a numeric or a character vector and whether it is ordered or unordered, the factor levels are internally represented by numbers, as we can see when we take a peek using the function `str()`:

```
str(country)
```

---

[3]The data come from the Wikipedia article on the four constituent countries, https://en.wikipedia.org/wiki/Countries_of_the_United_Kingdom, accessed on 16 April 2020.

```
Factor w/ 4 levels "England","Wales",..: 4 1 2 3 1 1 1 4 1 1 ...
```

If one is interested in this numeric representation, one can use the function `as.numeric()`:

```
as.numeric(country)
```

```
 [1] 4 1 2 3 1 1 1 4 1 1 1 1 1 1 1 1 1 1 1 4 1 1 1 1 2 1 3 4 1 3 1 1
[32] 1 1 1 1 1 1 1 1 1 1 2 1 1 4 1 1 1 1 1
```

Occasionally, factor labels appear longer than one desires, but fortunately one can change these labels, as illustrated by the following line of code:

```
levels(country) <- c("EN","NI","SC","WL")
table(country)
```

```
country
EN NI SC WL
39  3  3  5
```

The internal codes of factors are in general not used by R for anything other than distinguishing the levels. To simplify the internal aspects of the software, these codes are restricted to a sequence of successive positive integer numbers that start with 1. In practical survey research, the numbers used to code survey respondents do not always conform to such restrictions. For example, valid responses may be coded by numbers between 1 and 10, while invalid responses (the respondent does not know how to answer a survey question, refuses to give a response, etc.) are coded into numbers between 90 and 99 or into negative numbers (see e.g. Heath et al., 1983). To handle these kinds of data, an extension package is needed, one of which being the *memisc* package created by the author (Elff, 2019). Handling such survey response data is discussed in a dedicated chapter later in this book.

━━━━━━ Overview Box 2.1 ━━━━━━

Vectors, factors, operators: key concepts

Numeric vector: a sequence of numbers. This is the way in which numeric data are represented in R. Numeric vectors can be operands for operators, such as +, *; arguments for arithmetic functions, such as `exp()` or `log()`; or statistical functions, such as `mean()` or `var()`.

Logical vector: a sequence of logical values (either **TRUE** or **FALSE**). They can be the results of comparisons, like a == 0, or operands of logical operators, such as & ('and') and | ('or').

Character vector: a sequence of character strings. Character vectors can be used to represent textual data, but, more importantly, they can be used to document other kinds of data, in particular by attaching names to the elements of numeric vectors, logical vectors, or other data structures.

(Continued)

Factor: a data structure used to represent categorical data in R. A factor has a limited number of prespecified 'levels' that represent the categories of the data. R knows two kinds of factors, *ordered* and *unordered* ones. They usually differ in the way they are translated into dummy or contrast indicator variables.

Missing and non-finite values: In order to represent a generic missing value, R uses the symbol NA. For $+\infty$ and $-\infty$, R uses the symbols Inf and $-$Inf. The symbol NaN represents a result of an arithmetic operation that is neither finite nor equal to $+\infty$ or $-\infty$. Numeric, logical, and character vectors can have elements that are missing (i.e. that are NA).

Recycling: Arithmetic operators (e.g. + or *), comparisons (e.g. == or !=), and logical operators (e.g. & or |) can be applied to vectors of different lengths. To make this possible, the length of the shorter vector is increased to match the length of the longer vector by repeating their elements. This adaptation of the length of shorter operands to longer ones is called *recycling* in the terminology of R. There are also some functions that recycle their arguments to the same length, if necessary.

▬▬▬▬ Overview Box 2.2 ▬▬▬▬

Some important functions for the management of vectors and factors

`length()` This function reports, as its name suggests, the length of a numeric, logical, or character vector or of a factor; that is, the number of elements it has. The return value is a one-element numeric vector. With an assignment of the form

```
length(x) <- v
```

the length of a vector can be changed. If the new length is greater than the old length, new elements of the vector are created with NA as the value.

`names()` This function returns a character vector that contains the names attached to the elements of another vector. With an expression like

```
names(x) <- v
```

the names attached to the elements of a vector **x** can be (re-)defined.

`levels()` This function reports the (names of the) levels of a factor. The return value is a character vector with the names of the factor levels.

`nlevels()` This function reports the *number* of the levels of a factor and has a one-element numeric vector as return value.

`is.finite()` This function returns a logical vector, the elements of which indicate whether the elements of its argument are finite and non-missing:

```
is.finite(x)
```

gives a vector that is **TRUE** for every element that is a finite number and **FALSE** for every element that is **NA, NaN, Inf**, or **−Inf**.

is.na() This function returns a logical vector; that is, it indicates for each element of its argument whether it is **NA** or **NaN**. It is *not* the negation of **is.finite**, because **is.na(x)** equals **FALSE** for elements of **x** that are **Inf** or **−Inf**, even though **is.finite(x)** is also **FALSE**.

2.2 Basic data manipulations

2.2.1 Extracting and replacing elements of vectors

It is often convenient or even necessary to restrict analysis or other operations on a subset of the observations that are represented by a numeric, logical, character, or other kind of vector. The most basic operator used for the extraction of such subsets is the bracket operator, [ ]. To obtain a subset of a vector (whether it is numeric, logical, or character) stored in a variable, say **x**, one appends a pair of brackets to the variable name and inserts an *index vector*, or an expression that results in a vector of index values, between the brackets.

If the index vector consists of positive integer numbers, it selects elements of a vector according to their position in the main vector. For example, if we define the following vector

```
x <- c(10, 12, 30, 14, 50)
```

we get the first element with

```
x[1]
```

```
[1] 10
```

and the fifth element with

```
x[5]
```

```
[1] 50
```

With a length 3 index vector, we get three elements of the main vector:

```
x[c(2,4,6)]
```

```
[1] 12 14 NA
```

Indices (i.e. the values of index vectors) need not be unique. It is well possible to extract the same elements repeatedly. For example, to get the first element of **x** three times and the second element two times, we use the code

```
x[c(1,1,1,2,2)]
```

```
[1] 10 10 10 12 12
```

If the index vector consists of negative integer numbers, all the elements *other* than those specified by the positive counterparts of the index values are selected:

```
x[-c(1,3,5)]
```

```
[1] 12 14
```

If the index vector is logical, then all the elements of the main vector are selected for which the index vector is **TRUE**. For example,

```
x[c(FALSE,TRUE,FALSE,TRUE,FALSE)]
```

```
[1] 12 14
```

gives the second and the fourth element of the previously defined vector **x** because the index vector is **TRUE** for the first and the fourth argument and **FALSE** for the others.

Logical index vectors are typically used to extract elements of a vector that satisfy certain conditions. For example, to get all the elements greater than 20, we use the code

```
x[x>=20]
```

```
[1] 30 50
```

which gives the third and the fifth element of **x**, because these are greater than 20.

Character index vectors can be used when a vector has names. The index vector will then select those elements of a main vector where the attached names equal the elements of the index vector. This can be demonstrated if we attach names to the previously defined vector **x**:

```
names(x) <- c("a","b","c","d","e")
```

To select the first and the third element of **x** based on their name, we can now use the code

```
x[c("a","c")]
```

```
 a  c
10 30
```

With the bracket operator we just encountered, it is possible to not only extract single elements or a subset of the elements of a vector but also replace elements or subsets of elements. This is achieved by putting an expression with brackets on the left-hand side of an assignment, as in the following example.

We first create a new vector **y** of 12 random numbers:

```
y <- rnorm(n=12)
```

To illustrate the replacement by numeric index vectors, we replace the first four elements of **y** with 0:

```
y[1:4] <- 0
y
```

```
 [1]   0.00000000 0.00000000  0.00000000 0.00000000 -0.47335746
 [6]   0.21739728 0.06292205 -0.87782986 0.56368979 -0.03432728
[11] -0.22631292 1.38657787
```

Logical index vectors can also be used in element replacements. This is particularly useful to replace elements of a vector that satisfy certain criteria. For example, to replace all negative numbers in the recreated vector of random numbers by 0,

```
y <- rnorm(n=12)
```

we can use the code

```
y[y < 0] <- 0
```

so that the vector after the replacement looks like this:

```
y
```

```
[1] 0.0000000 0.0000000 1.4013312 0.3196224 1.0058453 0.0000000
[7] 0.0000000 1.6502536 1.4374338 0.0000000 0.0000000 0.0000000
```

2.2.2 Reordering the elements of a vector

R provides facilities to sort the elements of a numeric or character vector, where the elements can be ordered in either ascending (smallest element first) or descending (greatest element first) order.

There are two ways of sorting the elements of a vector. The first is the function `sort()`, which returns a sorted copy (as the name suggests) of the vector given as argument. Elements of numeric vectors then are ordered according to the mathematical relations 'less than' ($<$) and 'greater than' ($>$).

For example, if we create a vector of random numbers called **x**,

```
x <- rnorm(n=10)
x
```

```
[1] -0.53310192 -2.31166378 -0.95419786 0.26251575 -0.47335746
[6]  0.21739728  0.06292205 -0.87782986 0.56368979 -0.03432728
```

we can produce a sorted copy with `sort()`

```
x.srt <- sort(x)
```

which looks like this:

```
x.srt
```

```
[1] -2.31166378 -0.95419786 -0.87782986 -0.53310192 -0.47335746
[6] -0.03432728  0.06292205  0.21739728  0.26251575  0.56368979
```

With the optional argument **decreasing=TRUE**, we can instead get a copy with the elements sorted in decreasing order:

```
sort(x,decreasing=TRUE)
```

```
[1]  0.56368979  0.26251575  0.21739728  0.06292205 -0.03432728
[6] -0.47335746 -0.53310192 -0.87782986 -0.95419786 -2.31166378
```

Character vectors are sorted in 'lexicographical' order. This is the alphabetical order among lower-case and upper-case characters. Further, lower-case letters are considered as lesser than upper-case letters. But a lower-case 'b' is greater than an upper-case 'A'.[4] How longer strings are sorted is less easy to describe, so it is illustrated in one of the following examples:

```
stex <- c("1","11","A","a","Ab","AB","ab","aB","B","b","bb")
sort(stex)
```

```
[1] "1"  "11" "a"  "A"  "ab" "aB" "Ab" "AB" "b"  "B"  "bb"
```

The second way to obtain a sorted copy of a vector is by using the function **order()**. This function does not return a sorted copy of its argument but a vector of numbers that, when used as an index vector with the bracket operator, gives a sorted copy of the original vector. This has two advantages: first, it allows the user to 'undo' the sorting; and second, it allows one to sort a different vector according to the original vector. We demonstrate these two advantages of using the **order()** function by creating two vectors **x** and **y**, sorting both vectors according to the first vector **y**, and undoing the sort.

First, we create two vectors of random numbers:

```
x <- rnorm(6)
x
```

```
[1] 0.6549052 -0.2099869 -0.6148580 -0.2740271 -0.7234317
[6] 1.4371483
```

```
y <- rnorm(6)
y
```

---

[4]This differs from the order in terms of the encoding of the letters. According to Latin-1 or UTF-8 encoding, the order would be "a" < "b" < "A" < "B", instead of "a" < "A" < "b" < "B".

```
[1] -0.09385485 -0.05070594 0.77188553 0.36295090 1.12152639
[6] 0.72011916
```

Then we obtain an ordering index vector using `order()`

```
ii <- order(x)
```

and sort **x** and **y** with the help of the index vector:

```
x.ordered <- x[ii]
y.ordered <- y[ii]
x.ordered
```

```
[1] -0.7234317 -0.6148580 -0.2740271 -0.2099869 0.6549052
[6] 1.4371483
```

```
y.ordered
```

```
[1] 1.12152639 0.77188553 0.36295090 -0.05070594 -0.09385485
[6] 0.72011916
```

Using the comparison operator and `all()`, we verify that ordering/sorting with the index vector worked:

```
all(x.ordered == sort(x))
```

```
[1] TRUE
```

To get back from the sorted vector to the vector in its original order, we use `order()` on the index vector:

```
jj <- order(ii)
```

Finally, we verify that using `jj` as index vector on **x.ordered** and **y.ordered** gives us the original vectors:

```
all(x.ordered[jj] == x)
```

```
[1] TRUE
```

```
all(y.ordered[jj] == y)
```

```
[1] TRUE
```

2.2.3 Regular sequences and repetitions

Earlier in this chapter, we encountered ':', the colon operator. It can be used to create a sequence of integer values from a start to an end. To get sequences of a more general kind

with different step sizes, lengths, end points, or starting points, one can use the function
`seq()`. To get the sequence of integers from 1 to 10, we can use

```
1:10
```

```
[1]  1  2  3  4  5  6  7  8  9 10
```

while the explicit way of using `seq()` would be

```
seq(from=1,to=10)
```

```
[1]  1  2  3  4  5  6  7  8  9 10
```

We can vary the step size with the **by=** argument

```
seq(from=2,to=10,by=2)
```

```
[1]  2  4  6  8 10
```

and we can also let `seq()` figure out the correct starting point for a sequence with a given
end point, length, and step size:

```
seq(to=49,length.out=5,by=7)
```

```
[1] 21 28 35 42 49
```

Another kind of regular sequence can be created by repeating the elements of a given vector.
To create such a vector of repeated elements, one can use the function **rep()**, which allows
one to repeat a given sequence as a whole or the elements of the sequence individually. For
example, to repeat the sequence `1:5` three times, one can write

```
rep(1:5,3)
```

```
[1] 1 2 3 4 5 1 2 3 4 5 1 2 3 4 5
```

If instead one wants to repeat each element three times, one can specify this with the argument **each=**, as in

```
rep(1:5,each=3)
```

```
[1] 1 1 1 2 2 2 3 3 3 4 4 4 5 5 5
```

2.2.4 Sampling from vector elements

There are a variety of techniques in statistics that rely on drawing a sample from an existing
set of units or observations. One of these techniques is the non-parametric bootstrap (Efron

and Tibshirani, 1994), where from an existing sample new samples of the same size are drawn (with replacement). The idea behind this is that the new samples have in every respect the same distribution as the original sample. Another example is randomized experiments, where experimental subjects are selected into two groups, a 'treatment' group and a 'control' group. Finally, social surveys are based on sampling from a finite population (Levy and Lemeshow, 2013). To get all these kinds of (sub)samples, R provides the function `sample()`.

If `sample()` is called with only a vector as argument, the result is a random permutation of its arguments, for example

```
sample(1:9)
```

```
[1] 8 6 4 1 7 2 9 5 3
```

In most applications, `sample()` is really used to draw a sample from an artificial population or a subsample from an existing sample. In such cases, one will usually specify a sample size, with a `size=` argument. For example, to draw a sample of size 20 from the numbers from 1 to 1000, one can use the following code:

```
sample(1:1000,size=20)
```

```
 [1]    658 171 191 428 806 768 307 120 506 340 190 962 437 274 477
[16] 935 363 469 933   79
```

Unless specified otherwise, samples drawn with the function `sample` are *without* replacement; that is, every element of the 'population' can occur only once in the sample. Sampling *with* replacement is also possible with the optional argument `replace=TRUE`. In this case, the sample can even be larger than the population. The simulation of throwing a die is an example: the population is the set of integer numbers from 1 to 6, from which each sampled number corresponds to the throw of the die. Thus, throwing a die 10 times is simulated by the code

```
sample(6,size=10,replace=TRUE)
```

```
[1] 4 5 3 2 1 5 1 6 1 2
```

━━━━━━━ Overview Box 2.3 ━━━━━━━

Key operators and functions for the basic manipulation of vectors and factors

Bracket-operator, [ ] The bracket operator can be used to select or replace elements of a vector. To select elements of a vector, one uses an expression of the form

```
x[i]
```

(Continued)

where **x** is a (numeric, logical, or character) vector and **i** is a numeric, logical, or character vector or an expression that results in such a vector. Such a vector is referred to as an index vector. Numeric index vectors select elements of **x** according to their position in **x**, logical index vectors select each element for which the index value is **TRUE**, while character index vectors select elements from **x** according to the names attached to them. With an expression of the form

```
x [i] <- new_values
```

the elements of the vector **x** are replaced with **new_values** (which can be another vector of appropriate length or an expression resulting in such a vector).

sort() This function returns a sorted copy of the vector passed as first argument (the original vector is unaffected). If called as follows,

```
sort(x)
```

returns the elements in increasing order (lesser elements first, greater elements later). A sorted vector in *decreasing* order can be obtained by

```
sort(x,decreasing=TRUE)
```

order() This function returns a numeric vector that can be used to obtain a sorted copy of a vector. For example, with a vector **x**, the two expressions

```
ii <- order(x)
x[ii]
```

can be used.

seq() This function returns a regular sequence of numbers. For example, to obtain the sequence of all integer numbers from **a** to **b**, one can use an expression like

```
seq(from=a,to=b)
```

With other arguments, a different step size or a different total length of the resulting sequence can be specified.

sample() This function creates a vector of sample values. If the first argument is a vector, then a random sample is drawn from the elements of the vector. If the first argument is a number, then a sample from the integer numbers less than or equal to this number is drawn. Whether sampling with replacement is used is determined by the optional argument **replace=** (by default, sampling *without* replacement is used). The optional argument **size=** determines the size of the sample. If omitted, the sample is as large as the original vector; that is, the value of the function is the original vector in random order.

2⬤3 The construction of more complex data types: lists, attributes, and classes

Previously, we discussed four fundamental data types relevant for social science data management: (1) numeric vectors, (2) logical vectors, (3) character vectors, and (4) factors. R knows some more fundamental data types, but these rarely become relevant for the purposes of social science data management.[5] There are, however, quite a few data types discussed later in the book that are constructed from the four fundamental data types with the help of two mechanisms: (1) by combining objects into *lists* and (2) by attaching attributes to objects. These ways of constructing complex data types are discussed below.

2.3.1 Lists

The three fundamental data types introduced earlier – numeric vectors, logical vectors, and character vectors – are collections of values that are all of identical type (numeric, logical, or character string) and which in R cannot exist independently from the vectors that contain them. So far, the three fundamental data types are irreducible or, in R terminology, 'atomic'. The data type *list* differs from atomic data types in so far as lists are collections of objects that can exist independently and that can differ from one another in terms of their type. Thus, a list may contain not only numeric vectors, logical vectors, or character vectors but also other lists. This is why in R terminology they are referred to as 'recursive' data types.[6] At the same time, lists also have commonalities with numeric, logical, and character vectors: they have a well-defined length, their elements have a well-defined order, and one can extract elements or subsets of the elements of a list. Last but not least, one can attach names to the elements of a list.

A list can be created from atomic objects using the function `list()`. The elements need not have the same data type:

```
AList <- list(1:5,
              letters[1:6],
              c(TRUE,FALSE,FALSE,TRUE))
AList
```

```
[[1]]
[1] 1 2 3 4 5

[[2]]
[1] "a" "b" "c" "d" "e" "f"

[[3]]
[1] TRUE FALSE FALSE TRUE
```

As can be seen, the elements of the list are marked in the output with double brackets.

---

[5]These data types include 'pairlist', 'language', 'symbol', 'expression', 'environment' objects, and so on, which are quite useful for advanced programming but not relevant for the kinds of data management this book is concerned with. For those advanced aspects, see Chambers (2008).

[6]There are other recursive data types, which are discussed either later in this book or not at all, depending on their relevance for social science data management.

A list is 'vector-like' in so far as it has a length and its elements are sequentially ordered. However, in contrast to numeric vectors, logical vectors, or character vectors, the elements of a list can 'exist' outside it. For this reason, there are two variants of bracket operators. First, the single-bracket operator returns a list irrespective of whether it is called with a single-element index vector or a longer index vector, as in

```
AList[1:2]
```

```
[[1]]
[1] 1 2 3 4 5

[[2]]
[1] "a" "b" "c" "d" "e" "f"
```

```
AList[1]
```

```
[[1]]
[1] 1 2 3 4 5
```

Second, the double-bracket operator returns a single element of a list, which often is not a list (unless the list contains a list as element):

```
AList[[2]]
```

```
[1] "a" "b" "c" "d" "e" "f"
```

Using the double-bracket operator with a longer index vector leads to unexpected results

```
AList[[1:2]]
```

```
[1] 2
```

(here the second element of the first list element is returned) or an error:

```
AList[[1:3]]
```

```
Error in AList[[1:3]]: recursive indexing failed at level 2
```

Like a vector, a list has a length. The length of the example list **AList** that we just created is

```
length(AList)
```

```
[1] 3
```

List elements can have names attached to them. These names can be attached or requested explicitly using the **names()** function, as in

```
FDR <- list(c("John","Delano"),
            c("Roosevelt"))
names(FDR) <- c("first.name","last.name")
```

Alternatively, the names can be specified by tagging the arguments of a call to the `list()` function:

```
FDR <- list(first.name=c("John","Delano"),
            last.name=c("Roosevelt"))
FDR
```

```
$first.name
[1] "John" "Delano"

$last.name
[1] "Roosevelt"
```

Now if a list is printed, the elements are not marked with double brackets but with dollar signs, which indicates that they are extracted using the dollar operator ($):

```
FDR$last.name
```

```
[1] "Roosevelt"
```

This is equivalent to using the double-bracket operator with a character string index:

```
FDR[["last.name"]]
```

```
[1] "Roosevelt"
```

With lists, it is possible to collect various properties of a set of real objects into a comprehensive data object, something also known as a 'data set' in other software. A minimal data set could, for example, look like this:[7]

```
UK <- list(
    country.name = c("England","Northern Ireland","Scotland",
                                            "Wales"),
    population     = c(54786300,1851600,5373000,3099100),
    area.sq.km     = c(130279,13562,77933,20735),
    GVA.cap        = c(26159,18584,23685,18002))
UK
```

```
$country.name
[1] "England" "Northern Ireland" "Scotland"
[4] "Wales"
```

---

[7]The data come from the Wikipedia article on the four constituent countries of the United Kingdom, https://en.wikipedia.org/wiki/Countries_of_the_United_Kingdom, accessed on 16 April 2020.

```
$population
[1] 54786300 1851600 5373000 3099100

$area.sq.km
[1] 130279 13562 77933 20735

$GVA.cap
[1] 26159 18584 23685 18002
```

In fact, the object class **"data.frame"**, which is used in R to represent data sets, is a special kind of list.

2.3.2 Attributes

Combining atomic vectors and/or other objects into lists is one way of creating more complex data structures; another is attaching *attributes* to existing data structures. An attribute is a piece of information attached to an object that contains data, and this attached information can itself be a numeric, logical, or character vector, or a more complex data type, such as a list. These attributes can be accessed and manipulated using the functions **attributes()** and **attr()**, the former for the complete list of attributes and the latter for individual attributes.

We have already encountered attributes several times in this chapter. For example, the names that are attached to the elements of a vector or a list are attributes: when we create a named vector, that is a vector with names attached to its elements,

```
onetofour <- c(first=1,second=2,third=3,fourth=4)
```

the attribute list contains an element named **"names"** that contains the names:

```
attributes(onetofour)
```

```
$names
[1] "first" "second" "third" "fourth"
```

Other examples of attributes are the labels associated with the levels of a factor, and the **"class"** attribute,[8] which indicates that a certain object is indeed an ordered or unordered factor:

```
satisfaction <- sample(1:4,size=20,replace=TRUE)
satisfaction <- ordered(satisfaction,
                        levels=1:4,
                        labels=c(
                            "not at all",
                            "low",
```

---

[8]Since the names of attributes are character strings and not variables, they are written throughout this book in quotation marks to avoid confusion. For the same reason, the content of the **"class"** attribute is also put in quotation marks.

```
                              "medium",
                              "high"))
attributes(satisfaction)
```

```
$levels
[1] "not at all"  "low"          "medium"          "high"

$class
[1] "ordered"  "factor"
```

As can be seen, the attributes of the ordered factor **satisfaction** are collected in a list with two elements, named **"levels"** and **"class"**.

Since the attributes of the factor play a special role, there are special functions to access them. That is, the following lines of code are equivalent:

```
attr(satisfaction,"levels")
```

```
[1] "not at all" "low"          "medium"       "high"
```

```
levels(satisfaction)
```

```
[1] "not at all" "low"          "medium"       "high"
```

By the same token, the following lines are also equivalent:

```
attr(satisfaction,"class")
```

```
[1] "ordered" "factor"
```

```
class(satisfaction)
```

```
[1] "ordered" "factor"
```

2.3.3 Generic functions, classes, and methods

Many functions in R are *generic* in so far as they may return different values or create different output for different kinds of objects but where the return values or the output created is analogous or similar enough so that it is still practical that the same function is involved. For example, if the call to the function **print()** is made, the created output will differ, depending on the **"class"** attribute of the object **x**.

When the argument of the call of a generic function has a **"class"** attribute, then a specialization of this function is called, given that it is defined. Such a specialization is called a *method* of the generic function. In the terminology of the R function, the move from a generic function to a method is called *method dispatch*.

There are two major variants of classes and methods dispatch – the older, 'S3' variant and the newer, 'S4' variant. In the older variant, the method functions are functions with a name that is composed of the name of the generic function and the name of a class. In the newer variant, the method dispatch is a bit more flexible and complex: it is not restricted to a single argument of the generic function. Instead, if the generic function allows for several arguments, methods can be defined for each combination of object classes these arguments may have.

An important example of the S3 variant is the function `print()`. If it is called with the object `x` as first argument, then

```
print(x)
```

is equivalent to

```
print.data.frame(x)
```

if `x` has a `"class"` attribute that equals `"data.frame"`. If `x` has a `"class"` argument that instead equals `"ts"`, then the call `print(x)` is equivalent to

```
print.ts(x)
```

If `x` does not have a `"class"` attribute, then the call `print(x)` is equivalent to

```
print.default(x)
```

That `print()` is an 'S3-generic' function is indicated by the fact that it contains the line

```
UseMethod("print")
```

in its definition. It should be noted that R packages can provide S3 methods without making the method functions available for calling explicitly. For example, if `x` has the `"class"` attribute `"ts"`, `print(x)` dispatches to the function `print.ts()` inside the *stats* package, but it is not possible to call `print.ts(x)` explicitly (this would to the error message that the function `print.ts` cannot be found).

The other major variant of generic functions and methods dispatch is the S4 variant. In order to work with this, a class has to be explicitly declared with the function `setClass()`, 'S4-generic' functions need to be explicitly declared with the help of the function `setGeneric()`, while methods have to be declared with `setMethod()`. The S4 variant has other features, such as the capability to declare the composition of members of a class and to provide validity checks for them. However, this is clearly beyond the scope of this book, and interested readers are referred to Chambers (2008) or Chambers (2016).

━━━━━━━━━ **Overview Box 2.4** ━━━━━━━━━

The construction of complex data structures: key concepts

List: a sequential data structure that has - like numeric, logical, or character vectors - elements and a length, but in contrast to these vectors, the elements of lists can be of various types and can exist on their own as objects in R memory. There are two variants of the bracket operator, and they have different results when applied to a list: the single-bracket operator, `[]`, extracts a subset of a list, which itself is a list; the double-bracket operator, `[[]]`, can be used to extract a single element from a list, which in turn may be of a data type different from the list. When the index used with the double-bracket operator is a vector of length 2, then it extracts the element of an element of a list (if this is possible), and so on. Many of the more complex data types – for example, those that represent results from a linear regression – are built as lists.

Attribute: information attached to an object and provided with a name. This information could exist on its own as an object in R memory but, instead, is used to document or extend the object to which it is attached. For example, the names attached to the elements of a vector are in fact contained in a character vector attached as a `"names"` attribute.

Class of an object: a character string attached to it as its `"class"` attribute. It is possible to define specific methods for the `print()` function or other generic functions for the object that belong to a specific class or to adapt/define arithmetic operators for such objects. Classes and class attributes are thus powerful mechanisms by which the capabilities of R can be extended.

■━━━━━━━ **Overview Box 2.5** ━━━━━━━■

Concepts of S3 methods dispatch

Generic function: a function that returns different kinds of values or creates different kinds of output depending on the class membership of the arguments with which it is called.

Method: a specialization of a generic function that is called (or 'dispatched') if the argument of the generic function call has the appropriate `"class"` attribute.

Default method: a specialization of a generic function that is used if the main argument does not have a `"class"` attribute or if no method function for the class of the main argument exists.

3

Rectangles of Variables and Observations: Data Frames and Their Management

The present chapter discusses the data structures that social scientists are most likely to work with in their research-related data management activities and the structures' basic representation in R. These are structures that organize data in rows and columns, giving them a rectangular or tabular structure. Often, such data structures are referred to as *data sets*. The rows of data sets usually represent cases, observations, or, more generally, objects in the real world. The columns represent properties by which these cases, observations, or objects are described and compared. These columns are typically referred to as *variables*.[1] The most basic representations of such data structures in R are *data frames*. While data frames are supported by base R, extension packages provide additional data structures, which either add capabilities to data frames or are alternatives that are more useful for some purposes. Some of these extensions are discussed in later chapters.

3 ● 1 The structure of data frames

Social scientists analysing data with R will rarely enter data by hand; rather, they will use data obtained from other sources, be they public data repositories, commercially acquired data, or data collected by a polling or survey institute on their behalf. Nevertheless, to better understand what is possible with data frames and what is not, it helps knowing how they are constructed.

In general, a data frame is just a list composed of vectors and factors. Since these vectors and factors are all used to represent aspects of the same set of cases, observations, or objects in the real world, they all must have the same length.[2] Apart from these vectors and factors, a data frame contains two additional pieces of information: (1) a vector of character strings that contains the names of the variables that the data frame contains in its columns and (2) a vector of character strings that contains names for the rows. These row names may be actual names of observations, but quite often they are simply running numbers.

Data frames can be constructed from vectors and factors using the eponymous function `data.frame()`. This function does not expect a fixed set of arguments; instead, one can call the function with as many arguments as the resulting data frame should have columns. The function also makes it quite easy to assign names to the columns of the resulting data frame. For example, if we have the following data vectors all with the same length

---

[1]It should be noted that this terminology leads to some ambiguity: in R terminology, one uses the term *variable* more generally to refer to symbols that may refer to any data structure in the R workspace.

[2]In fact, lists of the appropriate lengths can also be columns of a data frame. That way, some of the more complex structures that we encounter in later chapters can be represented. But for the usual kinds of data analysis, data frames with lists as columns are likely to be too 'messy'. Since they, nevertheless, may be the result of a more complex process of data acquisition, there is at least one pacakge that deals with this kind of messy data, which will be discussed in a later chapter. It should also be noted that data frames may also contain matrices, which then must have exactly the same number of rows as the vectors and factors in the data frame have elements. Such matrices are not discussed in this book. While they play a central role in the computation of many estimators, they are very rarely a topic of data management.

```
population   <- c(54786300,1851600,5373000,3099100)
area.sq.m    <- c(130279,13562,77933,20735)
GVA.cap      <- c(26159,18584,23685,18002)
```

then constructing a data frame is easy:

```
UK <- data.frame(population,area.sq.m,GVA.cap)
UK
```

```
  population area.sq.m GVA.cap
1   54786300    130279   26159
2    1851600     13562   18584
3    5373000     77933   23685
4    3099100     20735   18002
```

We can now see that the vectors from which the data frame is constructed make the columns of the resulting data frame named UK. From the 'header' of the data frame, it becomes apparent that the function **data.frame()** conveniently created the data frame variables from the original variables from which it is constructed. We can check this by using the **names()** function:

```
names(UK)
```

```
[1] "population" "area.sq.m" "GVA.cap"
```

If we are not satisfied with the names thus provided, we can change them explicitly:

```
names(UK) <- c("Population","Area","GVA")
UK
```

```
  Population   Area   GVA
1   54786300 130279 26159
2    1851600  13562 18584
3    5373000  77933 23685
4    3099100  20735 18002
```

If we enquire the attributes of the data frame UK,

```
attributes(UK)
```

```
$names
[1] "Population" "Area"       "GVA"

$class
[1] "data.frame"

$row.names
[1] 1 2 3 4
```

we see that it has a `"row.names"` attribute. We can enquire it and set it explicitly using the `row.names()` function – for example, to indicate to which constituent country the rows in the UK data frame refer:

```
row.names(UK) <- c("England",
                   "Northern Ireland",
                   "Scotland",
                   "Wales")
UK
```

```
                  Population   Area   GVA
England             54786300 130279 26159
Northern Ireland     1851600  13562 18584
Scotland             5373000  77933 23685
Wales                3099100  20735 18002
```

It is also possible to set the names and row names in the data frame in a single step when the data frame is constructed:

```
UK <- data.frame(
          Population = c(54786300,1851600,5373000,3099100),
          Area       = c(130279,13562,77933,20735),
          GVA        = c(26159,18584,23685,18002),
          row.names  = c("England",
                         "Northern Ireland",
                         "Scotland",
                         "Wales"))
UK
```

```
                  Population   Area   GVA
England             54786300 130279 26159
Northern Ireland     1851600  13562 18584
Scotland             5373000  77933 23685
Wales                3099100  20735 18002
```

Often, one wants to check how many observations a data frame contains or how many variables. The number of observations corresponds to the number of rows of the data frame and can be enquired by `nrow()`, while the number of variables corresponds to the number of columns and can be enquired by `ncol()`. In the present case, `nrow(UK)` results in

```
[1] 4
```

while `ncol(UK)` results in

```
[1] 3
```

Data frames are actually lists with an additional set of attributes – the `"class"`, `"names"`, and `"row.names"` attributes that we just encountered. Hence, it is possible to access and change single variables in a data frame in the same way as one accesses or changes the elements of a list, by using the dollar ($) and double-bracket ([[]]) operators. To get a data frame with a subset of variables, we can use the double-bracket operator, [[]].

For example, to get the values of the Population in the data frame UK, we can just write

```
UK$Population
```

```
[1] 54786300   1851600   5373000   3099100
```

but we can also write UK[["Population"]] to the same effect.

To get a data frame consisting only of the first two variables in UK, we can write

```
UK[1:2]
```

```
                  Population    Area
England           54786300 130279
Northern Ireland   1851600  13562
Scotland           5373000  77933
Wales              3099100  20735
```

but we can also get a 'partial' data frame with the variables Population and Area by

```
UK[c("Population","Area")]
```

```
                  Population    Area
England           54786300 130279
Northern Ireland   1851600  13562
Scotland           5373000  77933
Wales              3099100  20735
```

Since the data in data frames are arranged in rows and columns, it can be useful to access these rows and columns. For this, one can use the bracket operator together with a comma: an index (a numeric, logical, or character vector) between brackets but before the comma then refers to rows, while an index after the comma refers to columns.

Thus, to obtain a data frame that contains only the first two rows of the UK data frame, we can use the line

```
UK[1:2,]
```

```
                  Population  Area    GVA
England           55619400 50301 28096
Northern Ireland   1885400  5460 20000
```

and to get the lines referring to Scotland and Wales, one can make use of the row names and write

```
UK[c("Scotland","Wales"),]
```

	Population	Area	GVA
Scotland	5424800	30090	24800
Wales	3125000	8023	19900

To get a data frame of the first two columns, one can use

```
UK[,1:2]
```

but here one might as well drop the comma because this has the same result as `UK[1:2]`.

━━━━━━━━━━━━ **Overview Box 3.1** ━━━━━━━━━━━━

Data frames: key concepts of this chapter

A **data frame** is an R data structure designed to contain data in a rectangular arrangement, where the rows correspond to *observations* and the columns correspond to *variables*. Parts and aspects of a data frame can be enquired using the following functions and operators:

data.frame() This function can be used to construct a data frame from individual vectors and/or factors.

names() With this function, it is possible to obtain a character vector that contains the names of the variables in a data frame.

row.names() This function can be used to get a character vector with the names attached to the rows of a data frame.

nrow(), ncol(), dim() These functions can be used to get the number of rows, number of columns, and total dimensions (number of rows and columns) of a data frame.

$, [[]] Since a data frame is also a list, the dollar operator and the double-bracket operator can be used to extract a vector or factor that forms a column of the data frame.

[,] The single-bracket operator with comma can be used to extract rows and/or columns from a data frame. Indices (which can be numeric, logical, or character) before the comma are used to select rows; indices after the comma are used to select columns.

To get a data frame composed of the rows of **dataf** indexed by **i**, one uses

```
dataf[i,]
```

To get a data frame composed of the columns of **dataf** indexed by **j**, one uses

```
dataf[,j]
```

To get a data frame composed of the intersection of the rows indexed by **i** and the columns indexed by **j**, one uses

```
dataf[i,j]
```

Accessing and changing variables in data frames

Data frames are useful for putting together several variables that refer to the same set of cases or observations and to encapsulate them into a single object. While it is possible to access the variables in a data frame in the way described above, this can become tedious if one wants to obtain summaries of several variables or create new variables within a data frame from computations based on other variables. Fortunately, R already has functions that facilitate the creation of such data summaries and data modifications, namely the functions `with()` and `within()`. Besides these functions, R also has the function `attach()`, by which the variables inside a data frame can be made available for use as if they were defined in the global workspace. Yet using `attach()` can become error-prone because one needs to keep track of which data frames are currently 'attached' by this function. This is illustrated in the following.

In this example, we use data from the 2010 British Election Study (BES), contained in a file named `"bes2010feelings-prepost.RData"`:

```
load("bes2010feelings-prepost.RData")
```

The file contains two objects: a data frame from the pre-election wave and a data frame from the post-election election wave of the study. Both contain the same variables.

Using the dollar operator, we can get variables from the pre-election data frame and compute the average feelings towards various party leaders. But this is a bit tedious because we have to write down the name of the data frame `bes2010flngs_pre` several times:

```
c(
    Brown   = mean(bes2010flngs_pre$flng.brown,na.rm=TRUE),
    Cameron = mean(bes2010flngs_pre$flng.cameron,na.rm=TRUE),
    Clegg   = mean(bes2010flngs_pre$flng.clegg,na.rm=TRUE),
    Salmond = mean(bes2010flngs_pre$flng.salmond,na.rm=TRUE),
    Jones   = mean(bes2010flngs_pre$flng.jones,na.rm=TRUE)
)
```

```
   Brown   Cameron    Clegg  Salmond     Jones
4.339703  5.090708 4.557366 4.505660  4.235949
```

Somewhat more convenient, but quickly getting messy, is the use of `attach()`. First, we attach the data frame from the pre-election wave and compute the pre-election average feelings. For added convenience, we also define a function `Mean()`:

```
Mean <- function(x,...) mean(x,na.rm=TRUE,...)
attach(bes2010flngs_pre)
c(
    Brown   = Mean(flng.brown),
    Cameron = Mean(flng.cameron),
    Clegg   = Mean(flng.clegg),
    Salmond = Mean(flng.salmond),
    Jones   = Mean(flng.jones)
)
```

```
    Brown   Cameron     Clegg  Salmond     Jones
 4.339703 5.090708 4.557366 4.505660 4.235949
```

Next, we attach the data frame from the post-election wave and compute the post-election average feelings:

```
attach(bes2010flngs_post)
```

```
The following objects are masked from bes2010flngs_pre:

    flng.bnp, flng.brown, flng.cameron, flng.clegg, flng.cons,
    flng.green, flng.jones, flng.labour, flng.libdem, flng.pcym,
    flng.salmond, flng.snp, flng.ukip, region
```

```
c(
    Brown   = Mean(flng.brown),
    Cameron = Mean(flng.cameron),
    Clegg   = Mean(flng.clegg),
    Salmond = Mean(flng.salmond),
    Jones   = Mean(flng.jones)
)
```

```
    Brown   Cameron     Clegg  Salmond     Jones
 4.448116 5.206120 5.001756 4.228707 4.509317
```

A notification is displayed when the second data frame is attached, to remind us that we have already attached another data frame with the same variables. But we still need to keep in mind where the variables that we refer to come from. Suppose we detach one of the data frames

```
detach(bes2010flngs_post)
```

but the other data frame is still attached. As a consequence, the following code gives the result

```
c(
    Brown   = Mean(flng.brown),
    Cameron = Mean(flng.cameron),
    Clegg   = Mean(flng.clegg),
    Salmond = Mean(flng.salmond),
    Jones   = Mean(flng.jones)
)
```

```
    Brown   Cameron     Clegg  Salmond     Jones
 4.339703 5.090708 4.557366 4.505660 4.235949
```

though the result would have been different had we first detached the other data frame, `bes2010flngs_pre`. For housekeeping, after finishing this example we detach the other data frame:

```
detach(bes2010flngs_pre)
```

Since attaching and detaching can easily go wrong – the result of `Mean(flng.cameron)`, and so on, depends on the order in which the data frames `bes1010flngs_pre` and `bes2010flngs_post` are attached and/or detached – it is preferable to use `with()` as a much safer alternative.

The function `with()` takes two arguments, a data frame and an expression (or a compound expression, where several expressions are enclosed in curly brackets/braces, i.e. { and }). By using `with()`, we basically tell R to evaluate the expression given as second arguments, with variables from the data frame given as first argument (if these variables exist there).

For example, with the following code we tell R to compute the averages of several variables in the data frame `bes2010flngs_pre`:

```
with(bes2010flngs_pre,c(
     Brown    = Mean(flng.brown),
     Cameron = Mean(flng.cameron),
     Clegg    = Mean(flng.clegg),
     Salmond = Mean(flng.salmond),
     Jones    = Mean(flng.jones)
))
```

```
   Brown  Cameron    Clegg  Salmond    Jones
4.339703 5.090708 4.557366 4.505660 4.235949
```

Then, we do the same with (the variables in) the data frame `bes2010flngs_post`:

```
with(bes2010flngs_post,c(
     Brown    = Mean(flng.brown),
     Cameron = Mean(flng.cameron),
     Clegg    = Mean(flng.clegg),
     Salmond = Mean(flng.salmond),
     Jones    = Mean(flng.jones)
))
```

```
   Brown  Cameron    Clegg  Salmond    Jones
4.448116 5.206120 5.001756 4.228707 4.509317
```

The advantage of using `with()` should have become clear by this example: it is relatively easy to copy and modify code written to obtain averages for the pre-election wave to obtain code to obtain averages for the post-election wave. At the same time, we avoid the potential confusion that may arise if we forget to `detach()` a data frame or if we `attach()` data frames in the wrong order.

The functions `attach()` and `with()` can be used to access the variables in a data frame to compute summaries of them but not to modify them or create new variables from them. It is possible to do this with the dollar operator, but this can quickly become tedious. Fortunately, there is a function, `within()`, that allows one to avoid such tedium. A call to the function `within()` has the same structure as a call to the function `with()`, but the result is different: while `with()` returns the result of the expression given as second argument after evaluating it with the variables in the data frame, `within()` returns a data frame which is a modified copy of its first argument with new or modified variables. Or more simply put, while using the function `with()` tells R to 'compute the following summaries with the variables in this data frame', using the function `within()` tells R to 'make the following modifications to the variables *within* this data frame'.

For an illustration of the use of `within()`, we create within the data frame `bes2010flngs_pre` a set of new variables that represent the 'relative' affective evaluation of the various candidates by the respondents, which we define as the average of the evaluations of the leaders of the three major parties. (For simplicity, we ignore the leaders of Plaid Cymru and the SNP [Scottish National Party], the parties that run candidates only in a part of the UK.)

For this purpose, we first create a variable with the average evaluation of Gordon Brown, David Cameron, and Nick Clegg. We then subtract this average from the evaluation of these three leaders.

```
bes2010flngs_pre <- within(bes2010flngs_pre,{
    ave_flng <-   (flng.brown + flng.cameron + flng.clegg)/3
    rel_flng.brown    <- flng.brown - ave_flng
    rel_flng.cameron <- flng.cameron - ave_flng
    rel_flng.clegg    <- flng.clegg - ave_flng
})
```

The code with the same effect but using the dollar operator is quite tedious:

```
bes2010flngs_pre$ave_flng <- (bes2010flngs_pre$flng.brown +
                              bes2010flngs_pre$flng.cameron +
                              bes2010flngs_pre$flng.clegg)/3
bes2010flngs_pre$rel_flng.brown    <- (bes2010flngs_pre$flng.brown
                                   - bes2010flngs_pre$ave_flng)
bes2010flngs_pre$rel_flng.cameron <- (bes2010flngs_pre$flng.cameron
                                   - bes2010flngs_pre$ave_flng)
bes2010flngs_pre$rel_flng.clegg    <- (bes2010flngs_pre$flng.clegg
                                   - bes2010flngs_pre$ave_flng)
```

It contains no less than 13 applications of the dollar operator. Apart from its tediousness, code like this is difficult to maintain. For example, to adapt this code for the post-election wave, one has to take care to replace all 13 instances of '`bes2010flngs_pre$`'.

━━━━━━ **Overview Box 3.2** ━━━━━━

Functions to conveniently access and modify variables in a data frame

`attach()` This function attaches an object to the 'search path' of R; that is, R will look inside this object if some code uses the name of a variable not present in the global workspace. If `dataf` is the name of a data frame, then after `attach(dataf)`, the variables in this data frame can be referred to without using the dollar operator. For example, instead of `print(dataf$some.var)`, one can simply write `print(some.var)`.

`detach()` This function removes an object from the 'search path', so that R no longer will look inside this object for variables.

`with()` This function makes the variables in a data frame temporarily available for use in the expressions that appear as the second argument to the function, as in

```
with(dataf,mean(x)+mean(y))
```

The return value of `with()` is the result of such an expression. This is the recommended way of accessing variables in a data frame if these variables are not being modified.

`within()` This function makes it possible to create or modify variables in a data frame without having to use the dollar operator. These creations and modifications are done in the expressions that form the second argument to the function, as in

```
dataf <- within(dataf, z <- x + y )
```

The return value of `within()` is a modified data frame.

3●3 Manipulating data frames

3.3.1 Subsetting

Often, one is interested in working with a subset of the available data. For example, if one has a data set about political attitudes and party preferences in Germany, one may be interested in the particular patterns of politics in East Germany. Usually, such subsets are defined by a logical condition: for example, that an East–West variable has a value indicating that certain observations belong to East Germany. Also, it is not always the full set of variables in a given data frame that are of real interest to the researcher, who therefore might want to work with just a selection of the variables in it. The function `subset()` can be used for both purposes. It allows for up to three arguments: first, the data frame from which the subset is obtained; second, a logical vector or an expression resulting in a logical vector, which usually involves variables in the data frame; and a third argument, usually tagged with `select=`, with which the variables of interest can be selected.

We illustrate the use of `subset()` by looking again at the 2010 BES data. In this example, we form a subset with the respondents in Scotland and the variables that refer to the affective evaluations of the parties and their leaders:

```
bes2010flngs_pre_scotland <- subset(bes2010flngs_pre,
                            region=="Scotland",
                            select=c(
                                    flng.labour,
                                    flng.cons,
                                    flng.libdem,
```

```
                                      flng.snp,
                                      flng.brown,
                                      flng.cameron,
                                      flng.clegg,
                                      flng.salmond
                              ))
```

The second argument selects observations from Scotland using the comparison `region==` `"Scotland"`, while the third argument, tagged with `select=`, selects the variables concerning the parties that run candidates in Scotland, that is `flng.labour`, `flng.cons`, `flng.libdem`, and `flng.snp`, and their leaders, that is `flng.brown`, `flng.cameron`, `flng.clegg`, and `flng.salmond`. We can now compare the average feeling about Gordon Brown in the whole sample

```
with(bes2010flngs_pre,mean(flng.brown,na.rm=TRUE))
```

```
[1] 4.339703
```

with the average in the subsample from Scotland

```
with(bes2010flngs_pre_scotland,mean(flng.brown,na.rm=TRUE))
```

```
[1] 5.395
```

Of course, the same result can also be achieved using the bracket operator discussed earlier, but the code there is considerably more tedious. Here, we use the expression `bes2010flngs_` `pre$region=="Scotland"` to select the rows by writing it between the square brackets but before the comma, and the character vector with the names of the desired variables after the comma:

```
bes2010flngs_pre_scotland <- bes2010flngs_pre[
bes2010flngs_pre$region=="Scotland",c(
                        "flng.labour",
                        "flng.cons",
                        "flng.libdem",
                        "flng.snp",
                        "flng.brown",
                        "flng.cameron",
                        "flng.clegg",
                        "flng.salmond"
)]
```

3.3.2 Combining data on different variables about the same observations: merging data frames

A quite common task of data management is to join data sets about the same range of cases or observations coming from different sources. This task is commonly referred to as *merging*. Here, one can distinguish between a one-to-one merge and a hierarchical, one-to-many, or many-to-one merge. In the first variant, two data sets are joined in such a way that each row in the first data set is combined (if possible) with a row in the other data set that refers to the same case or observation. In the second variant, a data set of individual (or lower-level) observations is joined with another data set of the contexts in which the individual-level observations are nested or embedded (e.g. voters within voting districts or citizens within countries). In both variants, information is needed on which rows of the first data set are to be combined with which rows of the second. Figure 3.1 illustrates these two variants of merging data sets.

The function needed to merge data frames in R is appropriately named `merge()`. This function requires at least two arguments, namely the two data frames being merged. In addition, it allows for an (optional) argument tagged with `by=`, which indicates the variables whose values identify the matching rows in the two data frames. If these variables have different names in both data frames, one can instead use the optional arguments `by.x=` and `by.y=`, where the first of these identifies variables in the first data frame and the second identifies variables in the second data frame. The following example illustrates the use of this function with 'real-world' data. The data used in these examples again come from the 2010 BES. To be specific, they are data from the pre-election wave with different variables and data about the electoral districts of the 2010 general election. They are contained in the file `"bes2010feel-ings-prepost-for-merge.RData"`:

```
load("bes2010feelings-prepost-for-merge.RData")
```

The first example pertains to a one-to-one merging of data frames that pertain to the same set of observations but differ in the variables. The data frames are `bes2010flngs_parties_pre` and `bes2010flngs_leaders_pre`. The variable names differ, but the numbers of observations are the same.

```
str(bes2010flngs_parties_pre)
```

```
'data.frame':  1935 obs. of 12 variables:
 $ id          : num  40103 40107 40109 40110 40111 ...
 $ refno       : num  312 312 312 312 312 312 312 312 312 312 ...
 $ vote        : Factor w/ 9 levels "Labour","Conservatives",..: NA
      NA NA 1 1 1 3 1 3 ...
 $ flng.labour : num  5 1 3 6 8 5 6 2 8 3 ...
 $ flng.cons   : num  6 6 4 6 4 1 3 3 3 3 ...
 $ flng.libdem : num  4 7 5 5 5 4 0 5 4 9 ...
 $ flng.snp    : num  NA NA NA NA NA NA NA NA NA NA ...
 $ flng.pcym   : num  NA NA NA NA NA NA NA NA NA NA ...
 $ flng.green  : num  7 6 5 5 4 4 1 5 5 5 ...
 $ flng.ukip   : num  3 0 0 3 NA 0 NA 2 3 1 ...
 $ flng.bnp    : num  0 0 0 2 2 0 0 0 0 0 ...
 $ region      : Factor w/ 3 levels "England","Scotland",..: 1 NA 1
      1 NA 1 1 1 1 1 ...
```

```
str(bes2010flngs_parties_pre)
```

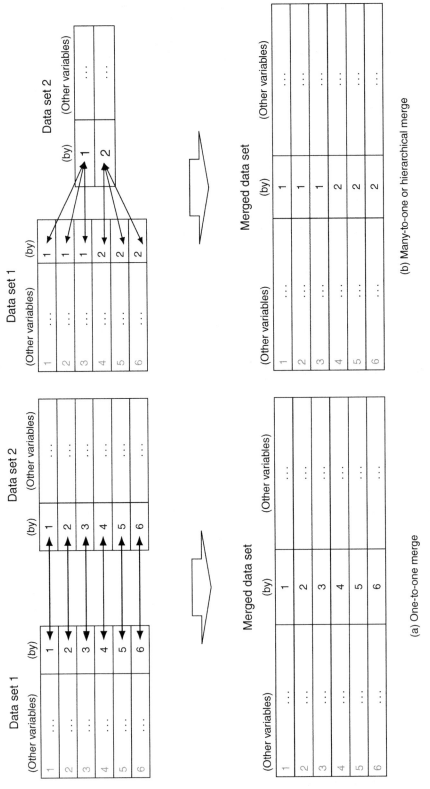

Figure 3.1 Illustration of two variants of merging data sets

```
'data.frame':     1935   obs. of 12 variables:
 $ id           : num   40103 40107 40109 40110 40111 ...
 $ refno        : num   312 312 312 312 312 312 312 312 312 312 ...
 $ vote         : Factor w/ 9 levels "Labour","Conservatives",..: NA
         NA NA 1 1 1 3 1 3 ...
 $ flng.labour  : num   5 1 3 6 8 5 6 2 8 3 ...
 $ flng.cons    : num   6 6 4 6 4 1 3 3 3 3 ...
 $ flng.libdem  : num   4 7 5 5 5 4 0 5 4 9 ...
 $ flng.snp     : num   NA NA NA NA NA NA NA NA NA NA ...
 $ flng.pcym    : num   NA NA NA NA NA NA NA NA NA NA ...
 $ flng.green   : num   7 6 5 5 4 4 1 5 5 5 ...
 $ flng.ukip    : num   3 0 0 3 NA 0 NA 2 3 1 ...
 $ flng.bnp     : num   0 0 0 2 2 0 0 0 0 0 ...
 $ region       : Factor w/ 3 levels "England","Scotland",..: 1 NA 1
         1 NA 1 1 1 1 1 ...
```

Both data frames share a variable `id` that identifies individual respondents, so we use the name of this variable in the `by=` argument to match rows:

```
bes2010flngs_pre_merged <- merge(
    bes2010flngs_parties_pre,
    bes2010flngs_leaders_pre,
    by="id"
)
```

If the variables used for matching the rows have different names, one would have to name arguments `by.x=` and `by.y=` instead. On the other hand, if the matching variable is the only variable that is present in both data frames, it is automatically selected for matching rows, so the following code works as well:

```
bes2010flngs_pre_merged <- merge(
    bes2010flngs_parties_pre,
    bes2010flngs_leaders_pre
)
```

We check whether we were successful by looking at the structure of the resulting data frame:

```
str(bes2010flngs_pre_merged)
```

```
'data.frame':     1935 obs. of   17 variables:
 $ id           : num   40103 40107 40109 40110 40111 ...
 $ refno        : num   312 312 312 312 312 312 312 312 312 312 ...
 $ vote         : Factor w/ 9 levels "Labour","Conservatives",..: NA
         NA NA 1 1 1 3 1 3 ...
 $ flng.labour  : num   5 1 3 6 8 5 6 2 8 3 ...
 $ flng.cons    : num   6 6 4 6 4 1 3 3 3 3 ...
 $ flng.libdem  : num   4 7 5 5 5 4 0 5 4 9 ...
 $ flng.snp     : num   NA NA NA NA NA NA NA NA NA NA ...
 $ flng.pcym    : num   NA NA NA NA NA NA NA NA NA NA ...
 $ flng.green   : num   7 6 5 5 4 4 1 5 5 5 ...
```

```
$ flng.ukip     : num  3 0 0 3 NA 0 NA 2 3 1 ...
$ flng.bnp      : num  0 0 0 2 2 0 0 0 0 0 ...
$ region        : Factor w/ 3 levels "England","Scotland",..: 1 NA 1
   1 NA 1 1 1 1 ...
$ flng.brown    : num  6 3 8 4 5 5 5 4 7 4 ...
$ flng.cameron  : num  3 7 7 4 5 0 3 6 2 2 ...
$ flng.clegg    : num  3 5 4 3 5 4 2 7 4 8 ...
$ flng.salmond  : num  NA NA NA NA NA NA NA NA NA NA ...
$ flng.jones    : num  5 3 10 7 5 1 7 1 6 4 ...
```

The second example is a many-to-one merge in which we match individual-level observations with data on electoral districts. The data frame `constwin` contains data about the electoral districts. Both the individual-level data frame and the district-level data frame contain a variable named `refno`, which we use as the matching variable.

```
bes2010pre_merged <- merge(
    bes2010flngs_pre_merged,
    constwin,
    by = "refno"
)
```

We use `str()` again to see whether we were successful:

```
str(bes2010pre_merged)
```

```
'data.frame':    1935 obs. of 22 variables:
$ refno         : num  1 1 1 1 1 1 1 1 1 1 ...
$ id            : num  77920 57911 57905 57906 57910 ...
$ vote          : Factor w/ 9 levels "Labour","Conservatives",..: 5
   NA 1 1 2 2 1 NA 1 NA ...
$ flng.labour   : num  6 5 10 10 0 8 5 9 7 4 ...
$ flng.cons     : num  5 3 0 0 9 9 2 5 4 0 ...
$ flng.libdem   : num  5 3 3 4 3 6 2 2 2 0 ...
$ flng.snp      : num  NA NA NA NA NA NA NA NA NA NA ...
$ flng.pcym     : num  7 3 5 3 3 5 4 5 1 3 ...
$ flng.green    : num  7 4 3 0 6 5 4 5 6 0 ...
$ flng.ukip     : num  5 0 4 6 2 6 NA 7 0 NA ...
$ flng.bnp      : num  5 0 0 0 10 5 NA 5 6 0 ...
$ region        : Factor w/ 3 levels "England","Scotland",..: 3 3
   3 3 NA 3 NA NA 3 ...
$ flng.brown    : num  0 6 8 10 0 4 5 0 6 7 ...
$ flng.cameron  : num  8 5 0 0 9 8 3 0 4 0 ...
$ flng.clegg    : num  NA 5 4 0 0 6 NA NA 2 0 ...
$ flng.salmond  : num  NA NA NA NA NA NA NA NA NA NA ...
$ flng.jones    : num  4 6 0 10 0 7 5 NA 7 0 ...
$ seat          : Factor w/ 632 levels "Aberavon","Aberconwy",..: 1
   1 1 1 1 1 1 1 1 1 ...
$ win05         : Factor w/ 6 levels "Conservative",..: 2 2 2 2 2 2
   2 2 2 2 ...
```

```
$ win10        : Factor w/ 7 levels "","Conservative",..: 3 3 3 3 3
      3 3 3 3 3 ...
$ maj05        : num   46.3 46.3 46.3 46.3 46.3 46.3 46.3 46.3 46.3 46.3 ...
$ maj10        : num   35.7 35.7 35.7 35.7 35.7 35.7 35.7 35.7 35.7 35.7 ...
```

We can see that the order of the observations in the merged data frame differs from the order in the individual-level data frame. The observations are ordered by the matching variable **refno** instead.

One cannot always be sure that each row of the first data frame finds a matching row in the second data frame, and vice versa. What happens in such cases is determined by the optional arguments **all.x=** and **all.y=**. This is illustrated by the following code, which uses artificial data for reasons of simplicity (the artificial data are contained in the data frames **df1** and **df2**):

```
df1 <- data.frame(
    x = c(1,3,2,4,6,5),
    y = c(1,1,2,2,2,4)
)
df1
```

```
  x y
1 1 1
2 3 1
3 2 2
4 4 2
5 6 2
6 5 4
```

```
df2 <- data.frame(
    a = c(51,42,22),
    b = c(1,2,3)
)
df2
```

```
   a b
1 51 1
2 42 2
3 22 3
```

In the first attempt at merging, the data frames do not share any variables; hence, there is no way of determining which of the rows of the two data frames 'belong together'. In such a case, each row of the first data frame is matched with each row of the second data frame. Hence, the number of rows of the result equals the products of the numbers of rows of the two data frames.

```
df12 <- merge(df1,df2)
df12
```

```
    x y  a b
1  1 1 1 51 1
2  3 1 51 1
3  2 2 51 1
4  4 2 51 1
5  6 2 51 1
6  5 4 51 1
7  1 1 42 2
8  3 1 42 2
9  2 2 42 2
10 4 2 42 2
11 6 2 42 2
12 5 4 42 2
13 1 1 22 3
14 3 1 22 3
15 2 2 22 3
16 4 2 22 3
17 6 2 22 3
18 5 4 22 3
```

In the second attempt, we explicitly specify the variables used for matching, and the result is different. It contains only rows for which matches can be found in both data frames:

```
merge(df1,df2,by.x="y",by.y="b")
```

```
  y x  a
1 1 1 51
2 1 3 51
3 2 2 42
4 2 4 42
5 2 6 42
```

With the optional argument `all.x=TRUE`, the result has a row for each row from the first data frame, whether or not a match for it is found; missing information (from non-existing rows of the second data frame) is filled up with 'NA':

```
merge(df1,df2,by.x="y",by.y="b",
      all.x=TRUE)
```

```
  y x  a
1 1 1 51
2 1 3 51
3 2 2 42
4 2 4 42
5 2 6 42
6 4 5 NA
```

With `all.y=TRUE`, the result contains all rows from the second data frame:

```
merge(df1,df2,by.x="y",by.y="b",
      all.y=TRUE)
```

```
  y  x   a
1 1   1 51
2 1   3 51
3 2   2 42
4 2   4 42
5 2   6 42
6 3 NA 22
```

The argument setting `all=TRUE` is equivalent to `all.x=TRUE` and `all.y=TRUE`:

```
merge(df1,df2,by.x="y",by.y="b",
      all=TRUE)
```

```
y x      a
1 1   1 51
2 1   3 51
3 2   2 42
4 2   4 42
5 2   6 42
6 3 NA 22
7 4   5 NA
```

3.3.3 Appending

In the previous section, we looked at merging pairs of data frames that contain different kinds of information (in different variables) about the same set of observations or cases into a single data frame. A different kind of data management task is to combine data frames that contain this same set of variables but that differ in the range of the observations or cases. This task of *appending* or *concatenating* data frames may appear simple in comparison with merging. It is usually much easier to check whether the variables of two data frames are the same than whether the rows of two data frames can be combined, not least because the number of variables in a data frame is much smaller than the number of observations or cases. To combine a series of data frames with the same variables into a single data frame, R provides the function `rbind()` (for 'bind together row-wise').[3] This function requires as arguments just the data frames to be combined. These data frames are expected to have the same variable names, not necessarily in the same order. If there are some variables present in one data frame that are not present in the other, an attempt to combine them with `rbind()` will fail.[4] This is demonstrated in the following example.

We start this example by loading some example data from the BES 2010:

---

[3]There is also a function `cbind()` for a 'column-wise binding' of its arguments. Yet this function is difficult to use correctly because it is usually not that easy to ascertain that the data frames so combined contain the same set of observations.

[4]Here, it is assumed that variables with the same name also have the same meaning. If this is not the case, the result of `rbind()` will be misleading.

```
load("bes2010feelings-for-append.RData")
```

We now have two data frames for the BES 2010, one from the pre-election wave and another from the post-election wave. They contain the same variables but in a different order:

```
str(bes2010flngs_pre)
```

```
'data.frame':   1935 obs. of  14 variables:
 $ flng.brown  : num  6 3 8 4 5 5 5 4 7 4 ...
 $ flng.cameron: num  3 7 7 4 5 0 3 6 2 2 ...
 $ flng.clegg  : num  3 5 4 3 5 4 2 7 4 8 ...
 $ flng.salmond: num  NA NA NA NA NA NA NA NA NA NA ...
 $ flng.jones  : num  5 3 10 7 5 1 7 1 6 4 ...
 $ flng.labour : num  5 1 3 6 8 5 6 2 8 3 ...
 $ flng.cons   : num  6 6 4 6 4 1 3 3 3 3 ...
 $ flng.libdem : num  4 7 5 5 5 4 0 5 4 9 ...
 $ flng.snp    : num  NA NA NA NA NA NA NA NA NA NA ...
 $ flng.pcym   : num  NA NA NA NA NA NA NA NA NA NA ...
 $ flng.green  : num  7 6 5 5 4 4 1 5 5 5 ...
 $ flng.ukip   : num  3 0 0 3 NA 0 NA 2 3 1 ...
 $ flng.bnp    : num  0 0 0 2 2 0 0 0 0 0 ...
 $ region      : Factor w/ 3 levels "England","Scotland",..: 1 NA 1
          1 NA 1 1 1 1 1 ...
```

```
str(bes2010flngs_post)
```

```
'data.frame':   3075 obs. of  14 variables:
 $ flng.jones  : num  NA NA NA NA NA NA NA NA NA NA ...
 $ flng.labour : num  5 2 9 7 0 2 6 5 7 2 ...
 $ flng.ukip   : num  NA NA NA NA NA NA NA NA NA NA ...
 $ flng.libdem : num  4 5 4 4 6 NA 4 4 7 7 ...
 $ flng.brown  : num  5 2 5 7 0 2 3 2 5 2 ...
 $ flng.bnp    : num  NA NA NA NA NA NA NA NA NA NA ...
 $ flng.snp    : num  NA NA NA NA NA NA NA NA NA NA ...
 $ flng.salmond: num  NA NA NA NA NA NA NA NA NA NA ...
 $ flng.pcym   : num  NA NA NA NA NA NA NA NA NA NA ...
 $ flng.cons   : num  5 5 3 10 10 3 3 8 7 7 ...
 $ flng.cameron: num  5 6 5 3 8 10 7 8 8 7 ...
 $ flng.green  : num  NA NA NA NA NA NA NA NA NA NA ...
 $ flng.clegg  : num  NA 4 3 NA 6 3 5 4 7 6 ...
 $ region      : Factor w/ 3 levels "England","Scotland",..: 1 1 1
          1 1 1 1 1 1 ...
```

If the variables in the two data frames differ, trying to use rbind() to append the data frames fails:

```
bes2010flngs_prepost <- rbind(bes2010flngs_pre[-1],
                          bes2010flngs_post[-1])
```

```
Error in match.names(clabs, names(xi)): names do not match previous
      names
```

However, if the variables in the two data frames are the same but differ in their order, then `rbind()` is successful and the variables in the resulting data frame ordered as in the first data frame:

```
bes2010flngs_prepost <- rbind(bes2010flngs_pre,
                              bes2010flngs_post)
```

To check the result of `rbind()`, we compare the tail ends of the resulting data frame `bes2010flngs_prepost` and the data frame given as second argument to `rbind()`. The tail ends are identical except for the order of the variables.

```
tail(bes2010flngs_prepost)
```

	flng.brown	flng.cameron	flng.clegg	flng.salmond	flng.jones
79219.2	2	8	7	NA	5
79220.2	0	5	5	NA	4
79621.2	8	4	7	NA	5
79622.2	8	5	3	NA	6
80019.2	5	8	6	NA	5
80020.2	7	6	8	NA	6

```
tail(bes2010flngs_post)
```

	flng.jones	flng.labour	flng.ukip	flng.libdem	flng.brown
79219.2	5	3	4	7	2
79220.2	4	3	0	4	0
79621.2	5	7	4	6	8
79622.2	6	8	4	4	8
80019.2	5	3	6	5	5
80020.2	6	7	2	7	7

If a data frame results from appending a set of data frames, the source or origin of the observations in the data frame – that is, which of the appended data frames they come from – can be identified only if all of the combined data frames contain a variable that has a single and unique value for each of them. Yet some R packages provide variants of `rbind()` that add the information needed to identify the source of the observations. For example, the *gdata* package (Heath et al., 2017) provides the function `combine()`, and the *memisc* package (Elff, 2019) provides the function `collect()`. These functions add information about the source of the observations being combined. The latter function can be used as illustrated in the following example:

```
library(memisc)
bes2010flngs_prepost <- collect(Pre=bes2010flngs_pre,
                                Post=bes2010flngs_post,
                                sourcename="wave")
```

In this example, the same data frames are combined as in the example for `rbind()`, but with the `sourcename=` argument, we create a variable that describes the 'origin' of the data. We compare the frequency distribution of this variable with the lengths of the data frames that we combined:

```
table(bes2010flngs_prepost$wave)
```

```
 Pre Post
1935 3075
```

```
c(
    Pre=nrow(bes2010flngs_pre),
    Post=nrow(bes2010flngs_post)
)
```

```
 Pre Post
1935 3075
```

As can be seen, the table of frequencies and the combined row numbers are identical.

3.3.4 Reshaping

Panel data or data with repeated measurements can be considered to have two proper layouts: one layout is the 'long format', in which different measurement occasions or item responses in different interview waves are placed in different rows of a data set, so that the objects or individuals about which the measures were taken are the 'contexts' of the rows in the data set. The other layout is the 'wide format', in which different measurement occasions or item responses in different interview waves are placed in different columns of the data set, so that the objects or individuals are the rows. Other kinds of data that can be arranged in a wide and a long format are choice data (if all choosers face the same set of alternatives). For example, it is possible to represent individuals' choices from a set of alternatives in a 'compressed' wide format, where the choices are recorded in a factor variable (with a factor level for each alternative), or in a long format, where each alternative is represented by a row and where a dummy variable indicates whether the alternative is chosen by the individual or not. These two layouts are illustrated in Figure 3.2.

		x			y		
		$t = 1$	$t = 2$	$t = 3$	$t = 1$	$t = 2$	$t = 3$
id	v	x_1	x_2	x_3	y_1	y_2	y_3
1	35	1.1	1.2	1.3	2.5	2.7	2.9
2	42	2.1	2.2	2.3	3.5	3.7	3.9
⋮	⋮	⋮	⋮	⋮	⋮	⋮	⋮

(a) Wide format

id	v	t	x	y
1	35	1	1.1	2.5
1	35	2	1.2	2.7
1	35	3	1.3	2.9
2	42	1	2.1	3.5
2	42	2	2.2	3.7
2	42	3	2.3	3.9
⋮	⋮	⋮	⋮	⋮

(b) Long format

Figure 3.2 Illustration of wide and long arrangements of the same data

Since both data layouts contain the same information (but only arranged in different ways), it should be possible to change or reshape data from wide format into long format, and vice versa. For this, R provides a function aptly named **reshape()**. This function requires, apart from the data frame being reshaped, information about the variables that correspond to multiple measures of variables in long format and information about the variable that distinguishes the measurement occasions in the long format. The information about the multiple measures is given as arguments to the function with tags **varying=** and **v.names=**. The **varying=** argument is expected to be a list of variable names corresponding to multiple measurements in the wide format, while the **v.names=** argument is expected to be a vector of variable names corresponding to multiple measurements in the long format. The information about the measurement occasions is given by function arguments with the tags **times=** and **timevar=**, respectively. Finally, the function needs information about whether the data are to be reshaped from wide into long format or from long into wide format. The following example illustrates the use of the function **reshape()** with the artificial data of Figure 3.2. In this example, we construct the data frame, the first rows of which appeared in the previous illustration:

```
example.data.wide <- data.frame(
    id = 1:2,
    v  = c(35,42),
    x1 = c(1.1,2.1),
    x2 = c(1.2,2.2),
    x3 = c(1.3,2.3),
    y1 = c(2.5,3.5),
    y2 = c(2.7,3.7),
    y3 = c(2.9,3.9))
example.data.wide
```

```
   id  v  x1   x2   x3   y1   y2   y3
1   1 35 1.1  1.2  1.3  2.5  2.7  2.9
2   2 42 2.1  2.2  2.3  3.5  3.7  3.9
```

We now call **reshape()** to cast the data into long format:

```
example.data.long <- reshape(data=example.data.wide,
                        varying=list(
                            # The first group of variables
                            # in wide format
                            c("x1","x2","x3"),
                            # The second group of variables
                            # in wide format
                            c("y1","y2","y3")
                        ),
                        v.names=c("x","y"),
                        timevar="t",
                        times=1:3,
                        direction="long")
example.data.long
```

```
      id  v t   x    y
1.1   1 35 1 1.1  2.5
2.1   2 42 1 2.1  3.5
1.2   1 35 2 1.2  2.7
2.2   2 42 2 2.2  3.7
1.3   1 35 3 1.3  2.9
2.3   2 42 3 2.3  3.9
```

In order to change the data from long to wide format, we can use almost the same function call, the only difference being the `direction=` argument:

```
example.data.wide.a <- reshape(data=example.data.long,
                      varying=list(
                          # The first group of variables
                          # in wide format
                          c("x1","x2","x3"),
                          # The second group of variables
                          # in wide format
                          c("y1","y2","y3")
                          ),
                      v.names=c("x","y"),
                      timevar="t",
                      times=1:3,
                      direction="wide")
```

However, the second call of **reshape()** does not completely revert the first call, because the order of the variables is now different:

```
example.data.wide.a
```

```
      id  v  x1  y1   x2  y2   x3  y3
1.1   1 35 1.1 2.5 1.2 2.7 1.3 2.9
2.1   2 42 2.1 3.5 2.2 3.7 2.3 3.9
```

Although the names of the arguments of **reshape()** suggest as much, it is not necessary that the multiple measurements are made at different points in time. The following example shows that multiple measurements may also concern the relations that individuals may have with certain objects or the feelings they may have towards such objects. In this example, we rearrange the data frame **bes201flngs_pre**, which we already encountered in earlier examples, from the wide into the long format, where the feelings towards the parties and their leaders are considered as multiple measurements. A complication that arises here is that no questions about the leaders of the Greens (Green Party), UKIP (United Kingdom Independence Party), and BNP (British National Party) were asked in the election study. We deal with this by creating a variable **na**, which has missing values for all respondents and is used to 'stand in' for the questions not asked.

```
bes2010flngs_pre_long <- reshape(
                    within(bes2010flngs_pre,
                        na <- NA),
```

```
            varying=list(
                # Parties
                c("flng.cons","flng.labour","flng.libdem",
                  "flng.snp","flng.pcym",
                  "flng.green","flng.ukip","flng.bnp"),
                # Party leaders
                c("flng.cameron","flng.brown","flng.clegg",
                  "flng.salmond","flng.jones",
                  # The variable "na" stands in for the
                  # questions not asked in the survey
                  "na","na","na")
            ),
            v.names=c("flng.party",
                    "flng.leader"),
            times=c("Conservative","Labour","LibDem",
                    "SNP","Plaid Cymru",
                    "Green","UKIP","BNP"),
            timevar="party",
            direction="long")
str(bes2010flngs_pre_long)
```

```
'data.frame':   15480 obs. of  5 variables:
 $ region      : Factor w/ 3 levels "England","Scotland",..: 1 NA 1
      1 NA 1 1 1 1 ...
 $ party       : chr  "Conservative" "Conservative" "Conservative"
      "Conservative" ...
 $ flng.party : num  6 6 4 6 4 1 3 3 3 ...
 $ flng.leader: num  3 7 7 4 5 0 3 6 2 2 ...
 $ id          : int  1 2 3 4 5 6 7 8 9 10 ...
 - attr(*, "reshapeLong")=List of 4
  ..$ varying:List of 2
  .. ..$ : chr  "flng.cons" "flng.labour" "flng.libdem" "flng.snp" ...
  .. ..$ : chr  "flng.cameron" "flng.brown" "flng.clegg" "flng.
      salmond" ...
  ..$ v.names: chr  "flng.party" "flng.leader"
  ..$ idvar  : chr "id"
  ..$ timevar: chr "party"
```

The data are not in the most sensible order: the variable **id**, which refers to the original rows in wide format, runs the fastest and is 'nested' within the variable **party**. It makes more sense to have the values of **party** nested in **id**, which corresponds to the comparisons (potentially) made by the respondents. With the individual observations nested in time points, the rows of the data set in long format may not be in the most convenient order. In the next section, we will see how the rows of a data frame can be sorted in the desired way.

An alternative to the function **reshape()** from the standard package *stats* is the function **Reshape()**, available from the *memisc* package (Elff, 2019). It simplifies the specification of repeated measurement variables and of the variable that identifies measurement occasions. It expects as first argument (or as argument tagged with **data=**) the data frame to be reshaped, as second argument (or as argument tagged with **spec=**) a list that describes the measurement variables and measurement occasions, and as third argument (or as argument tagged with `direction=`) a character string that indicates whether the data frame is to be reshaped from wide into long or from long into wide format. Those elements of the list that are vectors of variable names (i.e. symbols without quotation marks) are interpreted as variable names denoting repeated measures, and the names attached to the list denote the variables containing repeated measures in long format. There should be only a single list element that is a numeric or a character vector. This will be used to designate the measurement occasions. The simplifications made possible by the use of `Reshape()` are illustrated in the following example. We start the example by activating the *memisc* package:

```
library(memisc)
```

The example replicates the previous example, only with `Reshape()` instead of `reshape()`. It demonstrates a convenient feature of the function by allowing one to specify measurement occasions that are to be filled with `NA` for certain variables, in the present case the affective evaluation of party leaders who were not asked about in the questionnaire:

```
bes2010flngs_pre_long <- Reshape(bes2010flngs_pre,
        flng.leaders=c(flng.cameron,flng.brown,
                        flng.clegg,flng.salmond,
                        flng.jones,,,),
        flng.parties=c(flng.cons,flng.labour,
                        flng.libdem,flng.snp,
                        flng.pcym,flng.green,
                        flng.ukip,flng.bnp),
        party=c("Conservative","Labour","LibDem",
                "SNP","Plaid Cymru",
                "Green","UKIP","BNP"),
        direction="long")
```

The function `Reshape()` also differs from `reshape()` in how the observations are sorted – that is, measurement occasions (the party variable) are nested within individuals:

```
str(bes2010flngs_pre_long)
```

```
'data.frame':    15480 obs. of  5 variables:
 $ region       : Factor w/ 3 levels "England","Scotland",..: 1 1 1
        1 1 1 1 NA NA ...
 $ party        : Factor w/ 8 levels "Conservative",..: 1 2 3 4 5 6
        7 8 1 2 ...
 $ flng.leaders: num  3 6 3 NA 5 NA NA NA 7 3 ...
 $ flng.parties: num  6 5 4 NA NA 7 3 0 6 1 ...
 $ id           : int  1 1 1 1 1 1 1 1 2 2 ...
 - attr(*, "reshapeLong")=List of 4
  ..$ varying:List of 2
  .. ..$ flng.leaders: chr  "flng.cameron" "flng.brown" "flng.clegg"
        "flng.salmond" ...
  .. ..$ flng.parties: chr  "flng.cons" "flng.labour" "flng.libdem"
        "flng.snp" ...
  ..$ v.names: chr  "flng.leaders" "flng.parties"
  ..$ idvar  : chr "id"
  ..$ timevar: chr "party"
```

As with **reshape()**, reshaping from long into wide format takes (almost) the same syntax as reshaping from wide into long format:

```
bes2010flngs_pre_wide <- Reshape(bes2010flngs_pre_long,
        flng.leaders=c(flng.cameron,flng.brown,
                       flng.clegg,flng.salmond,
                       flng.jones,,,),
        flng.parties=c(flng.cons,flng.labour,
                       flng.libdem,flng.snp,
                       flng.pcym,flng.green,
                       flng.ukip,flng.bnp),
        party=c("Conservative","Labour","LibDem",
                "SNP","Plaid Cymru",
                "Green","UKIP","BNP"),
        direction="wide")
```

After reshaping into wide format, the variables that correspond to multiple measures of the same variable are grouped together:

```
str(bes2010flngs_pre_wide)
```

```
'data.frame':   1935 obs. of  15 variables:
 $ region      : Factor w/ 3 levels "England","Scotland",..: 1 NA 1
    1 NA 1 1 1 1 ...
 $ id          : int  1 2 3 4 5 6 7 8 9 10 ...
 $ flng.cameron: num  3 7 7 4 5 0 3 6 2 2 ...
 $ flng.cons   : num  6 6 4 6 4 1 3 3 3 3 ...
 $ flng.brown  : num  6 3 8 4 5 5 5 4 7 4 ...
 $ flng.labour : num  5 1 3 6 8 5 6 2 8 3 ...
 $ flng.clegg  : num  3 5 4 3 5 4 2 7 4 8 ...
 $ flng.libdem : num  4 7 5 5 5 4 0 5 4 9 ...
 $ flng.salmond: num  NA NA NA NA NA NA NA NA NA NA ...
 $ flng.snp    : num  NA NA NA NA NA NA NA NA NA NA ...
 $ flng.jones  : num  5 3 10 7 5 1 7 1 6 4 ...
 $ flng.pcym   : num  NA NA NA NA NA NA NA NA NA NA ...
 $ flng.green  : num  7 6 5 5 4 4 1 5 5 5 ...
 $ flng.ukip   : num  3 0 0 3 NA 0 NA 2 3 1 ...
 $ flng.bnp    : num  0 0 0 2 2 0 0 0 0 0 ...
 - attr(*, "reshapeWide")=List of 5
  ..$ v.names: chr  "flng.leaders" "flng.parties"
  ..$ timevar: chr "party"
  ..$ idvar  : chr "id"
  ..$ times  : Factor w/ 8 levels "Conservative",..: 1 2 3 4 5 6 7
     8
  ..$ varying: chr [1:2, 1:8] "flng.cameron" "flng.cons" "flng.
     brown" "flng.labour" ...
  .. ..- attr(*, "dimnames")=List of 2
  .. .. ..$ : chr  "flng.leaders" "flng.parties"
  .. .. ..$ : NULL
```

3.3.5 Sorting

When the data being analysed come from a simple random sample, the order in which observations occur in a data frame does not matter. If the data are from repeated measurement and are arranged in long format, the sorting order may still not matter for data analysis functions if the temporal structure or nesting structure is explicitly stated in terms of function arguments. But it is possible that, as in the example at the end of the previous section, one sorting order is better suited for data inspection than another. Thus, one may want to sort a data frame into a particular order.

One can arrange a data frame into a desired order with the 'basic' facilities of R alone – that is, without the need for installing an additional add-on package. This is possible with the help of the function `order()`, which we already encountered in the previous chapter. Here, we use the function `order` to get a 'sorting index' that helps order the data first by the variable `id` and second by the variable `party` (nested within `id`):

```
ii <- with(bes2010flngs_pre_long,order(id,party))
```

Now we apply the sorting index with the bracket operator:

```
bes2010flngs_pre_long_sorted <- bes2010flngs_pre_long[ii,]
head(bes2010flngs_pre_long_sorted[c("party","id",
                              "flng.leaders","flng.parties")],
    n=15)
```

	party	id	flng.leaders	flng.parties
1.Conservative	Conservative	1	3	6
1.Labour	Labour	1	6	5
1.LibDem	LibDem	1	3	4
1.SNP	SNP	1	NA	NA
1.Plaid Cymru	Plaid Cymru	1	5	NA
1.Green	Green	1	NA	7
1.UKIP	UKIP	1	NA	3
1.BNP	BNP	1	NA	0
2.Conservative	Conservative	2	7	6
2.Labour	Labour	2	3	1
2.LibDem	LibDem	2	5	7
2.SNP	SNP	2	NA	NA
2.Plaid Cymru	Plaid Cymru	2	3	NA
2.Green	Green	2	NA	6
2.UKIP	UKIP	2	NA	0

The use of `order()` is a bit tedious. Sorting can be simplified either by defining a special-purpose function or by using a function from an extension package such as *memisc*. The following code defines such a special-purpose function:

```
Sort <- function(data,...){
    ii <- eval(substitute(order(...)),
                       envir=data,
```

```
                        enclos=parent.frame())
    data[ii,]
}
```

Using this function already makes sorting a bit easier – for example, with the long-format version of the BES data:

```
bes2010flngs_pre_long_sorted <- Sort(bes2010flngs_pre_long,
                            id,party)
```

While this example demonstrates that it is relatively straightforward to extend the capabilities of R if one has the right programming skills, this is not the only way to go.

Alternatively, one can use the **sort()** method function available from the *memisc* package (Elff, 2019), which adapts the generic **sort()** function to data frames. This method function allows one to specify the variables by which the data frame is to be sorted via a *formula* – that is, a language construct that contains a tilde (~) and variable names combined with a plus operator. (Formulae are also used to specify linear regression models to be fit with **lm()** or for the construction of a contingency table with **xtabs()**.) The order of the variables is interpreted such that the variable that comes first in the formula runs the fastest and is nested in the variable that comes second in the formula, and so on. In the following example lines of code, after sorting the values of the variable **party** run the fastest:

```
library(memisc)
bes2010flngs_pre_long_sorted <- sort(bes2010flngs_pre_long,
                            by=~party+id)
head(bes2010flngs_pre_long_sorted[c("party","id",
                            "flng.leaders","flng.parties")],
    n=15)
```

	party	id	flng.leaders	flng.parties
1.Conservative	Conservative	1	3	6
1.Labour	Labour	1	6	5
1.LibDem	LibDem	1	3	4
1.SNP	SNP	1	NA	NA
1.Plaid Cymru	Plaid Cymru	1	5	NA
1.Green	Green	1	NA	7
1.UKIP	UKIP	1	NA	3
1.BNP	BNP	1	NA	0
2.Conservative	Conservative	2	7	6
2.Labour	Labour	2	3	1
2.LibDem	LibDem	2	5	7
2.SNP	SNP	2	NA	NA
2.Plaid Cymru	Plaid Cymru	2	3	NA
2.Green	Green	2	NA	6
2.UKIP	UKIP	2	NA	0

3 4 Aggregating data frames

Often, researchers are not interested in data at the level of individuals but in certain group summaries. There may be several reasons for this. They may simply want to explore the data, they may be more interested in description than in model fitting or hypothesis testing, or they may want to analyse how the context (e.g. country-specific institutions) influences aggregate behaviour (e.g. the propensity to vote in elections in different age groups). For such research, one will usually have to aggregate the data by groups. In R, this can be done with the help of the function **aggregate()** and similar functions.

In the following, the use of two related functions, **aggregate()** and **Aggregate()**, is illustrated with an application to the 2010 BES data. In this example, we use a single data frame with the feelings towards parties and party leaders from both the pre- and the post-election waves of the 2010 BES, which is contained in the file **"bes2010feelings.RData"**:

```
load("bes2010feelings.RData")
```

The function **aggregate()** has been a part of R from early on. The original way of using this function is exemplified by the following code. It creates a data frame of averages of the variables **flng.brown**, **flng.cameron**, **flng.clegg**, and **flng.salmond** for each wave and each value of **region** (which distinguishes the four constituent countries of the UK):[5]

```
Mean <- function(x,...)mean(x,...,na.rm=TRUE)
aggregate(bes2010feelings[c("flng.brown","flng.cameron",
                            "flng.clegg","flng.salmond")],
          with(bes2010feelings,
               list(Region=region,Wave=wave)),
          Mean)
```

	Region	Wave	flng.brown	flng.cameron	flng.clegg	flng.salmond
1	England	Pre	4.092674	5.284810	4.618690	NaN
2	Scotland	Pre	5.395000	4.502591	4.405229	4.412371
3	Wales	Pre	4.328244	4.774194	4.592233	NaN
4	England	Post	4.140990	5.441454	5.160313	NaN
5	Scotland	Post	5.510769	4.539075	4.513793	4.228707
6	Wales	Post	4.307692	4.855895	4.814480	NaN

This old style of using **aggregate()** is not very convenient: first, there is no simple way to select the variables for which averages are to be computed; and second, even though the grouping factors are variables of the data frame from which the group summaries are computed, there is no direct way to use this to simplify the code.

---

[5]There is also a variable **flng.jones**, representing the feelings towards the leader of Plaid Cymru in 2010, but the aggregated data frame would not fit on the page if this variable were included in the example.

A more convenient way of calling the function **aggregate()** is with a **formula=** argument. On the left-hand side of the tilde (the symbol '~') appear the variables for which summaries are computed; on the right-hand side are the variables that are the grouping factors. Unfortunately, all observations for which the group result is a missing value for any of the variables on the left-hand side are dropped, so that the earlier example cannot be fully reproduced in this way:

```
aggregate(cbind(flng.brown,
                flng.cameron,
                flng.clegg,
                flng.salmond
                )~region+wave,
          data=bes2010feelings,
          Mean)
```

```
    region wave  flng.brown  flng.cameron  flng.clegg  flng.salmond
1 Scotland  Pre    5.466667      4.500000    4.460000      4.480000
2 Scotland Post    5.513986      4.513986    4.498252      4.270979
```

The function **Aggregate()** from the *memisc* package (Elff, 2019) also allows the user to make use of formulae to specify variables and grouping factors, but it handles missing values better and allows for more flexibility in the structure of the aggregated data frame. For example, it allows one to attach names to the variables in the aggregated data frame. For example, here we obtain a data frame of aggregates where the columns are named **Brown**, **Cameron**, **Clegg**, and **Salmond**:

```
library(memisc)
Aggregate(c(Brown=Mean(flng.brown),
            Cameron=Mean(flng.cameron),
            Clegg=Mean(flng.clegg),
            Salmond=Mean(flng.salmond))~region+wave,
          data=bes2010feelings)
```

```
    region wave    Brown  Cameron    Clegg  Salmond
1  England  Pre 4.092674 5.284810 4.618690      NaN
2 Scotland  Pre 5.395000 4.502591 4.405229 4.412371
3    Wales  Pre 4.328244 4.774194 4.592233      NaN
4     <NA>  Pre 4.507143 4.929870 4.426573 4.760563
5  England Post 4.140990 5.441454 5.160313      NaN
6 Scotland Post 5.510769 4.539075 4.513793 4.228707
7    Wales Post 4.307692 4.855895 4.814480      NaN
8     <NA> Post       NA       NA       NA       NA
```

Further, it allows one to use different aggregating functions at the same time (while with **aggregate()** only one aggregating function can be used). For example,

```
Var <- function(x,...) var(x,...,na.rm=TRUE)
Aggregate(c(Mean(flng.brown),Var(flng.brown))~region+wave,
          data=bes2010feelings)
```

	region	wave	Mean(flng.brown)	Var(flng.brown)
1	England	Pre	4.092674	7.287340
2	Scotland	Pre	5.395000	8.210025
3	Wales	Pre	4.328244	8.776042
4	<NA>	Pre	4.507143	7.754125
5	England	Post	4.140990	7.109491
6	Scotland	Post	5.510769	6.376617
7	Wales	Post	4.307692	7.647408
8	<NA>	Post	NA	NA

Other functions in the *memisc* package to produce groupwise summaries are `genTable()`, which has a syntax similar to that of `Aggregate()` but produces an array instead of a data frame, and `withGroups()`, which has a syntax oriented on the function `with()`.

Other packages that allow the user to produce data summaries for groups of observations in a data frame are *plyr* (Wickham, 2011) and *dplyr* (Wickham, Francois, et al., 2018). The latter package will be discussed in the next chapter as a member of the Tidyverse collection of packages. There are several other packages that allow one to produce such summaries, too many to discuss them all in a way that would do them justice here.

━━━━━ **Overview Box 3.3** ━━━━━

Functions that operate on data frames and return modified data frames

`subset()` This function creates a subset of a data frame. It takes a subset as first argument, and as further arguments it takes a logical condition that specifies the rows in the subset and/or a collection of names of the variables in the subset.

`merge()` This function combines two data frames 'horizontally' that contain information in different variables about the same set of observations. It takes at least two arguments: the data frames being joined or 'merged'. Further arguments may include the specification of variables that identify the rows that are matched and how to proceed with unmatched rows in one of the two data frames.

`rbind()`, `collect()`, `combine()` These functions allow one to append several data frames – that is, to join them 'vertically'. The appended data frames are expected to have the same variables. While `rbind()` appends the data frame as is, the other two functions add information to the rows in the combined data frame that identifies from which of the appended data frames each row comes. These functions are provided by extension packages `combine()` is in the *gdata* package, while `collect()` is in the *memisc* package. Neither of these two packages is a part of a standard R distribution, and they have to be explicitly installed as add-ons.

`reshape()` and `Reshape()` These functions rearrange the information in a data frame from wide into long format, and vice versa. Repeated measures are in different rows when the data frame is in long format and in different variables in the same row in wide format.

`sort()` This function allows one to reorder the rows of a data frame such that they are sorted (in increasing or decreasing order) by the values of a set of sorting variables. The function is available from base R, and to be applicable to data frames, the extension package *memisc* has to be activated.

aggregate() **and** **Aggregate()** These functions each return a data frame where each row contains summaries of variables for a group of rows or observations of an original data frame. The former only allows a single summary function for all the variables, while the latter allows one to use different summary functions for the same aggregate data set. The function **Aggregate()** is provided by the extension package *memisc*, which is not a part of the R standard distribution. There are now many other functions in other packages that allow one to create summaries for groups of observations in data frames.

3.5 Groupwise computations within data frames

The functions **with()** and **within()**, which we encountered earlier, can be used to summarize the values of variables or change them over the full range of rows of the data frame. Occasionally, one may prefer to summarize or change data within groups of observations – that is, groups of rows of a data frame. For groupwise data summaries, one can use the function **aggregate()** or similar functions discussed in the previous section. But, of course, these functions do not allow one to change data within groups, for example to centre variables groupwise – that is, to subtract from the values of a variable their averages for different groups. This is, however, possible to do in R, and again, there are several ways of doing it.

The basic way of changing data within groups of rows is to use **split()** and **unsplit()** in combination with **lapply()** and **within()**, as demonstrated in the following example, which again uses data from the 2010 BES. Here, we use the long-format data frame that we created earlier. With **split()**, we get a list of data frames distinguished by their values of the variable **id**:

```
bes2010flngs_pre_long.splt <- split(bes2010flngs_pre_long,
                                     bes2010flngs_pre_long$id)
```

To verify, we look at the first element of this list:

```
bes2010flngs_pre_long.splt[[1]]
```

```
                  region          party flng.leaders  flng.parties id
1.Conservative England Conservative               3             6  1
1.Labour       England       Labour               6             5  1
1.LibDem       England       LibDem               3             4  1
1.SNP          England          SNP              NA            NA  1
1.Plaid Cymru  England Plaid Cymru               5            NA  1
1.Green        England        Green              NA             7  1
1.UKIP         England         UKIP              NA             3  1
1.BNP          England          BNP              NA             0  1
```

To centre the variables **flng.party** and **flng.leader** within groups of rows defined by **id**, we use the function **lapply()** together with **within()**. The way **lapply()** is called here, it applies the function `within()` to each element of the list `bes2010flngs_pre_long.splt` with the expression (tagged with `expr=`) that describes the computation to be done for each list element:

```
Mean <- function(x,...) mean(x,...,na.rm=TRUE)
bes2010flngs_pre_long.splt <- lapply(
    bes2010flngs_pre_long.splt,
    within,expr={
        rel.flng.parties <- flng.parties - Mean(flng.parties)
        rel.flng.leaders <- flng.leaders - Mean(flng.leaders)
    })
```

The result is a modified copy of `bes2010flngs_pre_long.splt`, where in each element of this list, two new variables `rel.flng.parties` and `rel.flng.leaders` are present:

```
bes2010flngs_pre_long.splt[[1]]
```

	region	party	flng.leaders	flng.parties	id
1.Conservative	England	Conservative	3	6	1
1.Labour	England	Labour	6	5	1
1.LibDem	England	LibDem	3	4	1
1.SNP	England	SNP	NA	NA	1
1.Plaid Cymru	England	Plaid Cymru	5	NA	1
1.Green	England	Green	NA	7	1
1.UKIP	England	UKIP	NA	3	1
1.BNP	England	BNP	NA	0	1

	rel.flng.leaders	rel.flng.parties
1.Conservative	-1.25	1.8333333
1.Labour	1.75	0.8333333
1.LibDem	-1.25	-0.1666667
1.SNP	NA	NA
1.Plaid Cymru	0.75	NA
1.Green	NA	2.8333333
1.UKIP	NA	-1.1666667
1.BNP	NA	-4.1666667

The list can be recombined into a single data frame with a call to the function `unsplit()`, which undoes the effect of the previous call to `split()`:

```
bes2010flngs_pre_long <- unsplit(bes2010flngs_pre_long.splt,
                                 bes2010flngs_pre_long$id)
```

Using the facilities existing in standard R may appear a bit tedious, but there are packages that make it easier to change data within groups. The *memisc* package provides the function `withinGroups()`, which works like `within()`, except that it allows one to do computations separately within groups of observations in a data frame. This is illustrated by the following example. Here, we use `withinGroups()` to subtract from the variables `flng.party` and `flng.leader` their means for each group distinguished by the values `id`:

```
library(memisc)
Mean <- function(x,...)    mean(x,...,na.rm=TRUE)
bes2010flngs_pre_long <-   withinGroups(bes2010flngs_pre_long,
                                        ~id,{
     rel.flng.parties <-  flng.parties - Mean(flng.parties)
     rel.flng.leaders <-  flng.leaders - Mean(flng.leaders)
     })
```

Obviously, the code is considerably simpler than in the previous example.

It should be noted that the functions **group_by()** and **mutate()** in the *dplyr()* package can be used for similar purposes. These functions are discussed in Chapter 4.

3●6 Importing data into data frames
3.6.1 Importing data from text files

The most basic, if not most widespread, way of exchanging data in tabular arrangement is using text files – that is, files that, at least in principle, can be opened and changed using simple text editor software. The most important format for text files containing tabular data is the CSV format, where 'CSV' stands for comma-separated values. Except for an optional header line with variable names, each line in such a file corresponds to an observation or row of a data frame. All lines other than the header line contain the values of one or several variables, separated by commas. The header line, if it exists in the file, contains the names of the variables, separated by commas. The data in such a file can be read in and converted into a data frame with the function **read.csv()**. For example, the file **"ConstituencyResults2010. csv"** contains the constituency results for the major parties in Great Britain in the 2010 general election for the House of Commons of the UK. Each line contains a reference number that identifies a voting district and the results for the Conservative Party, Labour Party, Liberal Democratic Party, SNP, Plaid Cymru, Greens, BNP, and UKIP.

The function **readLines()** can be used to read in textual data line by line. We use this function here to look at the first five lines of a CSV file:

```
readLines("ConstituencyResults2010.csv",n=5)
```

```
[1] "refno,cons,lab,libdem,snp,plcym,green,bnp,ukip"
[2] "1,14.3,51.9,16.3,,7.1,,4.1,1.6"
[3] "2,35.8,24.5,19.3,,17.8,,,2.1"
[4] "3,12.4,44.4,18.6,22.2,,,1.7,"
[5] "4,20.7,36.5,28.4,11.9,,1.0,1.2,"
```

We can see that the first line contains variable names, while the remaining lines contain the values of these variables, separated by commas. This confirms that we can use **read.csv()** to read the contents of this file into a data frame:

```
ConstRes2010 <- read.csv("ConstituencyResults2010.csv")
```

Looking at the first five lines of the data frame, we see that reading the contents of the file was successful:

```
ConstRes2010[1:5,]
```

```
  refno cons  lab libdem  snp plcym green bnp ukip
1     1 14.3 51.9   16.3   NA   7.1    NA 4.1  1.6
2     2 35.8 24.5   19.3   NA  17.8    NA  NA  2.1
3     3 12.4 44.4   18.6 22.2    NA    NA 1.7   NA
4     4 20.7 36.5   28.4 11.9    NA     1 1.2   NA
5     5 30.3 13.6   38.4 15.7    NA    NA 1.1  0.9
```

This example also shows that missing values in CSV files are represented as empty spaces between two commas or as two commas immediately following each other. Such missing values are appropriately translated into **NA**.

Another common format used for data interchange is the *tab-delimited* format. Files in this format are also text files. The tab-delimited format differs from CSV in that fields are separated by tab characters instead of commas. For reading data from such a file, there is the R function **read.delim()**. The file **"ConstituencyResults2010.tsv"** also contains the constituency results for parties in Britain in the 2010 election for the House of Commons.

Again, we use the function **readLines()** to get a glimpse of the data:

```
readLines("ConstituencyResults2010.tsv",n=5)
```

```
[1] "refno\tcons\tlab\tlibdem\tsnp\tplcym\tgreen\tbnp\tukip"
[2] "1\t14.3\t51.9\t16.3\t\t7.1\t\t4.1\t1.6"
[3] "2\t35.8\t24.5\t19.3\t\t17.8\t\t\t2.1"
[4] "3\t12.4\t44.4\t18.6\t22.2\t\t\t1.7\t"
[5] "4\t20.7\t36.5\t28.4\t11.9\t\t\t1.0\t1.2\t"
```

We can see how this file differs from the CSV file we encountered earlier. Here, tab characters, represented by the backslash sequence '\t', separate the values in the lines of the file.

Here, we use **read.delim()** to read the contents of the file into a data frame and look at the first five lines of the data frame to confirm that we were successful:

```
ConstRes2010 <- read.delim("ConstituencyResults2010.tsv")
ConstRes2010[1:5,]
```

```
  refno cons  lab libdem  snp plcym green bnp ukip
1     1 14.3 51.9   16.3   NA   7.1    NA 4.1  1.6
2     2 35.8 24.5   19.3   NA  17.8    NA  NA  2.1
3     3 12.4 44.4   18.6 22.2    NA    NA 1.7   NA
4     4 20.7 36.5   28.4 11.9    NA     1 1.2   NA
5     5 30.3 13.6   38.4 15.7    NA    NA 1.1  0.9
```

As with CSV files, missing values appear as empty spaces between delimiters or as two delimiters immediately following each other.

In the previous examples, the data files started with a header line – that is, a line with variable names (or column names). Not all data files contain such a header line. Such header-less files also can be read in using `read.csv()` or `read.delim()`, but in such cases, the optional argument `header=FALSE` is required, as in the following example. Again, we look at the first five lines of the file with `readLine()`:

```
readLines("ConstituencyResults2010-nohdr.csv",n=5)
```

```
[1] "1,14.3,51.9,16.3,,7.1,,4.1,1.6"
[2] "2,35.8,24.5,19.3,,17.8,,,2.1"
[3] "3,12.4,44.4,18.6,22.2,,,1.7,"
[4] "4,20.7,36.5,28.4,11.9,,1.0,1.2,"
[5] "5,30.3,13.6,38.4,15.7,,,1.1,0.9"
```

We can see that the file does not contain a header line. We therefore call `read.csv()` with `header=FALSE`:

```
ConstRes2010 <- read.csv("ConstituencyResults2010-nohdr.csv",
                         header=FALSE)
ConstRes2010[1:5,]
```

	V1	V2	V3	V4	V5	V6	V7	V8	V9
1	1	14.3	51.9	16.3	NA	7.1	NA	4.1	1.6
2	2	35.8	24.5	19.3	NA	17.8	NA	NA	2.1
3	3	12.4	44.4	18.6	22.2	NA	NA	1.7	NA
4	4	20.7	36.5	28.4	11.9	NA	1	1.2	NA
5	5	30.3	13.6	38.4	15.7	NA	NA	1.1	0.9

We can see that the resulting data frame has column names (or variable names) that are automatically generated.

Both `read.csv()` and `read.delim()` expect that periods ('.') are used as decimal marks. This is the convention in the English-speaking world, but in many non-English-speaking countries, a different convention regarding the decimal marks exists, namely the comma (','). Of course, if the comma is used as a decimal separator, it is no longer possible to use it as a field separator. In such cases, the semicolon (';') is often used instead of the comma. To read in data from files where the comma is used as a decimal separator, the functions `read.csv2()` or `read.delim2()` have to be used instead of `read.csv()` or `read.delim()`.

The functions discussed so far are mainly front ends to a more general function named `read.table()`, which allows for files with any kind of field separators and decimal marks. However, there is not enough room in this volume to discuss all the possibilities provided by this function in detail.

It is not always the case that data in text files are in CSV or tab-delimited format or in any format where the data fields are clearly separated by certain characters. A different way to store text files is the fixed-width format. Also, in this format lines correspond to rows in a data frame; however, the values of different variables are not separated by any particular character. Instead, one will need information about the widths of the fields or in which columns the fields start in order to be able to distinguish them. Fortunately, there is also an R function, named `read.fwf()`, that allows one to read in data from files in this format. The use of this function is illustrated in the following example. The file `"ConstituencyResults2010-fwf.txt"` is yet another collection of constituency results, this time in fixed format. As inspection of the first few lines indicates, the file does not have a header line, and the lines do not have field separators.

```
readLines("ConstituencyResults2010-fwf.txt",n=5)
```

```
[1] "  114.351.916.3     7.1      4.1 1.6"
[2] "  235.824.519.3    17.8          2.1"
[3] "  312.444.418.622.2        1.7"
[4] "  420.736.528.411.9     1.0 1.2"
[5] "  530.313.638.415.7        1.1 0.9"
```

Without information about where each field starts and ends, it will not be possible to import these data into a data frame. At least the function `read.fwf()` allows, or rather requires, one to specify the widths of the fields and thereby where each field starts and ends. Here, we call the function with the appropriate widths given in the argument tagged `widths=`:

```
ConstRes2010 <- read.fwf("ConstituencyResults2010-fwf.txt",
                     widths=c(3,4,4,4,4,4,4,4,4))
```

An inspection of the resulting data frame suggests that we were successful in importing the data from this fixed-format file:

```
ConstRes2010[1:5,]
```

```
   V1   V2   V3   V4   V5   V6 V7  V8  V9
1   1 14.3 51.9 16.3   NA  7.1 NA 4.1 1.6
2   2 35.8 24.5 19.3   NA 17.8 NA  NA 2.1
3   3 12.4 44.4 18.6 22.2   NA NA 1.7  NA
4   4 20.7 36.5 28.4 11.9   NA  1 1.2  NA
5   5 30.3 13.6 38.4 15.7   NA NA 1.1 0.9
```

Since the file does not contain a header line, again automatic variable names are created for this data frame. It should be noted, however, that the function `read.fwf()` can also deal with files in fixed-width format that do have a header line.

3.6.2 Importing data from other statistics packages

Data sets in tabular arrangement, with rows representing cases or observations and columns representing variables the values of which describe these observations or cases, play a central role in conventional statistical software packages often used in the social sciences, such as SPSS (IBM, 2017), SAS (SAS Institute, 2013), and Stata (StataCorp, 2019). Accordingly, files created with these software packages contain data in this row-by-column layout. Although files created by SPSS, SAS, and Stata have a proprietary format specific for each of these software packages, they can be read into R data frames with the help of special-purpose functions provided by the *foreign* package (R Core Team, 2018) or other packages such as *haven* (Wickham and Miller, 2018), *memisc* (Elff, 2019), or *readstata13* (Garbuszus and Jeworutzki, 2018). The following example shows how to read in SPSS and Stata files with the help of the *foreign* package:

```
library(foreign)
```

To read in an SPSS 'system' file, we use the function `read.spss()`:

```
ConstRes2010 <- read.spss("ConstituencyResults2010.sav",
                          to.data.frame=TRUE)
```

For historical reasons, the function `read.spss()` returns a list and not a data frame, unless the argument `to.data.frame=TRUE` is given.

```
ConstRes2010[1:5,]
```

```
  refno cons  lab libdem  snp plcym green bnp ukip
1     1 14.3 51.9   16.3   NA   7.1    NA 4.1  1.6
2     2 35.8 24.5   19.3   NA  17.8    NA  NA  2.1
3     3 12.4 44.4   18.6 22.2   NA    NA 1.7   NA
4     4 20.7 36.5   28.4 11.9   NA     1 1.2   NA
5     5 30.3 13.6   38.4 15.7   NA    NA 1.1  0.9
```

An SPSS 'portable' file can also be read in with this function:

```
ConstRes2010 <- read.spss("ConstituencyResults2010.por",
                          to.data.frame=TRUE)
ConstRes2010[1:5,]
```

```
  REFNO CONS  LAB LIBDEM  SNP PLCYM GREEN BNP UKIP
1     1 14.3 51.9   16.3   NA   7.1    NA 4.1  1.6
2     2 35.8 24.5   19.3   NA  17.8    NA  NA  2.1
3     3 12.4 44.4   18.6 22.2   NA    NA 1.7   NA
4     4 20.7 36.5   28.4 11.9   NA     1 1.2   NA
5     5 30.3 13.6   38.4 15.7   NA    NA 1.1  0.9
```

The variable names are all upper case in this portable file. In fact, it is a requirement of the definition of the 'portable' format that all variable names are upper case.

To read in a Stata file, the appropriate function is `read.dta()`:

```
ConstRes2010 <- read.dta("ConstituencyResults2010.dta")
ConstRes2010[1:5,]
```

```
  refno cons  lab libdem snp plcym green bnp ukip
1     1 14.3 51.9   16.3  NA   7.1    NA 4.1  1.6
```

2	2 35.8 24.5	19.3	NA	17.8	NA	NA	2.1
3	3 12.4 44.4	18.6 22.2	NA	NA	1.7	NA
4	4 20.7 36.5	28.4 11.9	NA	1	1.2	NA
5	5 30.3 13.6	38.4 15.7	NA	NA	1.1	0.9

Since Stata version 13, the standard format in which files are saved by the software has changed. Unfortunately, the *foreign* package does not support Stata files in the newer versions. So the attempt to read the file "ConstResults2010-stata-new.dta" leads to

```
ConstRes2010 <- read.dta("ConstResults2010-stata-new.dta")
```

```
Error in read.dta("ConstResults2010-stata-new.dta"): not a Stata
    version 5-12 .dta file
```

Fortunately, the new Stata file format is supported by other packages, namely *readstata13* (Garbuszus and Jeworutzki, 2018), *haven* (Wickham and Miller, 2018), and *memisc* (Elff, 2019).

It should be noted that loading data from files in these formats is not completely frictionless because the way these software packages organize data is not fully compatible with how data frames are defined in R. In SPSS and Stata, it is possible to define labels for specific values of a variable – that is, to define so-called value labels. This is not completely dissimilar to factors in R; however, the values to which the labels of factor levels are associated are always consecutive positive integer values starting with 1. In SPSS, it is also possible to declare certain values of variables as representing particular types of missing information (e.g. that survey respondents either do not know how to answer an interview question or refuse to give an answer). These 'user-defined missing values' are not supported by R unless a certain extension package is activated. A later chapter discusses the meaning of these value labels and user-defined missing values in the context of data from survey interviews and how they can be handled with the extension package *memisc* (Elff, 2019).[6]

━━━━━━ **Overview Box 3.4** ━━━━━━

Functions to import data from external files into data frames

read.csv(), read.csv2 These functions can be used to read data from files in CSV format into data frames. They are available from the R standard distribution and are provided by the standard package *utils*. **read.csv()** can be used with files in which the period is used as a decimal marker and the comma as a field separator. **read.csv2()** is for files with the comma as a decimal marker and the semicolon as a field separator.

---

[6]There is also some support for these features in the packages *haven* (Wickham and Miller, 2018) and *labelled* (Larmarange, 2020), but the author of the present book would argue that *memisc* provides the most complete support for value labels and user-defined missing values.

read.delim(), read.delim2() These functions are also provided by the standard package *utils* and are to be used for *tab-delimited* files – that is, files in which the fields in a row are separated by tab characters instead of commas or semicolons. **read.delim2()** is for files where the comma, instead of the period, is used as a decimal marker. These functions are provided by the standard R package *utils*.

read.spss() This function can be used to read in files in SPSS format. **read.spss()** is provided by the standard package *foreign* and can be used to load data from files both in SPSS 'system' and in SPSS 'portable' format. It gives a list as return value; it gives a data frame as return value only if **read.spss()** is called with the optional argument **to.data.frame=TRUE**.

read.dta() This function can be used to read data from files created by Stata into data frames. **read.dta()** is provided by the standard package *foreign*. It cannot load data from files created by newer versions of Stata (version 13 or later). In order to read data from newer versions of Stata, some non-standard packages need to be used. Such packages are *haven*, *memisc*, and *readstata13*

4

Data Tables and the Tidyverse

A guide on data management would not be complete without a discussion of the *data.table* package (Dowle and Srinivasan, 2019) and the Tidyverse collection of packages (Wickham, 2017). While these packages are not indispensable for successful data management – in fact, the author has been able to survive many years without ever using one of them – they both have a large and committed following. The popularity of these packages is evident not only in the number of websites and online discussions related to them but also in the number of packages on CRAN that somehow build on them.

Both *data.table* and the Tidyverse are intended to make data management and computing data summaries more efficient by re-implementing most of the data functionality discussed in Chapter 3. However, their approaches to data management differ radically both from base R and from each other. The *data.table* package emphasizes improvements in speed and in memory requirement for data management operation. At the same time, the package tries to minimize the number of new functions that users will have to learn in order to use the package.

One characteristic of the Tidyverse is the aim to make data management code more transparent by introducing many new functions that each correspond to a verb that describes a particular data management task (e.g. `arrange()`, `group_by()`, or `summarize()`). Another characteristic is a particular 'coding idiom,' where function calls are concatenated using a 'pipe' operator.

There is already ample documentation available for these packages in both book form and online (e.g. Wickham and Grolemund, 2016). Therefore only the general ideas of *data.table* and the Tidyverse are introduced. Thereafter, the performance of the two approaches is compared with regard to a few typical data management and summary tasks. One particular package from the Tidyverse collection will be discussed in some detail at the end of this chapter, namely the *tidyr* package (Wickham and Henry, 2019), which provides the means to 'tidy up' 'messy' data that initially do not come in an orderly row-by-column form.

4.1 Data tables

The *data.table* package (Dowle and Srinivasan, 2019) derives its name from the class of objects defined therein, that is objects with the `"class"` attribute `"data.table"`, which are referred to as data tables in the following. In terms of their internal structure, they are extensions of data frames and can be created in a similar way as data frames. In Chapter 3, we created a data frame about the four constituent countries of the UK. In this example, we create the analogous data table:

```
library(data.table)
UK <- data.table(
          Population = c(55619400,1885400,5424800,3125000),
          Area = c(50301,5460,30090,8023),
          GVA = c(28096,20000,24800,19900),
          country = c("England",
                      "Northern Ireland",
                      "Scotland",
                      "Wales"))
UK
```

```
   Population   Area    GVA            country
1:   55619400 50301  28096            England
2:    1885400  5460  20000 Northern  Ireland
3:    5424800 30090  24800           Scotland
4:    3125000  8023  19900              Wales
```

```
class(UK)
```

```
[1] "data.table" "data.frame"
```

It should be noted that although data tables are also data frames, no non-standard row names are supported by `data.table()`. That is why we add the country identifiers as a variable instead of row names.

Since data tables are intended to potentially contain large amounts of data and one usually does not want to see all these data in the R output, the `print()` version of data tables limits the amount of data being shown. So if we create a large data table with as many as 1 million rows,

```
DT <- data.table(
    x = rnorm(1000000),
    y = rnorm(1000000))
```

only a few lines are shown:

```
DT
```

```
                  x             y
      1:   1.96384983   0.01989805
      2:   1.19915771  -1.19224257
      3:  -0.46569844  -2.29136786
      4:  -0.07881038   0.34171610
      5:  -0.03679889   0.87035428
     ---
 999996:   0.66092818   0.24537127
 999997:   0.54843496   0.88778605
 999998:  -0.86703128   0.77917531
 999999:   0.00621505  -0.42583447
1000000:   0.73969886  -1.56473598
```

To create a data table from a data frame, one can use `as.data.table()` or `setDT()`. These two ways differ in so far as the former creates a copy of the data frame, while the latter modifies the data frame in place. That is, if the data table created with `setDT()` is modified, this may also affect the original data frame. This is so because many data modification facilities implemented by the *data.table* package are implemented to work 'by reference'.

For several of the following examples in this chapter, we will make use of the BES data that were already discussed in Chapter 3. Here, we work with the data frame that covers both the pre- and the post-election wave of the 2010 BES:

```
load("bes2010feelings.RData")
```

With `setDS()`, we transform the data frame into a data table. After

```
setDT(bes2010feelings)
```

the object named `bes2010feelings` is a data table:

```
class(bes2010feelings)
```

```
[1] "data.table" "data.frame"
```

Almost all data management functionality provided by the *data.table* package is implemented by particular extensions to the bracket operator when applied to data tables. That is, if `DT` is a data table, then any code for data manipulation or summarizing data will take the general form

```
DT[i,j,by]
```

Here, `i` is an expression that selects or orders the rows of the data table, while `j` is an expression that selects the columns of the data table, defines data summaries computed from the data table, or creates new variables in it. The third possible argument `by=` defines variables that define the groups by which data summaries are computed or within which data manipulations are conducted. It should be noted that `i`, `j`, and `by` do not need to be always present. It is possible to apply the bracket operator only with `i` set, so that the application of the operator takes the form `DT[i]`. If only `j` is given, then the operator is used in the form `DT[,j]`, unless it is an expression that describes a computation based on the variables in `DT`.

For example, to obtain a subset of the data table `bes2010feelings`, one will use the code

```
sctl2010feelings <- bes2010feelings[region=="Scotland"]
```

A copy of `bes2010feelings` that is ordered by the variables **wave** and **region** can be obtained by

```
bes2010feelings.srtd <- bes2010feelings[order(wave,region)]
```

To obtain a data table that contains only the variables **flng.brown**, **wave**, and **region**, one can use the code

```
bes2010feelings.sub <- bes2010feelings[,.(flng.brown,wave,region)]
names(bes2010feelings.sub)
```

```
[1] "flng.brown" "wave"       "region"
```

Here, one has to be careful because

```
bes2010feelings.c <- bes2010feelings[,c(flng.brown,wave,region)]
```

will not create a data table but a vector that is the concatenation of the three variables:

```
str(bes2010feelings.c)
```

```
num [1:15030] 6 3 8 4 5 5 5 4 7 4 ...
```

that is, `bes2010feelings[,c(flng.brown,wave,region)]` is equivalent to `with(bes2010feelings,c(flng.brown,wave,region))`.

Finally, we use the bracket operator to get a data table that creates a subset of the observations and a subset of the variables. The observations are restricted to Scotland, and the variables are restricted to the survey wave information and the affective evaluation of the leaders of the major parties that run candidates in Scotland.

```
sctl2010feelings <- bes2010feelings[region=="Scotland",
                      .(wave,
                        flng.brown,
                        flng.cameron,
                        flng.clegg,
                        flng.salmond)]
```

To give an example of the use of a `j` index, the following lines of code give the mean affective evaluation of Gordon Brown, David Cameron, and Nick Clegg, together with the sample size:

```
Mean <- function(x) mean(x,na.rm=TRUE)
bes2010feelings[,.(Brown=Mean(flng.brown),
                   Cameron=Mean(flng.cameron),
                   Clegg=Mean(flng.clegg),
                   .N)]
```

```
     Brown   Cameron    Clegg     N
1: 4.406517 5.162484 4.850231 5010      ,
```

To obtain the means of these variables for the regions and waves in the 2010 BES, one can use the code

```
bes2010feelings[,.(Brown=Mean(flng.brown),
                   Cameron=Mean(flng.cameron),
                   Clegg=Mean(flng.clegg),
                   .N),
                by=.(wave,region)]
```

```
   wave   region   Brown   Cameron    Clegg     N
1:  Pre  England 4.092674 5.284810 4.618690 1159
2:  Pre     <NA> 4.507143 4.929870 4.426573  437
3:  Pre Scotland 5.395000 4.502591 4.405229  207
4:  Pre    Wales 4.328244 4.774194 4.592233  132
5: Post  England 4.140990 5.441454 5.160313 2175
6: Post Scotland 5.510769 4.539075 4.513793  665
7: Post    Wales 4.307692 4.855895 4.814480  235
```

The bracket operator can also be used to change the data table to which it is applied. To create a new variable or change an existing variable z in a data table such that it is the result of adding the values of the variable x and the values of the variable y, one can use the code

```
DT[,z:=x+y]
```

In contrast to the function within(), which was discussed in Chapter 3, this does not return a modified copy of the data table but modifies the data table 'in place' – that is, after such code DT itself will contain the new variable z. In fact, this can even have surprising side effects if more than one variable name refers to the same data table, as we can see in the following example.

We use the data table UK that we created earlier. To see the consequences of such side effects, we create another variable UK1 that also refers to the same data table:

```
UK1 <- UK
```

We now create a variable with the population density (i.e. population per area) in UK:

```
UK[,Density := Population/Area]
```

As a consequence, not only is UK modified

```
UK
```

	Population	Area	GVA	country	Density
1:	55619400	50301	28096	England	1105.7315
2:	1885400	5460	20000	Northern Ireland	345.3114
3:	5424800	30090	24800	Scotland	180.2858
4:	3125000	8023	19900	Wales	389.5052

but also UK1

```
UK1
```

	Population	Area	GVA	country	Density
1:	55619400	50301	28096	England	1105.7315
2:	1885400	5460	20000	Northern Ireland	345.3114
3:	5424800	30090	24800	Scotland	180.2858
4:	3125000	8023	19900	Wales	389.5052

even though the modifying code makes no explicit reference to UK1.

━━━━━━━ Overview Box 4.1 ━━━━━━━

The *data.table* package: main purposes and some data management strategies

Main purposes: The main purpose of *data.table* is to make data management more efficient. On the one hand, the intention is to make management of large amounts of data less demanding for the computer. On the other hand, the intention is to minimize the number of new functions that users have to learn when they adopt the package. This is achieved by implementing a modification of data frames, which are the objects in the **"data.table"** class.

Creating "data.table" objects: Objects can be created from vectors with the `data.table()` function and from data frames with the `as.data.table()` function.

Selecting observations: Objects are selected by using the bracket operator in the form

```
DT[i,]
```

or

```
DT[i]
```

where DT is a **"data.table"** object and `i` is a logical vector, a numeric vector, or an expression. If `i` is an expression, it can include variables in DT without the need to use the dollar operator.

Selecting variables: Objects are selected by using the bracket operator in the form

```
DT[,j]
```

To obtain a **"data.table"** object with the variables x, y, and z from the **"data.table"** object DT, one should use the bracket operator in the form

```
DT[,.(x,y,z)]
```

Changing variables: Variables can be changed by combining the bracket operator with the special-assignment operator :=. To assign the result of the function call `f(x,y)` to the variable z in the `data.table` object DT, one should use the bracket operator in the form

```
DT[,z := f(x,y)]
```

Here, one should be aware that the object DT is modified 'in place' and that this can have repercussions in so far as other variables referring to the same objects are also affected by the modification.

Merging "data.table" objects: Objects can be merged (where the result of a merge is analogous to the merging of data frames) also with the bracket operator. To merge **"data.table"** objects X and Y, where rows are matched based on the variable t, one should use the bracket operator in the form

```
X[Y,,on="t"]
```

4.2 The Tidyverse

The Tidyverse (Wickham, 2017) is a collection of packages that have been created to simplify the transformation of data into a regular pattern and to create summaries of such data. Each package in this collection is developed for a specific stage in the process of data analysis. For the first stage – importing data into R – the Tidyverse has the packages *readr* (Wickham, Hester, et al., 2018) and *haven* (Wickham and Miller, 2018). For the second stage – bringing data into a so-called tidy format, a data frame with observations in rows and properties in columns – the collection has the *tidyr* package (Wickham and Henry, 2019). For the third and the fourth stages – wangling and arranging data and creating descriptive summaries from them – the collection has the *dplyr* package (Wickham, Francois, et al., 2018). For producing graphical summaries, a part of the fourth stage, the collection has the *ggplot2* package (Wickham, 2016). All these packages, except for *ggplot2*, are based on the *tibble* package (Müller and Wickham, 2019), which provides an object class designed to contain 'tidy' data with the same name. A 'tibble' is a data frame with additional `"class"` attributes `"tbl"` and `"tbl_df"`. Yet the construction and display differ. When a tibble is displayed (using the function `print()`), then only the first 10 observations and the first few variables are shown, where the number of variables shown depends on the R option `"width"`. Finally, if a single column of a tibble is extracted using the single-bracket operator (`[]`), the result is still a tibble and not a vector (as would be the case if the bracket operator were applied to a data frame).

The reliance on tibble objects is one of the distinctive characteristics of the Tidyverse; another one is that it has its specific code idiom, which makes heavy use of the 'pipe operator' `%>%`. This operator allows the user to avoid nested function calls or the creation of variables for the storage of intermediate results. For example, if one wanted to apply the function `f()` to the data frame `dataf`, then apply the function `g()` on the result of `f()`, and finally apply the function `h()` on the result of `g()`, the 'ordinary' way to do this would be by using the code

```
result <- h(g(f(dataf)))
```

The multiple nested parentheses can be avoided by defining variables for the intermediate results, as in

```
f_dataf <- f(dataf)
g_dataf <- g(f_dataf)
result <- h(g_dataf)
```

In the Tidyverse idiom, one would write instead

```
result <- dataf %>% f() %>% g() %>% h()
```

or even

```
dataf %>% f() %>% g() %>% h() -> result
```

In the Tidyverse, such nested function calls would occur quite frequently if not for the pipe operator, because the functions that the Tidyverse packages provide are meant to represent minimal units of activity of data management that can be directly represented each by a single verb.

The pipe operator derives its name from an operator of the same name defined in several shells (command line user interfaces) of the Unix family of operating systems (this family includes the open source operating system Linux and the operating system of Apple computers, macOS).

This original pipe operator would be used to start two programs in parallel so that the output of the first program would be fed as input to the second program. The pipe operator used in the Tidyverse idiom works similarly in so far as when the calls of two functions are combined with the pipe operator %>%, the result of the first function is used as an argument of the second function.

It should be noted that the pipe operator is defined in the *magrittr* package (Bache and Wickham, 2014).[1] The fact that several Tidyverse packages import the pipe operator from *magrittr* and re-export it has led at least some users to believe that they would need the Tidyverse to use it. However, it is perfectly possible to use the pipe operator, as well as some of its extensions, without any other Tidyverse packages.

The core of the Tidyverse collection is arguably the *dplyr* package. Its main purpose is the preparation of data for analysis and the creation of data summaries. This package actually re-implements a range of facilities already available in the standard R packages *base* and *stats*. Yet these re-implementations follow a set of specific principles: each function focuses on exactly one particular activity of data preparation, and each function has a calling syntax that makes it suitable for combining it with others using the pipe operator (%>%). For example, the function **subset()** from the *base* package, which we encountered in an earlier chapter, can be used both to select rows from a data frame based on a logical condition and to select a set of variables from the data frame based on their names. For the same purpose, *dplyr* has two functions: **filter()** to select observations based on logical conditions, and **select()** to select variables from a data frame. For illustration, let us assume that **dataf** is a data frame that contains, among others, the variables **a**, **b**, **x**, and **y**.

To obtain a data frame with only the variables **x** and **y** and only the observations that satisfy the condition **a > 0**, one can write in standard R

```
dataf_sub <- subset(dataf,a>0,select=c(x,y))
```

The equivalent code in the idiom of *dplyr* is

```
dataf_sub <- dataf %>% filter (a>0) %>% select (x,y)
```

As a practical illustration, we replicate an earlier example and create a subset of the BES 2010 data about respondents' affective evaluation of parties and their leaders:

```
library(dplyr)
bes2010feelings.sub <- bes2010feelings %>%
                       filter(region == "Scotland") %>%
                       select(wave,
                              flng.brown,
                              flng.cameron,
                              flng.clegg,
                              flng.salmond)
```

---

[1] The name of this package is a play on the name of the Belgian surrealist artist René Magritte and his famous painting *Ceci "n'est" pas une pipe* (This Is Not a Pipe). Ironically, this painting does show a pipe, but *pipe* is not used in the sense of an element of plumbing (which inspired the name 'pipe operator') but in the sense of a smoking pipe.

Creating subsets is a common activity in the stage of data preparation; combining data from different sources is another one. To combine data sets with different variables on the same set of observations, the *base* package has the function `merge()`. The *dplyr* package has the functions `inner_join()`, `left_join()`, `right_join()`, and `full_join()`, which correspond to different settings of the arguments `all.x=` and `all.y=` of the function `merge()`.

To obtain data summaries, *dplyr* offers the function `summarise()` (or the synonym `summarize()`). The function does not provide a specific kind of summary but allows for a variety of them. Often, one is interested not just in simple descriptive summaries for a full data frame but in summaries for various groups (defined by variables in the data frame). To define such groups, the *dplyr* package has the function `group_by`, so that per-group summaries can be obtained by combining a call to this function with a call to `summarize()`, which then results in a tibble data frame with one row for each group. With the functions `group_by()` and `summarize()`, we can reproduce our earlier example where the average affective evaluations of Gordon Brown, David Cameron, and Nick Clegg are computed together with the sample size for each wave and region:

```
bes2010feelings %>% group_by(wave,region) %>%
summarize(Brown=Mean(flng.brown),
                        Cameron=Mean(flng.cameron),
                        Clegg=Mean(flng.clegg),
                        N=n())
```

```
# A tibble: 7 x 6
# Groups:   wave [2]
  wave   region   Brown Cameron Clegg     N
  <fct>  <fct>    <dbl>   <dbl> <dbl> <int>
1 Pre    England   4.09    5.28  4.62  1159
2 Pre    Scotland  5.40    4.50  4.41   207
3 Pre    Wales     4.33    4.77  4.59   132
4 Pre    <NA>      4.51    4.93  4.43   437
5 Post   England   4.14    5.44  5.16  2175
6 Post   Scotland  5.51    4.54  4.51   665
7 Post   Wales     4.31    4.86  4.81   235
```

The *dplyr* package contains its own function to change variables in or add variables to a data frame – the function `mutate`. It works similar to `within()` but has a different syntax. If we return to the example data `UK`, then the code that creates the variable `Density` to be the result of dividing `Population` by `Area` will be

```
UK %>% mutate (Density = Population/Area)
```

```
  Population  Area   GVA            country   Density
1   55619400 50301 28096           England 1105.7315
2    1885400  5460 20000 Northern Ireland  345.3114
3    5424800 30090 24800          Scotland  180.2858
4    3125000  8023 19900             Wales  389.5052
```

━━━━━━━━━━━━ **Overview Box 4.2** ━━━━━━━━━━

The main packages in the Tidyverse

tibble: This package defines the so-called tibbles, which are in fact objects from the class `"tbl_df"`. These objects are in fact a slight variation of data frames that differ mainly in terms of how they appear when printed to the R console and how character strings are handled when these objects are constructed.

readr: This package re-implements functions from the standard R package *utils* that can be used to read CSV files and other text files into tibbles (instead of data frames, as done by *utils*).

haven: This package re-implements functions from the R package *foreign* to import data from SAS, SPSS, or Stata files into tibbles. In contrast to *foreign*, the *haven* package allows one to import Stata files in the newer format. Variable labels and value labels are handled differently than by *foreign*.

tidyr: The main purpose of this package is to provide a means to bring data into a row-by-column format, where rows refer to cases or observations and columns refer to properties of these cases or observations. It therefore provides several functions that allow one to rearrange data within tibbles.

dplyr: This package re-implements a variety of functions that already exist in the standard packages *base*, *stats*, and *utils* with the help of which one can modify variables in data frames and tibbles, merge data frames or tibbles, and produce data summaries for a full set of observations in a data frame or for groups of observations.

━━━━━━━━━━━━ **Overview Box 4.3** ━━━━━━━━━━

Some data management strategies with *dplyr*

Selecting observations based on certain conditions: In order to obtain a subset of observations from a data frame, the package offers the function `filter()`. To obtain all observations of a tibble `tbl` that satisfy the condition `x > 0` (where `x` may be a variable in `tbl`), one can use the line

```
filter(tbl,x>0)
```

This code is mostly equivalent to `subset(tbl,x>0)`.

Selecting variables: In order to get a tibble or data frame that contains a subset of variables, one can use the function `select()`. For example, to obtain the tibble with the variables `x`, `y`, and `z` from the tibble `tbl`, one can use the line

```
select(tbl,x,y,z)
```

This code is equivalent to `subset(tbl,select=c(x,y,z))`.

(Continued)

Changing variables: The main function in *dplyr* to create new variables or modify variables in a data frame is `mutate()`. For example, to create a copy of the tibble `tbl` with the new variables `x.2` and `y.2`, which are the squares of the variables `x` and `y`, one can use the line

```
mutate(tbl, x.2 = x^2, y.2 = y^2)
```

The standard function `within()` can be used to the same effect.

Merging tibbles: The *dplyr* package contains several functions that correspond to variants of calling the *base* function `merge()`. Thus, if `A` and `B` are two tibbles or data frames, then `inner_join(A,B,by="id")` is roughly equivalent to `merge(A,B,by="id")`, `left_join(A,B,by="id")` is roughly equivalent to `merge(A,B,by="id",all.x=TRUE)`, `right_join(A,B,by="id")` is roughly equivalent to `merge(A,B,by="id",all.y=TRUE)`, while `right_join(A,B,by="id")` is roughly equivalent to `merge(A,B,by="id",all=TRUE)`.

A comparison of approaches

The typical tasks of preparing and summarizing data can be completed with standard R, with the extensions provided by *memisc*, *data.table*, or with the Tidyverse package *dplyr*. This leads to the question of which package one should use. To find an answer to this question, we look at the various approaches and compare them – how they can be used to complete specific, yet typical, data management tasks and how efficient they are in terms of computational efficiency (i.e. how quickly they can be done by a contemporary computer).

For the purposes of comparison, we use two artificial data sets. The first data set comprises a large number – 1 million – of observations and a moderate number – 100 – of variables and thus may be typical of a data set involved in 'big data' analytics. The second data set comprises a moderate number – 3000 – of observations and a large number – 1500 – of variables and thus has the dimensions of a typical social survey data set, such as those obtained from the American Election Study, the BES, or the German Longitudinal Election Study (GLES). An R script to create these artificial data sets can be obtained from the website that accompanies this book (https://www.elff.eu/Data-Management-in-R/).

With these two data sets, we conduct typical data management tasks not unlike those that arise in social science research: summaries for groups of observations and transforming several variables within each group of observations. These tasks are replicated 100 times using approaches based on base R, the *data.table* package, the Tidyverse package *dplyr*, and the functions `withGroups()` and `withinGroups()` from the *memisc* package.

Table 4.1(a) shows the timing results for various ways of computing group summaries. The timings were obtained with the help of the *rbenchmark* package (Kusnierczyk, 2012) on a computer with an Intel Core i7-8700T microprocessor with a nominal frequency of 2.8 GHz. The column group headings 'Big data' and 'Survey data' refer to the settings with 1 million observations and 100 variables and 3000 observations and 1500 observations, respectively. The column headed 'absolute' refers to absolute timings (i.e. the length of time in seconds that 100 replications take), while the column headed 'relative' refers to relative timings (i.e. how many times longer the replications take relative to the fastest approach). The line labelled **aggregate** refers to the function `aggregate()` – discussed in Chapter 3; the line **with + tapply** refers to using the function `with()` together with the function `tapply()` to compute group summaries; the line `data.table` refers to using the bracket operator to a `data.table` object; `group_by + summarize` refers to using the *dplyr* functions `group_by()` and `summarize()`; finally, `withGroups` refers to using the eponymous function from the *memisc* package. For the 'big data' setting, the techniques using base R are both the fastest (`with + tapply`) and the slowest (`aggregate`). For the 'survey data' setting, again a base R technique is the fastest. The performance of the *data.table* and *dplyr* packages is moderate at best.

Table 4.1 Benchmark results

	(a) Group summaries			
	Big data		Survey data	
	absolute	relative	absolute	relative
aggregate	54.46	11.96	0.55	4.55
with + tapply	4.55	1.00	0.12	1.00
data.table	17.04	3.74	0.89	7.29
group_by + summarize	14.00	3.08	0.36	2.97
withGroups	22.70	4.99	1.41	11.56
	(b) Within-group modifications			
within + ave	26.91	1.08	2.37	1.58
data.table	24.85	1.00	2.66	1.77
group_by + mutate	27.18	1.09	3.26	2.17
withinGroups	33.94	1.37	1.50	1.00

Table 4.1(b) compares the timings for the different approaches to conduct data modifications within groups of observations. The line labelled `within + ave` refers to using the function `within()` to make data modifications within data frames and the function `ave()` to subtract group means. The line `data.table` refers to using the bracket operator and the `:=` together with a `by=` argument to subtract group means in a data table. The line `group_by + mutate` refers to using the *dplyr* functions `group_by()` and `mutate()` to subtract group means, while the line labelled `withinGroups` refers to using the *memisc* function `withinGroups()` for the same purpose. The results are somewhat different from the results regarding the group summaries. In the 'big data' setting, it appears that `data.table()` performs best, whereas `withinGroups()` appears to perform the best in the 'survey data' setting.

If computational speed or efficiency is to be taken as the criterion, then it appears impossible to make a straightforward recommendation in favour of any of the packages compared by the benchmark studies. None of the packages performs best for all data management tasks in both settings. One conclusion to be drawn from this is that, at least in so far as social science applications are involved, there is no need to give up on the facilities of the standard packages of R, all the fashionableness of *data.table* and the Tidyverse notwith-standing. Therefore, the decision about whether to adopt the *data.table* or the Tidyverse approach may hinge on how convincing one finds the specific (or idiosyncratic) ideas about R that are embodied by these packages. That is, if one believes that it is a good idea to minimize the number of functions a user has to memorize because many things can be done by the particular ways in which the bracket operator is used, then *data.table* would be the appropriate choice. If, on the other hand, one believes that data summaries and data transformations should all be conducted by single-purpose functions that are to be inter-preted as 'verbs', because this would make the code transparent to other 'stakeholders' (i.e. the R non-experts, who happen to be one's managers, supervisors, or customers), then the Tidyverse seems to be the right choice. However, the Tidyverse is built on a multitude of packages that depend on one another. Installing just one package from this collection, say *dplyr*, will lead to the installation of several other packages. For academic research, however, using `with()`, `within()`, `withGroups()`, and `withinGroups()` seems preferable, because they make it convenient to combine a larger set of data transformations into a single step and add comments that clarify these transformations. (It should be noted, however, that as the creator of the *memisc* package, the author of this book may not be completely unbiased in his assessment of this matter.) Chapter 5 makes it clear how complex these transforma-tions can become. Yet before moving on to this, we should take a look at the *tidyr* package.

4●4 Tidying up data using *tidyr*

Data obtained from other sources do not always come in the neat row-by-column structure described earlier, where rows correspond to observations and columns correspond to prop-erties of these observations or variables. Even though data available for download from the website of the OECD (Organisation for Economic Co-operation and Development), Eurostat (European Statistical Office), or other providers of public data have a tabular format, these data may be 'misarranged' in so far as different properties or variables are located in different rows or different observations are located in different columns. To deal with such a situation, the Tidyverse collection includes the *tidyr* package. The name of this package comes from the term that the authors of the Tidyverse use for data in the regular row-by-column arrangement and for the activity of transforming data into this arrangement.

The two main functions of the *tidyr* package to change the arrangement of data are `gather()` and `spread()`. The function `gather()` can be used to change a tibble with different obser-vations in different columns into a tibble where different observations are located in different rows, whereas the function `spread()` can be used to change a tibble with different properties (or notional variables) in different rows into a tibble with different properties located in dif-ferent columns. Both functions are thus intended to transfer data in an 'untidy' arrangement into a 'tidy' arrangement. From version 1.0.0 of the package, the functions `pivot_wider()` and `pivot_longer()` are available as somewhat more flexible alternatives to `gather()` and `spread()`, respectively.

It should be noted that the functionality provided by this package already exists in the standard R package *stats*, though with a different name. To use the terminology of earlier chapters, the transformation of a tibble by `gather()` or `pivot_longer()` corresponds to *reshaping* it from *wide* format into *long* format. By the same token, the transformation of a tibble by `spread()` or `pivot_wider()` corresponds to reshaping it from long format into wide format. While `gather()`, `spread()`, `pivot_longer()`, and `pivot_wider()` thus provide functionality that already exists in the form of the function `reshape()`, discussed earlier, they have a crucial restriction in comparison with the latter: `gather()` and `spread()` can only rearrange data in a single variable, while `reshape()` allows one to rearrange data in several variables simultaneously. These restrictions are the costs of making the use of the *tidyr* package simpler than the use of `reshape()`.

Yet `reshape()` (or the interface to this function named `Reshape()`, available in the *memisc* package) is only suited to data frames that are already 'tidy', with well-defined rows and columns and unambiguous variable names. They are meant to change between different arrangements of tidy repeated measurements or choice data, which we encountered in a previous chapter. The strength of the functions in the *tidyr* package lies instead in dealing with 'messy' data. For example, `pivot_longer()` and `pivot_wider()` are more fault-tolerant than `reshape()` by allowing the user to deal with duplicate row or column names.

The following examples will demonstrate the use of the functions of the *tidyr* package. In the first example, we work with tabular data scraped from the OECD website (OECD, 2018). It is a file with 'tab-delimited' columns that correspond to values of the Gini Index, a measure of income inequality, for different years, namely the years from 2007 to 2017.

Before we try to import the data, we look at the data file. Since the lines may be long, we only look at the first 50 characters of the first five lines:

```
substr(readLines("gini-oecd.tsv",n=5),start=1,stop=50)
```

```
[1] "Data table for: Income inequality, Gini coefficien"
[2] "Location \t 2007\t2008\t 2009\t2010\t2011\t2012\t2013\t201"
[3] "Australia\t\t\t\t\t\t0.326\t\t0.337\t\t0.330\t"
[4] "Austria\t0.284\t0.281\t0.289\t0.280\t0.281\t0.275\t0.279\t"
[5] "Belgium\t0.277\t0.266\t0.272\t0.267\t0.270\t0.265\t0.265\t"
```

We use the *tidyverse* package *readr* to read in the data from the file:

```
library(readr)
```

We use the function `read_tsv` from the *readr* package. The first line is just a data set description, so we skip this line by using the argument `skip=1`:

```
gini.oecd <- read_tsv("gini-oecd.tsv",
                      skip=1)
gini.oecd
```

```
# A tibble: 42 x 12
   Location `2007` `2008` `2009` `2010` `2011` `2012` `2013` `2014`
   <chr>     <dbl>  <dbl>  <dbl>  <dbl>  <dbl>  <dbl>  <dbl>  <dbl>
```

```
 1 Austral~ NA      NA      NA      NA      NA       0.326 NA       0.337
 2 Austria   0.284  0.281   0.289   0.28    0.281    0.275  0.279   0.274
 3 Belgium   0.277  0.266   0.272   0.267   0.27     0.265  0.265   0.266
 4 Brazil    NA     NA      0.485 NA        0.483 NA         0.47  NA
 5 Canada    0.317  0.315   0.316   0.316   0.313    0.317  0.32    0.313
 6 Chile     NA     NA      0.48  NA        0.471 NA          0.465 NA
 7 China (~ NA      NA      NA      NA       0.514 NA        NA      NA
 8 Costa R~ NA      NA      NA       0.472   0.48     0.483  0.494   0.485
 9 Czech R~  0.256  0.259   0.257   0.259   0.257    0.253  0.259   0.257
10 Denmark   NA     NA      NA      NA       0.251    0.249  0.254   0.256
# ... with 32 more rows, and 2 more variables: `2016` <dbl>, `2017`
```

We now make sure that the *tidyr* package is activated:

```
library(tidyr)
```

Since yearly observations are in different columns, we use `gather()` to get a tidy tibble:

```
gini.oecd %>% gather(`2007`, `2008`, `2009`, `2010`, `2011`, `2012`,
                     `2013`, `2014`, `2015`, `2016`, `2017`,
                     key="year",value="gini") -> gini.oecd.long
```

Mentioning several year numbers in backticks is a bit tedious. A more concise way is to specify the variables that do *not* represent observations in long format:

```
gini.oecd %>% gather(-Location,
                     key="year",value="gini") -> gini.oecd.long
```

The newer function `pivot_longer()` does the same but has a slightly different syntax:

```
gini.oecd %>% pivot_longer(-Location,
                           names_to="year",
                           values_to="gini") -> gini.oecd.long
gini.oecd.long
```

```
# A tibble: 462 x 3
   Location  year   gini
   <chr>     <chr> <dbl>
 1 Australia 2007   NA
 2 Australia 2008   NA
 3 Australia 2009   NA
 4 Australia 2010   NA
 5 Australia 2011   NA
 6 Australia 2012    0.326
 7 Australia 2013   NA
 8 Australia 2014    0.337
 9 Australia 2015   NA
10 Australia 2016    0.33
# ... with 452 more rows
```

In the second example, we work with data downloaded in tab-delimited or 'tab-separated val-ues' format (instead of scraped) from the OECD website (OECD, 2018). The data file contains various measures of inequality, the Gini Index, and other measures, for the years 2007–17. The downloaded data are in long format, where not only the years but also the measurement variables appear in different rows. We thus have to distribute the different measurement vari-ables into different columns if we want to tidy up our data.

```
substr(readLines("inequality-oecd-downloaded.csv",n=5),
       start=1,stop=40)
```

```
[1] "\"LOCATION\",\"INDICATOR\",\"SUBJECT\",\"MEASUR"
[2] "\"AUS\",\"INCOMEINEQ\",\"P50P10\",\"RT\",\"A\",\"20"
[3] "\"AUS\",\"INCOMEINEQ\",\"P50P10\",\"RT\",\"A\",\"20"
[4] "\"AUS\",\"INCOMEINEQ\",\"P50P10\",\"RT\",\"A\",\"20"
[5] "\"AUS\",\"INCOMEINEQ\",\"P90P10\",\"RT\",\"A\",\"20"
```

The first line contains the variable names, so the standard way of reading in the data should work:

```
inequality.oecd.dld <- read_csv("inequality-oecd-downloaded.csv")
inequality.oecd.dld
```

```
# A tibble: 2,315 x 8
   LOCATION INDICATOR  SUBJECT MEASURE FREQUENCY   TIME Value `Flag Codes`
   <chr>    <chr>      <chr>   <chr>   <chr>      <dbl> <dbl> <chr>
 1 AUS      INCOMEINEQ P50P10  RT      A           2012 2.2   <NA>
 2 AUS      INCOMEINEQ P50P10  RT      A           2014 2.2   <NA>
 3 AUS      INCOMEINEQ P50P10  RT      A           2016 2.1   <NA>
 4 AUS      INCOMEINEQ P90P10  RT      A           2012 4.4   <NA>
 5 AUS      INCOMEINEQ P90P10  RT      A           2014 4.3   <NA>
 6 AUS      INCOMEINEQ P90P10  RT      A           2016 4.3   <NA>
 7 AUS      INCOMEINEQ P90P50  RT      A           2012 2     <NA>
 8 AUS      INCOMEINEQ P90P50  RT      A           2014 2     <NA>
 9 AUS      INCOMEINEQ P90P50  RT      A           2016 2.1   <NA>
10 AUS      INCOMEINEQ GINI    INEQ    A           2012 0.326 <NA>
# ... with 2,305 more rows
```

The data set has a 'super-long' format: not only are different measurement occasions (the years) located in different rows but so also are the different substantial variables. Some of the columns contain metadata; for example, the column headed 'INDICATOR' describes the general concept of which the variables are indicators, the column headed 'SUBJECT' describes the measurement variable itself, 'MEASURE' describes the kind of measurement (e.g. 'RT' for ratio), 'FREQUENCY' indicates how often measures are taken. We are only interested in the measurement variables, the years, and the locations (or countries).

`spread()` assumes that all variables other than the ones that appear in the `key=` and `value=` arguments can be used to identify observations exactly. Unfortunately, the variables INDICATOR and MEASURE mess up the result here:

```
inequality.oecd.dld %>% spread(key="SUBJECT", value="Value") -> inequality.oecd
inequality.oecd[-c(2,4,6)]
```

```
# A tibble: 771 x 9
   LOCATION MEASURE  TIME   GINI P50P10 P90P10 P90P50 PALMA S80S20
   <chr>    <chr>   <dbl>  <dbl>  <dbl>  <dbl>  <dbl> <dbl>  <dbl>
 1 AUS      INEQ     2012  0.326    NA     NA     NA    NA     NA
 2 AUS      INEQ     2014  0.337    NA     NA     NA    NA     NA
 3 AUS      INEQ     2016  0.33     NA     NA     NA    NA     NA
 4 AUS      RT       2012   NA     2.2    4.4     2   1.24    5.5
 5 AUS      RT       2014   NA     2.2    4.3     2   1.34    5.7
 6 AUS      RT       2016   NA     2.1    4.3    2.1  1.26    5.5
 7 AUT      INEQ     2007  0.284    NA     NA     NA    NA     NA
 8 AUT      INEQ     2008  0.281    NA     NA     NA    NA     NA
 9 AUT      INEQ     2009  0.289    NA     NA     NA    NA     NA
10 AUT      INEQ     2010  0.28     NA     NA     NA    NA     NA
# ... with 761 more rows
```

The problem can be circumvented by using a data subset with only the relevant variables:

```
inequality.oecd.sub <- select(inequality.oecd.dld,
                          LOCATION,SUBJECT,TIME,Value)
inequality.oecd.sub
```

```
# A tibble: 2,315 x 4
   LOCATION SUBJECT  TIME Value
   <chr>    <chr>   <dbl> <dbl>
 1 AUS      P50P10   2012  2.2
 2 AUS      P50P10   2014  2.2
 3 AUS      P50P10   2016  2.1
 4 AUS      P90P10   2012  4.4
 5 AUS      P90P10   2014  4.3
 6 AUS      P90P10   2016  4.3
 7 AUS      P90P50   2012  2
 8 AUS      P90P50   2014  2
 9 AUS      P90P50   2016  2.1
10 AUS      GINI     2012  0.326
# ... with 2,305 more rows
```

Now the result of **spread()** looks as desired:

```
inequality.oecd.sub %>% spread(key=SUBJECT, value=Value) -> inequality.oecd
```

pivot_wider() allows one to specify the identifying columns directly, so that the desired result can be obtained in a single step:

```
inequality.oecd.dld %>% pivot_wider(names_from=SUBJECT,
                           values_from=Value,
```

```
                                     id_cols=c(LOCATION,TIME)) ->
                                             inequality.oecd
inequality.oecd
```

```
# A tibble: 386 x 8
   LOCATION   TIME P50P10 P90P10 P90P50  GINI S80S20 PALMA
   <chr>     <dbl>  <dbl>  <dbl>  <dbl> <dbl>  <dbl> <dbl>
 1 AUS        2012    2.2    4.4    2   0.326    5.5  1.24
 2 AUS        2014    2.2    4.3    2   0.337    5.7  1.34
 3 AUS        2016    2.1    4.3    2.1 0.33     5.5  1.26
 4 AUT        2007    2      3.6    1.8 0.284    4.4  1
 5 AUT        2008    1.9    3.4    1.8 0.281    4.3  1
 6 AUT        2009    2      3.6    1.8 0.289    4.5  1.03
 7 AUT        2010    1.9    3.5    1.8 0.28     4.3  0.98
 8 AUT        2011    1.9    3.5    1.8 0.281    4.4  0.99
 9 AUT        2012    2      3.5    1.8 0.275    4.2  0.96
10 AUT        2013    1.9    3.4    1.8 0.279    4.2  0.99
# ... with 376 more rows
```

Apart from functions to reshape data frames, the *tidyr* package has a variety of additional functions that deal with other kinds of 'messiness' in the data. These functions are still under development and (at the time of writing) sufficiently novel so that they are not discussed in Wickham and Grolemund (2016) but only discussed in the documentation that accompanies the package. Since there is not enough room in this book to cover all of these functions, just a few examples are discussed here.

The first of these functions is `fill()`, which replaces missing values in a variable in a tibble with the preceding or following non-missing values. While this may not always be a good idea, this function has its uses when the missingness of data is a consequence of the way in which the data were imported from elsewhere, as illustrated in the following.

The following character string contains data as they would look after scraping from a table on the internet or in a book: each country is named only once, but the rows that follow the one with the country name also refer to the country. (Actually, these are fantasy countries named after supercontinents from the geological past.)

```
messy_data_str <- "
country,  year,var1, var2
Rodinia,  1297,  67, -3.0
,         1298,  69, -2.9
,         1299,  70, -2.8
Pannotia, 1296,  73, -4.1
,         1297,  74, -3.9
,         1298,  75, -3.9
Pangaea,  1296,  54, -1.2
,         1297,  53, -1.1
,         1298,  52, -1.0
,         1299,  51, -0.9
"
```

We use `read_csv()` to read the string `messy_dta_str` into the tibble `messy_data`:

```
messy_data_str %>% read_csv () -> messy_data
messy_data
```

```
# A tibble: 10 x 4
   country   year  var1  var2
   <chr>    <dbl> <dbl> <dbl>
 1 Rodinia   1297    67    -3
 2 <NA>      1298    69  -2.9
 3 <NA>      1299    70  -2.8
 4 Pannotia  1296    73  -4.1
 5 <NA>      1297    74  -3.9
 6 <NA>      1298    75  -3.9
 7 Pangaea   1296    54  -1.2
 8 <NA>      1297    53  -1.1
 9 <NA>      1298    52    -1
10 <NA>      1299    51  -0.9
```

Since we know that the missing entries for the country names can be filled with the preceding non-missing entry, we can use the function `fill()`:

```
messy_data %>% fill(country) -> filled_data
filled_data
```

```
# A tibble: 10 x 4
   country   year  var1  var2
   <chr>    <dbl> <dbl> <dbl>
 1 Rodinia   1297    67    -3
 2 Rodinia   1298    69  -2.9
 3 Rodinia   1299    70  -2.8
 4 Pannotia  1296    73  -4.1
 5 Pannotia  1297    74  -3.9
 6 Pannotia  1298    75  -3.9
 7 Pangaea   1296    54  -1.2
 8 Pangaea   1297    53  -1.1
 9 Pangaea   1298    52    -1
10 Pangaea   1299    51  -0.9
```

The second of these example functions is `complete()`, which changes a tibble such that implicit missing values become explicit values. Such implicit missing values occur when the data can be conceived of as representing a regular grid of observations. In the previous example, such a grid of observations would consist of the period from 1296 to 1299 for the three imaginary countries Rodinia, Pannotia, and Pangaea. We continue that example to demonstrate the use of `complete()`. The observations appear to be nested in countries and years. For each country and for each year in the range from 1296 to 1299, there is or there could have been an observation. Accordingly, we indicate it in the call to the function `complete()`:

```
filled_data %>% complete(crossing(country, year))
```

```
# A tibble: 12 x 4
   country   year  var1  var2
   <chr>    <dbl> <dbl> <dbl>
 1 Pangaea   1296    54  -1.2
 2 Pangaea   1297    53  -1.1
 3 Pangaea   1298    52  -1
 4 Pangaea   1299    51  -0.9
 5 Pannotia  1296    73  -4.1
 6 Pannotia  1297    74  -3.9
 7 Pannotia  1298    75  -3.9
 8 Pannotia  1299    NA  NA
 9 Rodinia   1296    NA  NA
10 Rodinia   1297    67  -3
11 Rodinia   1298    69  -2.9
12 Rodinia   1299    70  -2.8
```

There were no rows for Pannotia in 1299 and Rodinia in 1296; these are now filled in with NAs for **var1** and **var2**.

As demonstrated by these examples, the *readr* and *tidyr* packages can be extremely helpful in dealing with data that one has obtained from other sources and that are not in a format that is directly amenable to data analysis. The only downside of these packages is that they are entangled in the Tidyverse collection of packages – far from being self-contained, these two depend on several other add-on packages. At the time of writing, these are *BH, clipr, crayon, dplyr, ellipsis, glue, hms, magrittr, purrr, Rcpp, rlang, R6, stringi, tibble, tidyselect, vctrs,* and *life-cycle*. Such multiple dependencies can make it cumbersome to keep the installation of these packages up to date.

▬▬▬▬▬▬▬ Overview Box 4.4 ▬▬▬▬▬▬▬

Some notable functions in the *tidyr* package

gather() This function allows one to reshape a tibble such that the values in different variables appear in different observations of the same variable. It is similar but not equivalent to **reshape(...,direction="long")**. The syntax of **gather()** is simpler, but it allows the user to only rearrange the values of a single variable. This function will be superseded by the function **pivot_longer()** in later versions of the same package.

spread() This function allows one to reshape a tibble such that the values in different rows of the variable appear in different variables. It is similar but not equivalent to **reshape(..., direction="wide")**. The syntax of **spread()** is simpler, but it allows the user to rearrange the values of a single variable only. This function will be superseded by the function **pivot_wider()** in later versions of the same package.

fill() This function allows one to 'fill in' the place of missing values (NAs) by non-missing values from the same tibble, where the replacements follow certain patterns. For example,

(Continued)

missing values may be replaced by the last preceding non-missing value or the first succeeding non-missing value in the same variable. This function does not have an obvious equivalent in any of the standard R packages.

`complete()` This function allows one to expand the number of rows of a tibble in such a way that every combination of possible values of a set of variables is present in the resulting tibble. This function does not have an obvious equivalent in any of the standard R packages.

5

Handling Data from Social Science Surveys

5.1 The structure of data from opinion polls and social and political surveys

In Chapter 3, we looked at the basic R data structure used for representing empirical research data – data frames – and how to import such data into the R workspace. Chapter 4 discussed extensions to the `"data.frame"` class and various data management functions that build on them. So far, the data considered consisted of nothing more than a bunch of variables that all had the same length but could be of different data types – that is, consisting of numbers, character strings, or numeric values. Such data are almost 'ready to use', but the data that survey researchers in the social sciences deal with are often richer in structure and content.

Consider, for example, the data set of the British Election Study (BES) of 1983 (Heath et al., 1983) and in particular the variable Q46G in this data set. It contains the left–right self-placements of the survey participants. In the interviews, the respondents were asked to place themselves on a scale running from –10 to +10, where –10 indicated the leftist extreme, +10 indicated the rightist extreme, and 0 indicated a centrist position. Not all respondents in the sample gave a valid answer to the corresponding question. If a respondent refused to answer the question about his or her left–right self-placement, his or her response is represented by the code 96; if he or she did not know what answer to give, his or her response is represented by the code 98; and for some other kinds of invalid answers, the codes 95, 97, and 99 were used.

Such information is typically contained in a *codebook*, a document or part of a document that is included in the technical documentation that accompanies a survey data set made available by public data archives (e.g. the UK Data Archive, www.data-archive.ac.uk/; the ICPSR data archive, www.icpsr.umich.edu/; or the GESIS data archive, www.gesis.org/) or by the principal investigators themselves – as in the case of the BES. As an example, Figure 5.1 shows an excerpt of the codebook that accompanies the cross-sectional survey data set of the 1983 BES (Heath et al., 1983).

A researcher who wants to reuse the BES 1983 data set for secondary analysis will need the following information to be able to make proper use of the variable Q46G:

1   The *meaning of the variable*: that is, what question in the questionnaire it refers to and perhaps the question wording – in the present case, this would be the left-right self-placement of the survey respondents

2   The *meaning of the values* of the variables – in the present case, the code –10 refers to the left end and the code and +10 refers to the right end of the left-right self-placement scale

3   Which values of the variable represent valid information (i.e. are *valid values*), and which represent missing information of a certain kind of 'missingness' (i.e. are *missing values*) – in the present case, this means that values from to +10 refer to valid responses while the codes 95 to 99 refer to instances where respondents did not give a response that could be interpreted and used as a left-right self-placement.

The first kind of information is relevant because survey data sets can contain quite a large number of variables whose meaning usually is not immediately clear from their names. The variable name Q46G in the BES data set, which contains no less than 403 variables, reflects its

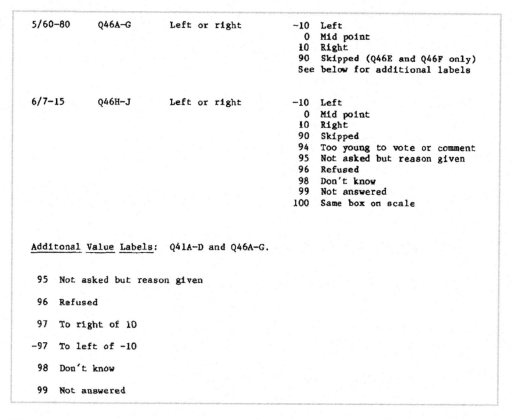

Figure 5.1 An excerpt from the codebook that accompanies the cross-sectional data set of the 1983 British Election Study

Note: The document file is available at the British Election Study website at www.britishelectionstudy.com/data-object/1983-bes-cross-section/

origin in the seventh item from the 46th question battery, but of course, it is impossible to 'read' from the variable name that it refers to the left–right self-placements of respondents. The second kind of information is relevant because of the fact that the range of valid values from –10 to +10 in the variable still allows for two different possibilities: that the scale runs from 'left' to 'right' or from 'right' to 'left'. The third kind of information is relevant because it would only be sensible to compute averages or other statistics from the valid values of the variable – that is, after dropping all observations where the variable has any other value than 1 between –10 and +10.

Operating on the 'raw values' of the variable without considering this additional information would end in misleading results, which is why survey data are usually accompanied by codebooks. In addition, data in files created with software like SPSS or Stata also include this additional information in the form of *variable labels*, *value labels*, and *missing value definitions*. Newer data files created with SPSS additionally may contain information about the intended *measurement level* of the variables in the data set. Figure 5.2 shows a codebook page for the variable Q46B reconstructed from the metadata information contained in the SPSS file that contains the data from the cross-sectional survey of the 1983 BES.

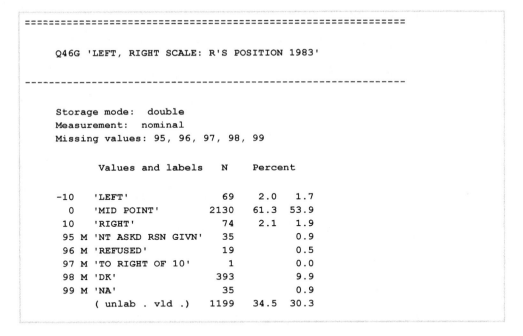

```
===================================================================

    Q46G 'LEFT, RIGHT SCALE: R'S POSITION 1983'

-------------------------------------------------------------------

    Storage mode:  double
    Measurement:   nominal
    Missing values: 95, 96, 97, 98, 99

            Values and labels   N      Percent

    -10    'LEFT'                69     2.0    1.7
     0     'MID POINT'         2130    61.3   53.9
    10     'RIGHT'               74     2.1    1.9
    95 M 'NT ASKD RSN GIVN'     35             0.9
    96 M 'REFUSED'              19             0.5
    97 M 'TO RIGHT OF 10'        1             0.0
    98 M 'DK'                  393             9.9
    99 M 'NA'                   35             0.9
            ( unlab . vld .)   1199    34.5   30.3
```

Figure 5.2 A codebook page created from metadata

Note: The output was created with the function `codebook()` from the R package *memisc* (Elff, 2019). The data set is available from the BES website, www.britishelectionstudy.com/data-object/1983-bes-cross-section/

A *variable label* is a character string attached to a variable in a data set that is typically longer than the name of the variable itself and is not subject to syntactical restrictions as to what kinds of characters are allowed in a variable name. In function calls for the construction of statistical models or statistical summaries, only variable names are used but not variable labels. Variable labels are supported by those statistical software packages that are widely used by survey researchers – that is, SPSS (IBM, 2017), and its open source clone PSPP (Pfaff, 2018), and Stata (StataCorp, 2019). R by itself does not support variable labels, but it is relatively easy to implement variable labels in the form of object attributes. The *memisc* package provides such an implementation (Elff, 2019). With *memisc*, the variable label `"LEFT,RIGHT SCALE: R'S POSITION 1983"` seen in Figure 5.2 could be attached to a variable Q46G with a code like this:

```
description(Q46G) <- "LEFT,RIGHT SCALE: R'S POSITION 1983"
```

Value labels are character strings associated with certain values a variable in a data set can have. It is common practice in the creation of social survey data sets that if a variable has value labels then all possible values have associated value labels. There are exceptions to this rule, however. In case of the left–right self-placement variable in the 1993 BES data set discussed above, only the values –10, 0, and +10 are labelled, as can be seen in Figure 5.2. More usual exceptions are variables that can take a large number of possible values, such as household or personal income (here only the missing values will usually be labelled) or survey weights (which are rarely labelled at all). Again, the commercial software packages SPSS and Stata provide for value labels, while R without extension packages does not. However, the *memisc* package as well as some other packages provide ways to create and manage value labels. If value labels were not already associated to the variable Q46G from the 1983 BES data set, value labels such as those seen in Figure 5.2 could be added to the variable by the following code:

```
labels(Q46G)  <- c("LEFT"              = -10,
                    "MID POINT"        =   0,
                    "RIGHT"            =  10,
                    "NT ASKD RSN GIVN"=  95,
                    "REFUSED"          =  96,
                    "TO RIGHT OF 10"   =  97,
                    "DK"               =  98,
                    "NA"               =  99)
```

Value labels should not be confused with the labels of factor levels. A *factor* in R is a data structure that is supposed to contain (ordered or unordered) categorical data. An example perhaps well known to most R users is the factor variable Species in the example data set iris. This factor has three distinct levels with the labels "setosa", "versicolor", and "virginica". The crucial difference between a factor and a variable with value labels is that the levels of a factor are always internally coded with successive numbers and these codes do not have any other substantive meaning than that they indicate the order of the factors. For example, the codes that are associated with the three levels of the factor Species in the data set iris are 1, 2, and 3. It is even impossible to use any other codes for a factor with n levels than the numbers from 1 to n. In contrast, there are no restrictions as to what values are labelled in the case of a variable with value labels. This discrepancy can make it tricky to adequately handle in R value labels metadata from data files created with SPSS or Stata. The next section will explore these problems further.

A *missing value declaration* is information associated with a variable that determines which of its values represent valid measurements, for example valid responses to interview questions, and which represent missing measurements, for example 'don't know' responses or refusals to give answers in an interview. Missing value definitions are rules about what observations to discard when the intention is to compute meaningful summary statistics, and so on. SPSS so far is the only commercial software package that supports missing value declarations directly. Stata allows the user to distinguish between different types of missing values, but these are not numbers. They are a bit like the general missing value NA in R but with different 'flavours' added to them. Again, missing value definitions are supported in R only with the help of extension packages such as *memisc*. In the case of the left–right self-placement variable Q46G from the 1983 BES data set, the missing values are 95, 96, 97, 98, and 99. Although possible in SPSS, there is no missing value definition attached to this variable. Using *memisc*, a missing value definition can be associated to Q46G with the following code:

```
missing.values(Q46G)  <- c(95,96,97,98,99)
```

Alternatively, all values within a certain range can be defined as representing missing values with the code

```
missing.range(Q46G)  <- c(95,99)
```

The same package also allows the converse of a missing value definition, a definition of which values of a variable are considered valid measurements. In the case of the left–right self-placement variable Q46G, all integers between −10 and +10 are valid values. This can be indicated using the code

```
valid.values(Q46G) <- -10:10
```

or

```
valid.range(Q46G) <- c(-10,10)
```

The *level of measurement* of a variable indicates what comparisons of and computations on its values make sense substantially. If the measurement level of a variable is *nominal*, different values of a variable merely reflect that objects are different with respect to the measured properties. For example, the variable Q9A in the BES 1983 data set, which contains coded responses to the question about which party the respondents voted for, has a nominal level of measurement: the variable equals 1 for respondents who voted for the Conservative Party, 2 for respondents who voted for the Labour Party, and so on. A variable has an *ordinal* level of measurement if the order between its values can be interpreted substantially. For example, the variable Q15A in the BES 1983 data set represents the responses to the question about how effective the respondents perceived Margaret Thatcher to be prime minister, with 1 representing the response 'very effective', 2 the response 'fairly effective', 3 the response 'fairly ineffective', and 4 the response 'very ineffective'. A variable has an *interval scale* level of measurement when the comparison of differences of values makes sense substantially, while a *ratio scale* level of measurement means that ratios of values can be sensibly compared. For example, the variable Q56 has not just an interval scale level but even a ratio scale level of measurement: it contains responses about respondents' age on their last birthday – one respondent can be twice as old as another respondent. For a mean or a variance of a variable to make sense, it needs to have at least an interval level of measurement. With the *memisc* package, it is possible to obtain or specify the level of measurement using the function `measurement()`. For example, to tell R that the intended level of measurement of the variable Q56 is ratio scaled, one can use the following code:

```
measurement(Q56) <- "ratio"
```

If the function `measurement()` is called before a specification of a measurement level, it will need to 'guess' it. In that case, `measurement()` will return `"nominal"` if it has value labels, otherwise it will return `"interval"`.

The objects in the class `"data.frame"`, introduced in Chapter 3, have a row-by-column structure, where the rows refer to cases or observations and the columns refer to variables (the ways in which the cases or observations differ systematically from one another). The *memisc* package defines the object class `"data.set"`, which is a variant of the `"data.frame"` class. The main difference is that the columns of a `"data.set"` class are expected to be variables with metadata about their variable labels, value labels, and/or missing values. While the columns of a data frame are vectors or factors, the columns of a `"data.set"` object are objects from the class `"item"`. If a `"data.set"` object is translated into a data frame with `as.data.frame()`, its columns are translated into numeric vectors or factors based on their declared measurement level. A column of a `"data.set"` object, which is an `"item"` object, is translated into a numeric vector with `as.numeric()` if its `"measurement"` attribute (i.e. whatever is returned by `measurement()`) equals either `"interval"` or `"ratio"`. It is translated into an ordered factor with `as.ordered()` if its `"measurement"` attribute equals `"ordinal"`, and it is translated into an unordered factor with `as.factor()` if the `"measurement"` attribute equals `"nominal"`.

In order to inspect the metadata of an `"item"` object as well as the distribution of its values, the *memisc* package provides the function `codebook()`. A call to this function will result in the creation of codebook pages such as those seen in Figure 5.2. The function `codebook()` can also be applied to entire `"data.set"` objects or to the similarly constructed `"importer"` objects, discussed in the next section. In this case, the result of `codebook()` will be a sequence of codebook pages, one page for each variable/item in the `"data.set"` object.

The present section has introduced the concepts of *variable labels*, *value labels*, *valid values*, and *missing values* and some functionality provided by the R extension package *memisc*. The key concepts are summarized in Overview Box 5.1. The functions from the *memisc* package are summarized in Overview Boxes 5.2–5.4. It should be noted that other packages, namely *gdata* (Warnes et al., 2017) and *haven* (Wickham and Miller, 2018), provide some support for value labels and user-defined missing values. Yet this support is relatively limited in comparison with that provided by the *memisc* package.

━━━━━━━━━━ Overview Box 5.1 ━━━━━━━━━━

Key concepts: the structure of data from opinion polls and social and political surveys

Variable name: a usually short character string that is used to refer to a variable in a data set.

Variable label: a character string attached to a variable in a data set that gives a somewhat more extensive description of what a variable and its values are supposed to mean.

Value labels: a set of character strings associated with a set of values that a variable can take. These strings describe the meaning of the values if they are coded responses. For example, in a social survey the values `"female"` and `"male"` may be coded by the numbers 1 and 2. The appropriate value labels would then be `"female"` for 1 and `"male"` for 2.

Missing value: a value of a variable in a data set – usually a number but possibly also a character string – that represents the absence of substantial information. For example, the number 98 can be used to indicate observations where a survey respondent did not know how to answer the relevant interview question.

System missing value: an internal code, not interpreted as a number, used by statistical software to represent the absence of information in a value of a variable. In the Stata system, missing values are symbolically represented by `.`, `.a`, and so on. In the SPSS system, missing values are symbolically referred to as `SYSMIS`. In R, the system missing value is `NA` (for 'not available' or 'not applicable').

(Continued)

Measurement level: an aspect of a variable that determines what comparisons of or computations with its values make sense substantially. The measurement level is `"nominal"`, which means that the values of the variable can only be used to make distinctions; `"ordinal"`, which means that the order between two different values can be interpreted; `"interval"`, which means that differences can be interpreted and compared; or `"ratio"`, which means that ratios can be interpreted and compared.

Codebook: a document that describes the contents of a data set. At least, it describes what the variables and their values mean. It usually associates variable labels with variable names and value labels with codes. If applicable, it also describes missing value definitions for the variables in the data set. Often, a codebook also shows some basic descriptive statistics, such as univariate frequency distributions, the number of missing values, and so on.

■■■■■ Overview Box 5.2 ■■■■■

Functions defined in the *memisc* package for handling variable labels and value labels

`description()` This function is used to get the label attached to a variable or attach a label to a variable. To get the label attached to a variable **var**, use, for example,

```
description(var)
```

To attach a label to a variable **var**, use, for example,

```
description(var) <- "String describing the variable"
```

`labels()` This function is used to get the *value labels* of a variable, the labels associated with codes that are used to represent certain response categories. To get the value labels of a variable **var**, use, for example,

```
labels(var)
```

To define value labels for a variable **var**, use, for example,

```
labels(var) <- c("one code"=1,
                 "another code"=2)
```

■■■■■ Overview Box 5.3 ■■■■■

Functions defined in the *memisc* package for handling user-defined missing values, declaring measurement levels, and creating codebooks

`missing.values()` This function can be used to find out which codes of a variable represent *missing values*. For example,

```
missing.values(var)
```

reports which values are declared missing. Conversely, to declare values 98 and 99 of a variable **var** as missing, use

```
missing.values(var) <- c(98,99)
```

valid.values(), **valid.range()** These functions can be used to declare all the non-missing (i.e. valid) values of a variable. For example, if one uses the code

```
valid.values(var) <- 1:5
```

then only the values 1, 2, 3, 4, and 5 of the variable **var** will be valid and all other values (e.g. 1.5 or 9) will be declared as missing. With

```
valid.range <- c(1,5)
```

all values between 1 and 5 inclusive are declared as valid and all values outside this interval will be declared as missing. In contrast to the previous example, 1.5 will now be a valid value, but 9 will still be a missing value.

measurement() This function can be used to obtain the *measurement level* declared or inferred for a variable. Its value is one (and only one) of the strings **"nominal"**, **"ordinal"**, **"interval"**, or **"ratio"**. For example, the measurement level of a variable **var** can be declared to be interval level with

```
measurement(var) <- "interval"
```

codebook() This function produces a codebook page (see e.g. Figure 5.2) if applied to a single **"item"** object, or a series of codebook pages if applied to a **"data.set"** object, in which case it gives one codebook page for each **"item"** object in the **"data.set"** object.

■■■■■■■■■ **Overview Box 5.4** ■■■■■■■■■

Object classes defined in the *memisc* package for handling variable labels, value labels, and user-defined missing values

An **"item"** **object** is an object that is a member of the class **"item"**. Such objects are created from ordinary vectors if value labels, valid values, or missing values are declared. When such an object is translated into a factor or numeric vector, its missing values are changed into NAs. If it is translated into a factor, then the value labels become labels of its factor levels.

A **"data.set"** **object** is an object that is a member of the class **"data.set"** that is similar in structure to a data frame. It is dedicated to contain **"item"** objects as columns. If a **"data.set"** object is translated into a data frame, then its columns are translated into unordered factors with **as.factor()**, into ordered factors with **as.ordered()**, or into numeric vectors with **as.numeric()**, depending on their respective measurement attribute.

5.2 Importing survey data from SPSS and Stata into R

As already discussed in Chapter 3, the 'standard' way of importing data from SPSS or Stata is by using the *foreign* package (R Core Team, 2018). If a data set imported in this way contains only numeric variables or only string variables, then importing such a data set into a data frame does not lead to a loss of information. However, data files coming from other statistical software, in particular if this software is written for social scientists working with survey data, such as SPSS and Stata, may contain metadata of the sort discussed in the previous section. What kind of metadata is used and supported by file formats from these statistical software packages is shown in Table 5.1. The handling of these metadata poses some challenges if the information contained in the metadata is to be retained, and the support provided by the *foreign* package quickly reaches its limits.

Table 5.1 Support for survey interview metadata in file formats of various commercial software systems

Software system	Variable labels	Value labels	Missing value declarations
SPSS	Yes	Yes	Yes
Stata	Yes	Yes	No
SAS	No	Limited	No

The function **read.spss()** from the *foreign* package handles all variables with value labels using the same set of rules. If all values that occur in a variable have labels, the variable is converted into a factor. If only some of the values have labels, then, depending on the setting of the option **add.undeclared.levels**, either all values are converted into factor levels or the variable is treated as a numeric vector. It is, however, not possible to convert the left–right self-placement into a factor and the age variable into a numeric vector if they are both part of the same data set. The function **read.dta()** from the *foreign* package is even more restrictive: depending on the option **convert.factors**, variables in a Stata data set that have value labels are either converted into factors, where all unlabelled values are translated into **NA**, or converted into numeric vectors.

Both **read.spss()** and **read.dta()** offer options to deal with missing values. In SPSS, it is possible to define certain values as missing, as discussed in the previous section. For example, in the 1983 BES data set in SPSS format, the (integer) values from 95 to 99 are defined to represent various forms of missing information. If **read.spss()** is called with the optional argument **use.missings= TRUE**, these values will be converted into **NA**s, otherwise they will be kept as is. In Stata files, different forms of missing information can be encoded in various non-numeric missing value codes, and the function **read.dta()** provides for ways to handle such missing values. Missing values in variables in Stata files are always converted into **NA**s, and if the optional argument **missing.type= TRUE**, additional information is attached to the resulting data frame that informs what missing values are present in the variables of the imported data set.

Finally, both **read.spss()** (with the optional argument **to.data.frame= TRUE**) and **read.dta()** return data frames with all metadata, like variable labels, value labels, and user-defined missing values attached to them in the form of special *attributes*. However, *foreign* does not provide specific facilities to handle these metadata attributes. Further, the names of the metadata attributes are inconsistent: variable labels from SPSS files are attached to the data frame as an attribute named **"variable.labels"**, while variable labels from Stata files are attached as an attribute named **"var.labels"**.

While the *foreign* package, at least since version 0.8-70, allows one to import data sets from SPSS, Stata, or SAS files in such a way that no metadata information is lost, it does not yet provide facilities to handle this information *after* the data are imported. Further, the way these functions deal with value labels and (where applicable) user-defined missing values is not very coherent and convenient and can be controlled with arguments to these functions that affect *all* variables in the data set.

The *memisc* package (Elff, 2019) improves upon the restrictions set by the *foreign* package. In addition, it helps in dealing with some aspects of social science data sets that would make working with them inconvenient. Data sets from major social science survey projects, such as the American National Election Study (ANES), the British Election Study (BES), the German Longitudinal Election Study (GLES), and the European Social Survey, often contain a large number of variables, a few hundred at least. Although such data sets with sizes between 5 and 100 megabytes would nowadays no longer be considered as 'big data', they can nevertheless become unwieldy because of the many variables contained in them. Further, the variables in such data sets (at least in the way they are offered by social science data archives, such as the ICPSR archive, the UK Data Archive, or the GESIS Data Archive) often have non-mnemonic names, such as V480001, V480002, and so on (as in the 1948 ANES data set; Campbell and Kahn, 2015) or Q1, Q2A, Q2B, and so on (as in the 1983 BES data set; Heath et al. 1983). Selecting the variables of interest for analysis from a data set with a large number of variables can thus be a considerable challenge.

The *memisc* package (Elff, 2019) follows an approach to importing data from an SPSS or Stata file that is different from that of the *foreign* (R Core Team, 2018) and *haven* (Wickham and Miller, 2018) packages. *memisc* makes it possible to examine the data in a data file *before* they are loaded into the main memory of R. Further, it enables one to manage value labels and user-defined missing values before a data set that contains such metadata is converted into a data frame. Following the approach taken by the *memisc* package, creating a data frame from data in an external file produced by SPSS or Stata involves several steps:

1   The declaration of a file containing data in a format used by SPSS or by Stata
2   The selection of those variables and cases/observations in the data file that are of interest for data analysis
3   The preparation of the selected variables and cases/observations for conversion into a data frame
4   The eventual creation of a data frame

While this multiple-step procedure may seem tedious at first glance, it allows one to avoid or at least to address some of the difficulties described above.

For the first step, the declaration of data files, the *memisc* package provides the functions **spss.system.file()**, **spss.portable.file()**, and **Stata.file()**. The function **spss.system.file()** can be used to make a data file in an SPSS 'system' format known to R. The system format is the binary format in which data are usually saved by SPSS if the command **SAVE FILE** is used. Such files usually have the filename extension '.sav'. Along the same lines, the function **spss.portable.file()** can be used to declare a file as containing data in SPSS 'portable' format, encoded in a textual format as ASCII or EBCDIC characters.[1] Such files usually have the filename extension '.por'. To declare a file as containing data in Stata binary format, the function **stata.file()** can be used. For example, to declare the file **"83BES.por"** as an SPSS portable file, one uses

```
BES.1983.por <- spss.portable.file("83BES.por")
```

The result of such a function call (stored in the variable **BES.1983.por**) is an object that contains only the location of the data in the file system and the associated metadata (value labels etc.) but not yet the data. This allows one to examine the structure of the data without actually loading them. To get an overview of all the variable labels in the data file, one can use in this example the code

```
description(BES.1983.por)
```

which creates the following output (only the 13th to the 24th lines are shown):

```
[...]
  Q1        'CARE WHICH PARTY WON'
  Q2A       'FOLLOWED ELECTION BROADCASTS'
  Q2B       'READ ABOUT CAMPAIGN IN NEWSPAPER'
  Q2C       '[IF READ NEWSPP] WHICH DAILY ON CAMPAIGN'
  Q2D       'HEARD CANDIDATE AT POLITICAL MEETING'
  Q2E       'CANVASSED FOR CANDIDATE'
  Q2F       'PUT UP POLITICAL PARTY POSTER'
  Q2G       'CANVASSER CALLED DURING CAMPAIGN'
  Q2H1      'CON CANVASSER CALLED'
  Q2H2      'LAB CANVASSER CALLED'
  Q2H3      'ALLIANCE CANVASSER CALLED'
  Q2H4      'LIB CANVASSER CALLED'
[...]
```

The function **description()** is useful, because it is impossible to keep in mind the meaning of all the variables, especially when the variable names do not reflect the concept that they are supposed to represent. It does not help very much if the variable names are related to the number of the corresponding question in the survey questionnaire, because it is no less difficult to keep the questionnaire in mind.

The second step of importing data using the *memisc* package would be the selection of the variables and observations that one actually needs for further data analysis. If one were working with a data set already imported into a data frame, such a selection would be done with

---

[1]ASCII is a standard for representing characters by 7-bit numbers. Many modern coding schemes, such as ISO 8859 or UTF-8, are extensions of it. EBCDIC is another 8-bit coding standard that used to be common in mainframe computers, but it is incompatible with ASCII.

the help of the function **subset()**. The *memisc* package allows one to create such a subset even before the full data set is imported because this may be more efficient than importing a large data set and then discarding a large fraction of it. For this purpose, there is a method for the generic function **subset()** that is applicable to the **"importer"** objects returned by functions like **spss.system.file()** or **Stata.file()**. As a measure of additional convenience, the **subset()** method function for **"importer"** objects also allows one to rename the variables selected for import, because the original variable names may be hard to remember. The use of the **subset()** method is illustrated with the 1983 BES as an example.

Overall, the 1983 BES data set (Heath et al., 1983) contains 3955 observations on 402 variables, and the SPSS 'portable' data set has a size of 3.5 megabytes. While a file of that size will not cause any problems for a contemporary computer (and not even for a contemporary smartphone), the large number of variables may be tedious to work with for the practical data analyst or data manager. Therefore, we apply the function **subset()** to load a subset of the variables from this external data file. We also rename some of the selected variables into something easier to remember. For example, the code

```
BES.1983.classvot <- subset(
    BES.1983.por,
    select=c(
        voted          = Q7A,
        vote           = Q9A,
        lrself         = Q46G,
        fglclass       = FGLCLASS,
        rglclass       = RGLCLASS,
        sglclass       = SGLCLASS,
        ethnicity      = Q64A,
        gender         = Q64B,
        age            = Q56,
        educ           = Q59A,
        religion       = Q63A,
        religatt       = Q63B
    ))
```

imports the variables Q7A, Q9A, Q46G, FGLCLASS, RGLCLASS, SGLCLASS, Q64A, Q64B, Q56, Q59A, Q63A, and Q63B into a data set object BES.1983.classvot; changes the names of the variable Q7A into voted, Q9A into vote, Q46G into lrself, Q64A into ethnicity, Q64B into gender, Q56 into age, Q59A into educ, Q63A into religion, and Q63B into religatt; and changes the names of the variables FGLCLASS, RGLCLASS, and SGLCLASS to lower case. Why these names of variables are chosen becomes obvious once the labels of these variables are obtained using

```
description(BES.1983.classvot)
```

which leads to the output

```
voted      'DID RESPONDENT VOTE 1983'
vote       '[IF VOTED] PARTY VOTED FOR'
lrself     'LEFT,RIGHT SCALE: R'S POSITION 1983'
```

```
fglclass    'FATHER'S GOLDTHORPE-LLEWELLYN CLASS'
rglclass    'RESPONDENT'S GOLDTHORPE-LLEWELLYN CLASS'
sglclass    'SPOUSE'S GOLDTHORPE-LLEWELLYN CLASS'
ethnicity   'RESPONDENT'S ETHNIC ORIGIN'
gender      'RESPONDENT'S SEX'
age         'RESPONDENT'S AGE LAST BIRTHDAY'
educ        'AGE RESPONDENT LEFT SCHOOL'
religion    'RESPONDENT'S RELIGION'
religatt    '[IF RELIGION] FREQUENCY OF ATTENDANCE'
```

The value of **voted** indicates whether the respective respondents have participated in the election, **vote** contains codes for the parties the respondents voted for, **lrself** contains the respondents' left–right self-placement (where they located themselves on a 21-point scale from 'left' to 'right'), **rglclass** contains the respondents' socio-economic class (obtained by recoding their current occupation using the Goldthorpe–Llewellyn class schema), **fglclass** contains the socio-economic class of the respondents' fathers, and **sglclass** contains the socio-economic class of the respondents' spouses.

The third step is optional but should always be considered: the preparation of the variables in the imported data set for conversion into a data frame. This conversion (the fourth step) is done using the **as.data.frame()** method function applied to the imported data set. The reason for the optional third step is that often the one-size-fits-all approach, in which either all or none of the variables with value labels are converted into factors, is unsuitable for most applications. In order to determine which of the variables in a data set are to be converted into factors and which are to be converted into numeric variables, one uses the **"measurement"** attribute of a variable in an object of class **"data.set"**.

The measurement attributes and their consequences for the final step of converting a data set object into a data frame are again illustrated with the 1983 BES data set, where we pick up after the creation of the **"data.set"** object **BES.1983.classvot**. All variables in this data set have value labels, so that they would be converted into factors with **as.data.frame(BES.1983.classvot)**, but this is not what we should intend. If we assume that the intended level of measurement of the respondents' left–right self-placement (**lrself**) is interval scaled, we can set the measurement attribute accordingly with

```
measurement(BES.1983.classvot$lrself) <- "interval"
```

The variable **age** is quite obviously interval scaled, as is the variable **educ**, which contains the respondents' age at the time they finish their education. To adapt the level of measurement of several variables in a data set, for example of **lrself**, **age**, and **educ** in the data set **BES.1983.classvot**, one can use the function **within()**, for example

```
BES.1983.classvot <- within(BES.1983.classvot,{
    measurement(lrself) <- "interval"
    measurement(age) <- "interval"
    measurement(educ) <- "interval"
})
```

or one can use the `foreach()` function in *memisc*:

```
BES.1983.classvot <- within(BES.1983.classvot,{
    foreach(var=c(lrself,age,educ),{
            measurement(var) <- "interval"
    })
})
```

As a consequence, the data frame that is the result of `as.data.frame()` applied to `BES.1983.classvot` will contain the factors `voted`, `vote`, `fglclass`, `rglclass`, `sglclass`, `ethnicity`, `gender`, `religion`, and `religatt` (because, in `BES.1983.classvot`, these variables have value labels defined for them) and the integer vectors `lrtest`, `age`, and `educ` (because we set the measurement level explicitly to interval scaled).

If we generate the codebook of the variable `age`

```
codebook(BES.1983.classvot["age"])
```

```
================================================================


   age 'RESPONDENT'S AGE LAST BIRTHDAY'


-----------------------------------------------------------------


   Storage mode: double
   Measurement: interval

        Values and labels    N     Percent

    99      'NA'            20     0.5   0.5
            (unlab.vld.)  3935   99.5  99.5


            Min:    18.000
            Max:    99.000
            Mean:   45.704
       Std.Dev.:    18.174
       Skewness:     0.362
       Kurtosis:    -0.757
```

we can see that the variable `age` has a single labelled value, the number 99, which is used to represent observations in which survey respondents did not give information about their age. Therefore, it would not make much sense to include observations where the age variable takes a value of 99 to compute an average. As described earlier, 99 can be declared as a missing value with the code

```
missing.values(BES.1983.classvot$age) <- 99
```

After studying the codebook of all variables in the data set **BES.1983.classvot**, one could declare the missing values of all of these with the code

```
BES.1983.classvot <- within(BES.1983.classvot,{
    missing.values(voted)      <- 9
    missing.values(vote)       <- 95:99
    missing.values(lrself)     <- 95:99
    missing.values(fglclass)   <- 0
    missing.values(rglclass)   <- 0
    missing.values(sglclass)   <- 0
    missing.values(ethnicity)  <- 9
    missing.values(gender)     <- 9
    missing.values(age)        <- 99
    missing.values(religion)   <- 99
    missing.values(religatt)   <- 7:9
})
```

Files created with SPSS often contain missing value declarations. In such cases, a declaration after importing the data is not necessary since the functions **spss.system.file()** and **spss.portable.file()** import these declarations in the same way as the variable labels and value labels contained in such a file.

Occasionally, data sets are not provided in SPSS or Stata format but in plain text format, accompanied by text files that contain code in SPSS syntax that defines variable labels, value labels, and missing value declarations. The data set from the 2008 cross-section of the ANES originally was available only in this format (ANES, 2015). The principal function for importing such fixed-column format data is **spss.fixed.file()**. To be able to use this function, one usually also has to specify a file with SPSS syntax that declares which columns in the data file correspond to which variables. This file is specified by the argument **columns.file=**. A data file of this type is often accompanied by further text files containing SPSS syntax defining variable labels, value labels, and missing values. These files can be specified with arguments **varlab.file=**, **codes.file=**, and **missval.file=**, respectively. For example, if the 2008 ANES data are in the fixed-column format file **"anes2008TS_dat.txt"**, the columns declarations in the file **"anes2008TS_col.sps"**, the variable labels declarations in the file **"anes2008TS_lab.sps"**, the value labels declarations in the file **"anes2008TS_cod.sps"**, and the missing value labels declarations in the file **"anes2008TS_md.sps"**, the code to create an importer for these data is

```
anes2008TS <- spss.fixed.file(
             "anes2008TS_dat.txt",
             columns.file = "anes2008TS_col.sps",
             varlab.file  = "anes2008TS_lab.sps",
             codes.file   = "anes2008TS_cod.sps",
             missval.file = "anes2008TS_md.sps")
```

━━━━━━━━━━ **Overview Box 5.5** ━━━━━━━━━━

Functions and concepts of the *memisc* package for importing data from various statistical packages: I. "`importer`" objects

An "`importer`" **object** is an R object that contains information about a data file - where the file is located, what variables are present in this file, and what metadata (about value labels etc.) are associated with these variables.

`spss.file()` reads the metadata from an SPSS 'system' or 'portable' file and returns an "`importer`" object. SPSS system files are binary files and have a name ending with '`.sav`', while SPSS portable files are text files encoded in ASCII or EBCDIC.

It requires a filename as first argument (or an argument tagged as `file=`).

Optionally, further arguments can be given with the tags `varlab.file=`, `codes.file=`, and `missval.file=`, which specify files that contain SPSS syntax defining variable labels, value labels, and missing values, respectively - in case these metadata are not already defined in the file. Occasionally, such additional syntax files are available from data archives.

Internally, `spss.file()` calls `spss.system.file()` for system files and `spss.portable.file()` for portable files.

`spss.fixed.file()` has two required arguments, an argument tagged `file=`, which specifies the data file, and an argument tagged `columns.file=`, which specifies the file that contains syntax that describes the correspondence between variables and columns in the data file. If a data archive provides a data file in fixed-column format together with SPSS syntax that defines the variables, it typically also provides syntax files defining variable labels, value labels, and missing value declarations. These files can be specified by arguments with the tags `varlab.file=`, `codes.file=`, and `missval.file=`, respectively.

Based on the `columns.file=`, `varlab.file=`, `codes.file=`, and `missval.file=`arguments, the function returns an `importer` object.

`Stata.file()` reads the metadata from a Stata file and returns an "`importer`" object. At the time of writing, files in the format specific to Stata version 13 or newer are not supported. However, files in an older Stata format can also be created with recent Stata versions.

━━━━━━━━━━ **Overview Box 5.6** ━━━━━━━━━━

Functions and concepts of the *memisc* package for importing data from various statistical packages: II. Creating "`data.set`" objects from "`importer`" objects

`subset()` is a generic function that can be applied not only to data frames and "`data.set`" objects but also to "`importer`" objects. With `subset()`, it is possible to obtain a subset of the data - a subset of observations and/or a subset of variables. `subset()` is particularly useful if an

(Continued)

importer refers to a large data file with many variables and many observations – in which case it is often undesirable to load the entire data set into a computer's memory.

`as.data.set()` is a generic function that translates ('coerces') the object given as its first argument into a `"data.set"` object. When applied to an `"importer"` object, it loads into memory the complete contents of the data file to which that object refers.

5.3 Recoding and similar transformations of survey items

Having imported a survey data set does not always mean that it is already ready for analysis. Quite often, the way certain variables are measured in a survey is much too detailed to be suitable for analysis. In such cases, one may want to combine several response categories so that they are encoded by a single number or a single 'code'. In other cases, one may simply change the order in which the response categories are encoded or may want to combine several variables into a single one. When the values of variables that encode survey responses or other categorical observations are changed in a systematic, rule-based manner, one talks about these variables as being *recoded*.

Take, for example, the vote variable in the 1983 BES, a codebook page of which is shown in Figure 5.3. The code plan used for this variable distinguishes between no less than 10 alternatives, of which 4 gained less than 10 votes in the sample. Further, it distinguishes between the Liberal Party, the Social Democratic Party, and the Alliance, which was an electoral alliance between the Liberals and the Social Democrats. Thus, it may be convenient for analysis and presentation to reduce the number of categories of the vote variable, by combining the codes 3–5 into a code for the Alliance and the codes 6–10 as well as 97 into a code for 'Other parties'. The following R code could be used to combine categories in such a way:

```
BES.1983.classvot <- within(BES.1983.classvot,{
    vote.new <- vote
    vote.new[vote %in% 3:5]          <- 3
    vote.new[vote %in% c(6: 10, 97)] <-4
})
```

With the function `recode()` from the *memisc* package, this can be done a bit more elegantly, in so far as the names of the relevant variables have to be used only once:

```
BES.1983.classvot <- within(BES.1983.classvot,{
    vote.new <- recode(vote,
                    3 <- 3:5,
                    4 <- c(6:10,97),
                    otherwise="copy"
                    )
})
```

Here, the operator '<-', normally used for assigning values to variables, is used to assign old values to new values. The argument `otherwise="copy"` tells the `recode()` function to copy all other values into the new variable if they are not mentioned in any of the recoding rules. Without `otherwise="copy"`, the variable `vote.new` would have an **NA** for all observations where **vote**, for example, is equal to 1, because the value 1 does not appear on the right-hand side of a recoding rule.

```
==================================================================

    vote '[IF VOTED ] PARTY VOTED FOR'

------------------------------------------------------------------

    Storage mode : double
    Measurement : nominal
    Missing values : 0, 95, 98, 99

        Values and labels    N    Percent

    0  M  'SKIPPED'         660         16.7
    1     'CON'            1432   44.7  36.2
    2     'LAB'             937   29.3  23.7
    3     'ALLIANCE'        416   13.0  10.5
    4     'LIB'             278    8.7   7.0
    5     'SOCIAL DEMOCR'    94    2.9   2.4
    6     'SNP'              33    1.0   0.8
    7     'PLAID CYMRU'       7    0.2   0.2
    8     'ECOLOGY PARTY'     2    0.1   0.1
    9     'NATNL FRONT'       2    0.1   0.1
   10     'COMNIST PARTY'     0    0.0   0.0
   95  M  'REFUSED'          92          2.3
   97     'OTHER PARTY'       2    0.1   0.1
   98  M  'DK'                0          0.0
   99  M  'NA'                0          0.0
```

Figure 5.3 The codebook page for the **vote** variable in the 1983 British Election Study data set

While for short recodings, as in the previous example, one may very well do without the function **recode()**, if more complex or comprehensive recodings are required, the function will be more effective. The following code changes all values of the **vote** variable so that they are all single-digit numbers and attaches somewhat better-looking labels to these numbers (instead of 'all-caps' labels, as present in the original data set):

```
BES.1983.classvot <- within(BES.1983.classvot,{
    vote.new <- recode(vote,
                    Conservative  = 1 <- 1,
                    Labour        = 2 <- 2,
                    Alliance      = 3 <- 3:5,
                    Other         = 4 <- c(6:10,97),
                    "Didn't vote" = 5 <- 0,
                    DK            = 8 <- 98,
                    Refused       = 9 <- 95)
})
```

Here, the equals sign '=' can be used to attach labels to the new codes.

While it is possible to combine codes in this way without the use of additional packages, it is a bit inconvenient. The *memisc* package provides for a simpler way of recoding such variables, by way of a dedicated function `recode()`, which can simplify recoding tasks, in particular if they are more complex. In fact, it is inspired by procedures in SPSS and Stata with the same name and similar semantics. The *car* (Fox and Weisberg, 2011) and *dplyr* (Wickham, Francois, et al., 2018) packages also provide their own versions of a `recode()` function.

Occasionally, one wants to construct a variable out of several other variables so that the values of the new variable are obtained from different variables based on various conditions. Consider, for example, a data set from an election study that is conducted in two waves, one survey wave conducted before the election – a so-called pre-election wave – and another survey wave conducted after the election – a so-called post-election wave. Such a data set, a *cumulation* of the pre- and post-election waves, typically contains a variable that indicates for each row in the data set whether it refers to an observation from the pre- or the post-election wave, while respondents' vote intentions in the pre-election wave and (recalled) vote decisions are recorded in different variables. If one wants to analyse vote intentions and vote decisions in combination, one needs to construct a new variable that contains, conditional on the value of the pre-/post-election wave indicator variable, the values of either the vote intention or the vote decision variable. If (as a hypothetical example) the wave indicator variable is named **wave**, with the value 1 for the pre-election wave and 2 for the post-election wave, and if the vote intentions of respondents in the pre-election survey are recorded in the variable **pre.voteint** and their vote decisions in the post-election survey are recorded in variable **post.votedes**, the combined variable can be constructed by the following syntax:

```
vote <- ifelse(wave == 1, pre.voteint, post.votedes)
```

The function `ifelse()` used in this code example is part of the core vocabulary of R and takes three arguments. The first argument, which should be a logical vector (e.g. the result of a comparison like **wave == 1**), determines whether the elements of the resulting vector come from the vector or value given as second argument or from the vector or value given as third argument.

Sometimes, the combination of variables one is interested in is more complicated. Consider, for example, the 2017 wave of the GLES, which combines a pre-election survey and a post-election survey (Roßteutscher et al., 2018). In the pre-election survey, the respondents were asked whether they intended to turn out to vote or if they had already cast a postal vote. In the post-election survey, the respondents were asked whether they had participated in the election or not. In all of these cases, they were asked about their vote intention or vote decision with regard to their first vote (for the district candidate of a party) or with regard to their second vote (for a party list at the level of the federal state). Thus, for the first and the second vote there are five cases that can be distinguished: (1) a voter was interviewed in the pre-election survey and had already cast his or her postal vote, in which case the combined variable should contain this postal vote; (2) he or she intended not to vote, in which case the combined variable should contain an appropriate missing value code; (3) he or she intended to cast a vote, in which case the combined variable should contain the vote intention; (4) a voter was interviewed in the post-election survey and did not participate in the election, in which case the combined variable should contain the appropriate missing value code; and finally (5) a voter was interviewed in the post-election survey and participated in the election, in which case the combined variable should contain the post-election vote decision. For such a complex distinction of cases, one could of course use the standard R function **ifelse()**. However, one would need five nested calls of this function, which would be cumbersome and is likely to be error-prone. To make it simple to deal with such distinctions of cases, the *memisc* package contains the function **cases()**. To combine vote intention and recalled vote decision in the manner just described, the following syntax can be used:

```
gles2017.vote <- within(gles2017.vote,{
  vote.first <- cases(
    survey == 0 & pre.turnout.int == 6 -> pre.postvote.first,
    survey == 0 & pre.turnout.int %in% 4:5 -> -85,
    survey == 0 & pre.turnout.int %in% 1:3 -> pre.voteint.first,
    survey == 1 & post.turnout ==1 -> post.vote.first,
    survey == 1 & post.turnout ==2 -> -85,
    TRUE -> -97
  )
  vote.second <- cases(
    survey == 0 & pre.turnout.int == 6 -> pre.postvote.second,
    survey == 0 & pre.turnout.int %in% 4:5 -> -85,
    survey == 0 & pre.turnout.int %in% 1:3 -> pre.voteint.second,
    survey == 1 & post.turnout ==1 -> post.vote.second,
    survey == 1 & post.turnout ==2 -> -85,
    TRUE -> -97
  )
})
```

Here, **gles2017.vote** is the data set that contains vote intentions and vote decisions, **survey** is the indicator variable that distinguishes between the pre-election and post-election surveys, **pre.turnout.int** is the variable that contains answers to the question about respondents' intention to turn out to vote asked in the pre-election survey, **post.turnout** is the variable that contains answers to the question about respondents' turnout asked in the post-election survey, **pre.postvote.first** and **pre.postvote.second** contain the (reported) first and second vote choices in the postal votes of respondents interviewed in the pre-election survey, **pre.voteint.first** and **pre.voteint.second** contain the vote intentions of respondents interviewed in the pre-election survey, and **post.vote.first** and **post.vote.second** contain the (reported) first and second vote choices of respondents interviewed in the post-election survey.

▬▬▬▬▬ Overview Box 5.7 ▬▬▬▬▬

Functions of the *memisc* package for recoding

recode() is a function that allows one to change the values of a variable according to rules – to *recode* the variable. Its first argument is the variable to be recoded. Its result is the variable with

(Continued)

changed values. The other arguments are expressions - for example, of the form `c(1:3,7) ->` `1` or `1 <- c(1:3,7)` - that define the rules by which values are changed. Those values that are not included in these rules are changed into `NA` or to a default value declared with the argument with the tag `otherwise=`.

The function `recode()` can also be used to add labels to values. For this, the recoding rules take a form like `lbl = 1 <- c(1:3,7)`.

It is also possible to recode numeric values into factor levels, with rules like `"a" <- 1:3`, or factor levels into factor levels, with rules like `"a" <- c("A","B")`.

`cases()` is a function that allows one to assign values to certain logical conditions. It can take any number of arguments, where each argument defines a rule for assigning values to these logical conditions. It is possible to assign either constant values - with a rule like `x > 0 -> 1`, where the result is `1` whenever `x` is greater than 0 (`x > 0`) - or values of a variable - with a rule like `x > 0 -> a`, where the result is the value of `a` whenever `x` is greater than 0 (`x > 0`).

With rules like `a = 1 <- x > 0`, it is possible to attach labels to the values that are assigned to logical conditions. Finally, if the arguments contain no explicit assignments, they are changed into factor levels that have the syntactical form of the logical conditions. For example,

```
cases(x < -1, -1 <= x & x < 1, 1 <= x)
```

results in a factor with the levels `"x < -1"`, `"-1 <= x & x < 1"`, and `"1 <= x"`.

6

Managing Data from Complex Samples

Large-scale surveys used in the social sciences are often based on complex samples when simple random sampling is infeasible. A typical instance is the multistage sample used in the recent waves of the German General Social Survey (Allgemeine Bevölkerungsumfrage der Sozialwissenschaften, or ALLBUS; see GESIS, 2017). In the first stage, a sample of municipalities (*Gemeinden*) is drawn (the *primary sampling units*, or PSUs), which is *stratified* according to regional criteria (federal states, administrative regions, etc.). That is, from each of the relevant regional units (i.e. each *stratum*), a separate sample is drawn, and these separate samples are then combined into a *stratified sample*. In the second stage, samples of individual persons are drawn from the registers of each of the sampled municipal units. As a consequence, the probability that a pair of individuals in the sample come from the same municipality is higher than under simple random sampling. This is a typical instance of *two-stage cluster sampling*. Further, in order to facilitate comparisons between eastern and western Germany, the eastern part is oversampled – that is, the proportion of people from the eastern part in the sample is greater than the corresponding proportion of people in the population. Obviously, if the intention is to compute countrywide statistics, one will have to correct for this oversampling by re-weighting. But weights may also be needed to take into account the different sizes of the strata.[1] Further adjustments to sample estimates and their standard errors are required to take into account that cluster sampling has been applied.

Another instance of a complex sample is the American National Election Study (ANES) of 2016 (ANES, 2019), which combines two independently drawn samples, one for the component that involves face-to-face interviews and one for the component that involves questionnaires filled in via the internet. For the face-to-face sample, counties or combinations of counties were used as PSUs.[2] From each PSU, four smaller areas were drawn, and from these secondary sampling units, households were selected at random using the Postal Service's address list. In the final stage, respondents were sampled from the households. Thus, apart from the consequences of the multistage sample design, a further complication arises because individuals living in larger households have a somewhat smaller chance to get into the sample than individuals living in smaller households. Again, re-weighting is needed to correct for this.

Survey data sets, such as those from ALLBUS or ANES, usually contain survey weights – that is, weights that are intended to correct for unequal sampling probabilities – as they arise intentionally due to stratification and oversampling or inevitably due to sampling of households instead of individuals within primary or secondary sampling units. Many statistical functions in R, such as `lm()` or `glm()`, allow for weighting observations. Consequently, unequal sampling probabilities can be taken into account and to some degree corrected for in statistical analyses. Yet the computation of survey weights is not always straightforward for complex samples. Further, statistical theory (e.g. Thompson, 1997) indicates that for accurate and efficient inference simple re-weighting is not sufficient and that the computation of accurate standard errors for complex samples can be quite complicated.

When it comes to the analysis of survey data from complex samples, in particular the estimation of population totals, means, and proportions, the *survey* package (Lumley, 2004, 2019) is

---

[1] This is so because, in a finite sample, the proportions of population strata can rarely be reproduced exactly in a stratified sample.

[2] In the case of Los Angeles, half-counties are used as PSUs because of the large population of LA County.

the first one to consider. The package not only provides for efficient estimators and accurate inference about them, but also introduces particular data structures that allow one to describe various sampling designs. These data structures are the focus of this chapter.

━━━━━━━━━ **Overview Box 6.1** ━━━━━━━━━

Core concepts

The following concepts that focus on survey research should be familiar to social scientists and social science students. For convenience and reference, they are described here anyway.

Simple random sample: In this kind of sample, individuals are drawn into the sample purely at random; that is, they are selected only by chance, and for each individual in the population, the probability of ending up in the sample is the same.

Stratified sample: This kind of sample is a composition of simple random samples from several population strata. A stratum is one of several groups in the population the sizes of which are known; each individual is a member of only one of these groups.

Cluster sample: In a single-stage cluster sample, the sampling units are not individuals in the population but groups of them. These groups may be defined in terms of administrative regions or organizational units. If a group is selected into the sample, all the individuals in the groups are in the sample.

Multistage sample: In a two-stage cluster sample, a sample of clusters or primary sampling units (PSUs) is drawn at random. From within each of these PSUs, a sample of individuals is drawn at random. This is generalized by a multistage sample, where secondary sampling units are drawn from the PSUs and, if applicable, tertiary sampling units are drawn from the secondary sampling units, and so on, before individuals are drawn from the tertiary or later-stage sampling units. The sample at the first stage may be a simple random sample or a stratified sample.

Sampling with and without replacement: In sampling without replacement, any sampling unit may end up in the sample at most once. In sampling with replacement, if a sampling unit is selected into the sample, it nevertheless stays in the pool of units available to be selected. As a consequence, there is a (however small) chance that a unit is selected into the sample twice or several times. The difference between sampling with and without replacement becomes negligible if the population is large or the clusters at the lowest level of a multistage design are large.

6●1 Survey design objects

Basic survey design objects are created using the function **svydesign()**. The result of the function is usually a data frame enhanced with information on the design of the sample from which the data are obtained. To mark such a data frame appropriately, its **"class"** attribute contains the string **"survey.design"**. Yet it is also possible that the data are stored in an SQL (Structured Query Language) database, in which case the object returned by **svydesign()** contains only information about the structure of the sample and a reference to the SQL database.

When it is used to create a survey design object from a data frame, **svydesign()** requires at least two arguments: an **id=** and a **data=** argument. The **id=** argument should be a formula that identifies the clusters (e.g. PSUs, secondary sampling units, etc.) – that is, a single variable name preceded by a tilde (the character ~), several variable names connected by +, or a data frame that contains such variables. The **data=** argument should be a data frame from which the survey design object is to be constructed. The function **svydesign** has further optional arguments, such as the **strata=** argument for the sampling strata (usually a formula), the **probs=** argument for the sampling probabilities, the **weights=** argument for the sampling weights, and the **fpc=** argument for finite sample correction.

The sampling probability π_i of a unit i in the sample is the probability at which it gets into the sample. In the case of a simple random sample of size n from a population of size N, this will be $\pi_i = n/N$. If N_i is the population stratum to which i belongs and n_i is the corresponding subsample size, the sampling probability will be $\pi_i = n_i/N_i$. If such sample probabilities are available, they are supposed to be passed to **svydesign** as the **probs=** argument. Alternatively, sampling weights can be supplied as the **weights=** argument, which should be the inverse of the sampling probabilities – that is, $w_i = 1/\pi_i$.

Data sets available from social science data archives – for example, the data set of the 2016 ANES – often do not contain inverse probability weights but sample-relative weights. That is, while the sum of the inverse probability weights over all units in the sample is the population size, the sum of the existing weights in such data sets is the sample size. Yet if the intention is to estimate population proportions or population averages, the difference between these two types of sample weights does not matter. It does matter, however, if the intention is to estimate population totals. This is illustrated in the following with an example data set that is supplied with the *survey* package (Lumley, 2019) and originally comes from the US (NHANES National Health and Nutrition Examination Survey, 2011). We start this example by activating the *survey* package:

```
library(survey)
```

Next we make the NHANES data set available (which is included as a data example in the *survey* package):

```
data(nhanes)
```

We can take a look at the data set and find that it has 7 variables and 8581 observations:

```
head(nhanes)
```

	SDMVPSU	SDMVSTRA	WTMEC2YR	HI_CHOL	race	agecat	RIAGENDR
1	1	83	81528.77	0	2	(19,39]	1
2	1	84	14509.28	0	3	(0,19]	1
3	2	86	12041.64	0	3	(0,19]	1
4	2	75	21000.34	0	3	(59,Inf]	2
5	1	88	22633.58	0	1	(19,39]	1
6	2	85	74112.49	1	2	(39,59]	2

```
nrow(nhanes)
```

```
[1] 8591
```

According to the documentation, the PSUs are identified by the variable **SDMVPSU**, the strata from which the PSUs are drawn are identified by the variable **SDMVSTRA**, and the sample weights are in the variable **WTMEC2YR**. The sum of the sample weights corresponds to the population size; this is because they are inverse probability weights:

```
with(nhanes,sum(WTMEC2YR))
```

```
[1] 276536446
```

Here, we create 'ordinary' sampling weights as they are common in social science data sets, which sum up to the total sample size:

```
nhanes <- within(nhanes,{
    smplw <- WTMEC2YR/sum(WTMEC2YR)*nrow(nhanes)
})
```

We now create a survey design object that involves the inverse probability weights:

```
design_pop <- svydesign(id = ~SDMVPSU, strata = ~SDMVSTRA,
                        weights = ~WTMEC2YR, data = nhanes)
```

```
Error in svydesign.default(id = ~SDMVPSU, strata = ~SDMVSTRA,
    weights = ~WTMEC2YR, : Clusters not nested in strata at top
    level; you may want nest=TRUE.
```

The first attempt fails: the clusters are not nested in the strata, in contrast to the default assumption made by the **svydesign()** function. The PSU numbers are not nested in the strata; that is, the enumeration of the PSUs starts anew within each stratum, and the same PSU identification numbers occur in several strata (although the numbers refer to different PSUs). We try again, calling the function with the optional argument with **nest = TRUE**

```
design_pop <- svydesign(id = ~SDMVPSU, strata = ~SDMVSTRA,
                        weights = ~WTMEC2YR, data = nhanes,
                        nest = TRUE)
```

For the purposes of comparison, we create a survey design object based on the same data but with the sample-relative weights:

```
design_smpl <- svydesign(id = ~SDMVPSU, strata = ~SDMVSTRA,
                         weights = ~smplw, data = nhanes,
                         nest = TRUE)
```

Now we estimate the proportion of the population with high cholesterol (i.e. the proportion for which `HI_CHOL==1`). Since a proportion is the mean of a binary variable, we can use **svymean()** to estimate the proportion:

```
svymean(~HI_CHOL, design=design_pop, na.rm=TRUE)
```

```
            mean       SE
HI_CHOL  0.11214  0.0054
```

```
svymean(~HI_CHOL, design=design_smpl, na.rm=TRUE)
```

```
            mean       SE
HI_CHOL  0.11214  0.0054
```

Here, it does not make a difference whether we use the population-size weights or the sample-size weights. What kinds of weights are used does make a difference, however, if we try to estimate the *total number* of people with high cholesterol.

```
svytotal(~HI_CHOL, design=design_pop, na.rm=TRUE)
```

```
            total        SE
HI_CHOL  28635245  2020711
```

```
svytotal(~HI_CHOL, design=design_smpl, na.rm=TRUE)
```

```
            total      SE
HI_CHOL    889.59  62.776
```

Obviously, we need the population-size weights for an unbiased estimate of the population total; otherwise, we just get a sample total.

The NHANES data set may not be representative of the data sets usually employed by social scientists since it contains explicit information about PSUs and also contains inverse probability weights. An example that is closer to what social scientists are used to working with is the ANES. In particular, we focus on the ANES 2016 Time Series Study. The sampling design of this survey has already been described at the beginning of this chapter. Strictly speaking, this is a three-stage sample with PSUs and secondary sampling units. However, the data set contains only information about PSUs and first-stage samples. The following example demonstrates how one can make do with this limited information. We start this example by activating the required packages: *memisc* for importing the ANES data, *magrittr* for the convenient **%<>%** operator, and the *survey* package.

```
library(memisc)
library(magrittr)
library(survey)
```

Having set the stage, we acquaint R with the ANES data file:

```
anes_2016_sav <- spss.file("anes_timeseries_2016.sav")
dim(anes_2016_sav)
```

```
[1] 4270 1842
```

The data set has 4270 observations and 1842 variables. We do not need all the variables for this example. (Anyway, for most typical analyses of electoral behaviour, we will not need the entire set of variables.) Also, to keep things simple, we restrict ourselves to the face-to-face interviews of the pre-election wave. That is, we form a subset of the data for which the condition `V160501 == 1` applies:

```
anes_2016_pre_work_ds <- subset(anes_2016_sav,
                        # Only pre-election face-to-face
                        # interview data
                        V160501 == 1,
                        select=c(
                            # According to docs, these are the
                            # sample weights for the
                            # face-to-face component
                            pre_w_f2f     = V160101f,
                            # Face-to-face strata
                            strat_f2f     = V160201f,
                            psu_f2f       = V160202f,
                            # Voting variables
                            pre_voted12   = V161005,
                            pre_recall12  = V161006,
                            pre_voted     = V161026,
                            pre_vote      = V161027,
                            pre_intov     = V161030,
                            pre_voteint   = V161031,
                        ))
```

Next, we construct the variables that contain the recalled vote from the 2012 election, the 2016 early votes, and the 2016 vote intentions, and we combine the latter two into the 2016 vote choice. The variables are constructed so that non-voters are counted as such instead of receiving a missing value. Here, we use the `%<>%` operator so that we do not have to write the name of the data object twice:

```
anes_2016_pre_work_ds %<>% within({
    # Setting up recalled votes of 2012
    # Since a "default" value for the remaining conditions
    # is used, we use 'check.xor = FALSE' to avoid warnings.
    recall12 <- cases(
        'No vote'   = 9 <- pre_voted12   == 2,
        'Obama'     = 1 <- pre_recall12  == 1,
        'Romney'    = 2 <- pre_recall12  == 2,
        'Other'     = 3 <- pre_recall12  == 5,
```

```
        'Invalid'      = 99 <- TRUE, check.xor = FALSE
    )
    # Early voters
    vote16_1 <- cases(
        'Clinton' = 1 <- pre_voted == 1 & pre_vote == 1,
        'Trump'   = 2 <- pre_voted == 1 & pre_vote == 2,
        'Other'   = 3 <- pre_voted == 1 & pre_vote %in% 3:5,
        'Invalid' = 99 <- TRUE, check.xor = FALSE)
    # Vote intentions
    vote16 <- cases(
        'Clinton' = 1 <- pre_intov == 1 & pre_voteint == 1,
        'Trump'   = 2 <- pre_intov == 1 & pre_voteint == 2,
        'Other'   = 3 <- pre_intov == 1 & pre_voteint %in% 3:6,
        'No vote' = 8 <- pre_intov %in% c(-1, 2),
        'Invalid' = 99 <- TRUE, check.xor = FALSE)
    vote16[] <- ifelse(vote16 == 99 & vote16_1 != 99,
                    vote16_1,
                    vote16)

})
```

Having set up the data, we translate the "data.set" object into a data frame for the construction of a survey design object and for data analysis:

```
anes_2016_prevote <- as.data.frame(anes_2016_pre_work_ds)
```

As a reference point for comparing weighted results, we create a cross-table with unweighted observations:

```
xtabs(~ vote16 + recall12,
      data=anes_2016_prevote)
```

```
          recall12
vote16    Obama Romney Other No vote Invalid
  Clinton   326     12     2      59       6
  Trump      29    242     5      70       8
  Other      30     28     7      16       4
  No vote    28     41     0     139       5
  Invalid    46     27     2      31      17
```

We now create a survey design object from the data frame, with **psu_f2f** as identifier of the PSUs, **strat_f2f** as stratum identifier, and **pre_w_f2f** as design weights:

```
anes_2016_prevote_desgn <- svydesign(id = ~psu_f2f,
                                     strata = ~strat_f2f,
                                     weights = ~pre_w_f2f,
                                     data = anes_2016_prevote,
                                     nest = TRUE)
anes_2016_prevote_desgn
```

```
Stratified 1 - level Cluster Sampling design (with replacement)
With (65) clusters.
svydesign(id = ~psu_f2f, strata = ~strat_f2f, weights = ~pre_w_f2f,
    data = anes_2016_prevote, nest = TRUE)
```

Then we create a cross-table from the weighted data. Since the sample weights are noninteger, the counts in a cross-table will also be noninteger. We therefore limit the number of digits after the decimal mark:

```
ops <- options(digits=2)
(tab <- svytable(~ vote16 + recall12,
                design = anes_2016_prevote_desgn))
```

```
          recall12
vote16    Obama Romney Other No vote Invalid
  Clinton 316.0   11.7   1.1    69.9     8.6
  Trump    35.9  228.8   4.2    73.0     5.1
  Other    34.1   24.4   6.6    13.9     5.3
  No vote  28.8   41.4   0.0   150.2     4.3
  Invalid  44.8   25.0   1.9    28.3    16.0
```

Since the weights sum to the sample size and not to the population size, the counts in the result of **svytable()** have roughly the same size as in the cross-table from the unweighted data.

We now create a table of percentages from the previous cross-table. For ease of interpretation, we drop the rows and columns that refer to invalid responses.

```
percentages(vote16 ~ recall12, data=tab[-5,-5])
```

```
          recall12
vote16    Obama Romney Other No vote
  Clinton  76.2    3.8   9.2    22.8
  Trump     8.6   74.7  35.5    23.8
  Other     8.2    8.0  55.2     4.5
  No vote   6.9   13.5   0.0    48.9
```

```
options(ops)
```

For housekeeping, we restore the original setting of the options.

The function **summary()** can be used to compute a statistical test of independence of the cross-classified factors. When used with survey-weighted data, it computes an F test, which uses the Rao–Scott second-order correction with a Satterthwaite approximation of the denominator degrees of freedom.

```
summary(tab)
```

```
            recall12
vote16     Obama Romney Other No vote Invalid
   Clinton   316     12    1      70       9
   Trump      36    229    4      73       5
   Other      34     24    7      14       5
   No vote    29     41    0     150       4
   Invalid    45     25    2      28      16


        Pearson's X^2: Rao & Scott adjustment

data:   svychisq(~vote16 + recall12, design =
    anes_2016_prevote_desgn,      statistic = "F")
F = 29.235, ndf = 9.3968, ddf = 310.0952, p-value < 2.2e-16
```

For the more conventional Pearson χ^2 test with design effect adjustment, the function summary() has to be called with the optional statistic= argument:

```
summary(tab, statistic="Chisq")
```

```
            recall12
vote16     Obama Romney Other No vote Invalid
   Clinton   316     12    1      70       9
   Trump      36    229    4      73       5
   Other      34     24    7      14       5
   No vote    29     41    0     150       4
   Invalid    45     25    2      28      16


        Pearson's X^2: Rao & Scott adjustment

data:   svychisq(~vote16 + recall12, design =
    anes_2016_prevote_desgn,      statistic = "Chisq")
X-squared = 778.41, df = 16, p-value < 2.2e-16
```

Since the sample size is quite large, both tests result in very small p values that are indistinguishable from one another.

■■■■■ Overview Box 6.2 ■■■■■

The construction of survey design objects

In order to construct a survey design object with the function **svydesign()**, the following pieces of information can be provided, in addition to the information about the data set:

Sampling units: The identifying numbers of primary, secondary sampling units, and so on, can be given with the argument **ids=**. For simple random sampling or single-stage stratified sampling, the argument should be **ids=~0** or **ids=~1**, respectively; otherwise, the argument should be a formula or a data frame.

Strata: The identification numbers of strata from which the PSUs or individuals (if there are no clusters) are given by argument **strata=**.

Sampling probabilities: If the sampling probabilities of the PSUs are unequal, they can be given with the `probs=` argument.

Sample weights: Inverse probability weights for the clusters or the individuals can be given with the `weights=` argument.

Finite sample correction: If sampling without replacement is used, sample statistics have a smaller variance than if sampling with replacement is used. This increase in precision depends on the size of the population or the strata. The relevant information can be given as the `fpc=` argument.

PPS sampling: If PPS (Probability Proportional to Size) sampling is used for the selection of PSUs, the PPS method can be given with the `pps=` argument.

The only mandatory argument of the `svydesign()` function is `ids=`. The remaining information is optional.

6●2 Survey replicate weights

Survey design objects as defined in the *survey* package are useful for the computation of Horvitz–Thompson estimators of totals and of means of quantities in finite populations, as well as estimates of their variance, and other estimators that allow a straightforward incorporation of sampling probabilities and sampling weights. They are also useful for the adjustment of estimators that can be implicitly defined as the solution of estimating equations (including maximum likelihood estimators) and for Rao–Scott adjustments for hypothesis tests (Lumley, 2010). For this, the package provides functions such as `svymean()`, `svytotal`, `svytable`, `svyglm`, `svymle`, and so on.

An alternative to these estimators is resampling-based estimators that involve replicate weights. There are two kinds of situations where one may want to use replicate weights. The first kind of situation arises when conventional sampling design adjustments provided by the methods mentioned above do not work, because the sample size is too small (or the number of PSUs is too small) or because the population quantities to be estimated are so complicated that linearization methods break down. The second kind of situation arises when information such as identifiers for PSUs and strata memberships is not available due to concerns about data protection (Lumley, 2010).

The basic idea of resampling-based estimators is that the variance of an estimator can be gauged by repeatedly drawing (sub)samples from the original sample. Straightforward subsampling approaches, such as balanced repeated replication or the jackknife, can be achieved by re-weighting the entire sample with weights that are equal to either 1 (for units in the current subsample) or 0 (for units not included in the current subsample). The weights used to construct these subsamples are known as *replicate weights*. In more complicated resampling approaches, they may be different from 0 or 1.

If one does not trust conventional sampling design adjustments (the first kind of situation described above), one may want to generate replicate weights from a known sampling design. If data publishers cannot provide the complete information about the sampling design for privacy reasons, they can instead publish the survey data accompanied by a set of replicate weights. For these cases, the *survey* package provides the `"survey.repdesign"` class of objects. Such an object can be created by the function **srvrepdesign()** from a data frame, replicate weights, and information on the type of these replicate weights. To create a survey replicate design object from a survey design object, one can use the function **as.srvrep-design()**. Usually, one uses **srvrepdesign()** for data that are accompanied by replicate weights, whereas one uses **as.srvrepdesign()** to generate replicate weights for an existing survey design object.

An example of a data set accompanied with replicate weights is the public use file of the California Health Interview Survey of 2005 (CHIS, 2007; Lumley, 2019). The following example demonstrates the specification of replicate weights. The CHIS data that we use in this example are in the file **"adult.dta"** – downloaded from the website of the Health Policy Institute of the University of California at Los Angeles (http://healthpolicy.ucla.edu/chis/data/Pages/GetCHISData.aspx) – which contains the 2005 wave of the survey.[3] We use the *foreign* function **read.dta()** to import this data set:

```
library(foreign)
adult_chis <- read.dta("adult.dta",
                       warn.missing.labels=FALSE)
```

The data set contains 80 sets of (raked) replicate weights. (We will discuss 'raking' later in this chapter.) They are in the variables named **rakedw1** through **rakedw80**. Raked sampling weights are in **raked0**.

We obtain the column numbers of the replicate weight variables, making use of patterns in the variable names:

```
repw <- which(names(adult_chis) %in% paste0("rakedw",1:80))
```

To specify replicate weights, we call the function **svrepdesgin**. The first argument specifies the variables that will be used for data analysis. The **weights=** argument specifies the sampling weights, while the argument **repweights=** specifies the replicate weights. The **data=** argument specifies the data frame where all the data come from. The **combined.weights=** argument is needed here because the replicate weights were constructed from sampling weights and 'pure' replicate weights. Since we do not know the way in which the replicate weights were constructed, we have to specify **type="other"**.

```
adult_chis_rd <- svrepdesign(adult_chis[-repw],
                    weights=~rakedw0,
                    repweights=adult_chis[repw],
                    data=adult_chis,
                    combined.weights=TRUE,
                    type="other",
                    scale=1,rscales=1)
```

[3]Redistribution of the data is prohibited, so the website that accompanies this book does not include this data set. Readers who want to reproduce the following example will need to download their own copy of the data set.

With **svymean()**, we get the estimated proportions of the various categories of health insurance status in California in 2005, along with the standard errors. By multiplying by 100, we get the percentages:

```
100*svymean(~instyp_p, design=adult_chis_rd)
```

	mean	SE
instyp_pUNINSURED	16.1204	0.0027
instyp_pMEDICARE & MEDICAID	4.0544	0.0011
instyp_pMEDICARE & OTHERS	9.5286	0.0010
instyp_pMEDICARE ONLY	2.0639	0.0007
instyp_pMEDICAID	8.5105	0.0018
instyp_pEMPLOYMENT-BASED	51.9316	0.0030
instyp_pPRIVATELY PURCHASED	6.0567	0.0017
instyp_pHEALTHY FAM/OTHER PUBLIC	1.7339	0.0011

With **svytotal**, we obtain estimates of how many people have which health insurance status:

```
svytotal(~instyp_p, design=adult_chis_rd)
```

	total	SE
instyp_pUNINSURED	4253792	72494
instyp_pMEDICARE & MEDICAID	1069871	28764
instyp_pMEDICARE & OTHERS	2514367	25892
instyp_pMEDICARE ONLY	544612	19018
instyp_pMEDICAID	2245709	48474
instyp_pEMPLOYMENT-BASED	13703511	79679
instyp_pPRIVATELY PURCHASED	1598225	45184
instyp_pHEALTHY FAM/OTHER PUBLIC	457527	27854

The CHIS sample is an example of the case where, for reasons of data protection, replicate weights are provided as part of the data set instead of complete sample design information. As indicated earlier, this is not the only reason why one may want to use replicate weights. Another reason may be that one does not want to rely on assumptions about the distribution of estimators or test statistics. We therefore look at how replicate weights can be obtained from a more or less fully specified sampling design and how these replicate weights can be used in the computation of certain statistics. Creating a replicate weights design object from a regular survey design object is quite straightforward if one requires jackknife replicate weights. Then, one does not need to specify the replicate weights explicitly because this type of replicate weight is the default setting.

```
anes_2016_prevote_jk <- as.svrepdesign(anes_2016_prevote_desgn)
```

The number of replicates is then determined by the number of clusters:

```
anes_2016_prevote_jk
```

```
Call: as.svrepdesign(anes_2016_prevote_desgn)
Stratified cluster jackknife (JKn) with 65 replicates.
```

An alternative are bootstrap replicates or, more specifically in the case of multistage survey samples, multistage rescaled bootstrap replicates. They are requested by calling as.svyrepdesign() with the argument type="mrbbootstrap":

```
anes_2016_prevote_boo <- as.svrepdesign(anes_2016_prevote_desgn,
                                         type="mrbbootstrap")
anes_2016_prevote_boo
```

```
Call: as.svrepdesign(anes_2016_prevote_desgn,
                     type = "mrbbootstrap")
Multistage rescaled bootstrap with 50 replicates.
```

By default, 50 sets of bootstrap replicate weights are created; however, one can change that. In the following lines, we set the number of replicates to 200:

```
anes_2016_prevote_boo <- as.svrepdesign(anes_2016_prevote_desgn,
                                         type="mrbbootstrap",
                                         replicates=200)
anes_2016_prevote_boo
```

```
Call: as.svrepdesign(anes_2016_prevote_desgn,
                     type = "mrbbootstrap",
                     replicates = 200)
Multistage rescaled bootstrap with 200 replicates.
```

We now demonstrate the use of both types of replicate weights for the computation of standard errors. In the present case, these are estimates of the sampling variance of the 'stayer percentage' – that is, the percentage of voters who voted for the candidate from the same party (either Democrat or Republican) in both US presidential elections.

In order to be able to use replicate weights, the relevant sample statistic has to be the function of a vector of weights and a data set from where the variables are obtained. Here, we define the function **StayerPerc**, which computes such a statistic:

```
StayerPerc <- function(weights,data){
    tab <- xtabs(weights~vote16+recall12,data=data)
    # Remove 'invalid' responses
    tab <- tab[-5,-5]
    # Table percentages
    ptab <- 100*prop.table(tab)
    # The diagonals are the percentages of 'stayers'
    # among the voters.
    # The first two elements of the diagonal are
    # the Democratic and Republican stayers.
    structure(diag(ptab)[1:2],
```

```
                names=c("Democratic",
                        "Republican"))
}
```

Using `withReplicates`, we get a sample value of the statistic along with an estimate of its sampling variance. First, we compute the jackknife standard errors:

```
withReplicates(anes_2016_prevote_jk,
               StayerPerc)
```

```
           theta     SE
Democratic 30.387 2.5651
Republican 21.998 1.6002
```

Second, we compute the bootstrap standard errors:

```
withReplicates(anes_2016_prevote_boo,
               StayerPerc)
```

```
           theta     SE
Democratic 30.387 2.6761
Republican 21.998 1.5797
```

Both standard errors agree with the first digit after the decimal point.

6.3 Post-stratification, raking, and calibration

Stratified sampling is often used to increase the precision of sample estimates of population characteristics. Sampling variability is reduced by, first, drawing samples from population strata that are roughly proportional in size and, second, by weighting the data such that the sample proportions match the population proportions in terms of the strata. For example, if separate samples were drawn from the various regions of England and if it is known that 5,479,615/55,977,178 = 9.789% of the population of England live in the region of Yorkshire and Humber, then weights can be applied such that 9.789% of the weighted sample are from that region.

Often, the distribution of certain properties in the population is well known, but it is not possible or practicable to draw samples from the groups distinguished by this property. Examples of such properties are sex, age group, or ethnicity, the distribution of which may be known from a population census. In such cases, it is still possible to apply weights to a sample in such a way that proportions in the weighted sample match proportions in the population. Weighting or re-weighting a sample in this way is called *post-stratification*. To obtain a post-stratified version of a sample design object, the *survey* package has the function `postStratify()`.

It is also possible to apply post-stratification in terms of several variables of which the distribution in the population is known – that is, in terms of ethnicity and age group. This, however, requires that not only is the marginal distribution of such variables known but also their joint distribution. This means, for example, that one has to know not only how many individuals in the US population are between 30 and 40 years old and how many individuals are of Korean American ethnicity, but also how many individuals are between 30 and 40 years old *and* have Korean American ethnicity. Such detailed information is not always available, and it may also be possible that the sample proportions of such cross-classifications are too small to allow reliable re-weighting. There are, however, several possibilities to re-weight a sample in such a way that it matches the marginal distribution of several properties simultaneously, without the need to take into account their joint distribution. That is, there are several ways to re-weight a sample in such a way that the distribution of age and of ethnicity matches the distribution in the population, without requiring knowledge about every combination of age and ethnic group.

A relatively straightforward way to achieve a match between several properties in the sample and the population is *raking*, a technique that involves the iterative application and refinement of post-stratification weights. Raking is a special case of a set of techniques known as *calibration* that create a match between sample and population distributions. For raking, the *survey* package has the function `rake()`; for calibration, the package has the function `calibrate()`. The latter function provides for a variety of techniques. These include a relatively straightforward technique based on linear regression, which is the default technique used by `calibrate()`, but they also include more complicated techniques that allow one to keep the calibration weights within bounds so that the weights of certain individuals do not get too large. For more information about these techniques, the reader is referred to Lumley (2010) and the literature cited therein. For the purposes of this book, it suffices to discuss an example of the use of `postStratify()`, `rake()` and `calibrate()` to demonstrate the practical issues in the application of these techniques with R.

■■■■■■■■ Overview Box 6.3 ■■■■■■■■

Post-stratification, raking, and calibration

Post-stratification: In a post-stratified sample, the units are re-weighted in such a way that the relative sizes of certain groups in the sample are equal to their relative sizes in the population. To get a post-stratified survey design object, one can use the function `postStratify()`.

Raking: This means that a sample is re-weighted in such a way that the relative group sizes distinguished by several grouping factors match those in the population, where the relevant weights are obtained by iterated proportional fitting. A raked survey design object can be obtained with the help of the function `rake()`.

Calibration: This means that a sample is re-weighted in such a way that the sample statistics (means, variances, quantiles, etc.) of one or several variables equal the statistics of these variables in the population. These variables need not be factors, they can also be metric variables. A calibrated sample can be obtained using the function `calibrate()`.

The following example makes use of the 2016 ANES data. Non-valid responses to survey questions do not have a counterpart in terms of population-level marginal frequencies. That is why we have to drop them from the sample.

```
anes_2016_vprevote <- subset(anes_2016_prevote,
                            vote16 != "Invalid" &
                            recall12 != "Invalid"
                            )
```

We also have to make sure that the empty factor levels are dropped:

```
anes_2016_vprevote <- within(anes_2016_vprevote,{
    recall12 <- recall12[,drop=TRUE]
    vote16 <- vote16[,drop=TRUE]
})
```

Now we set up a survey design object from the pre-election wave face-to-face interview sample:

```
anes_2016_vprevote_desgn <- svydesign(id = ~psu_f2f,
                            strata = ~strat_f2f,
                            weights = ~pre_w_f2f,
                            data = anes_2016_vprevote,
                            nest = TRUE)
```

For post-stratification and calibration, we need the population-level results of the 2012 and 2016 elections. Here, we collect the results of the 2012 US presidential election:

```
result.2012 = c(Obama   = 65915795,
                Romney = 60933504,
                # Other candidates are combined
                Other = sum(c(
                    Johnson = 1275971,
                    Stein  =  469627,
                    Others =  490510
                )))
```

We compute the number of non-voters from the sum of the results and census data on the population for voting age:

```
result.2012 <- c(result.2012,
                "No vote" = 235248000 - sum(result.2012))
```

We collect the results of the 2016 US presidential election:

```
result.2016 <- c(Clinton = 65853514,
                Trump   = 62984828,
                Other   = sum(c(
                    Johnson  = 4489341,
                    Stein    = 1457218,
                    McMullin =  731991,
                    Others   = 1154084
                )))
result.2016 <- c(result.2016,
                "No vote" = 250056000 - sum(result.2016))
```

Since the function **postStratify()** expects the population data in the form of data frames, another step of data preparation is required in which we put the population totals into data frames:

```
pop.vote16 <- data.frame(
    vote16=names(result.2016),
    Freq=result.2016)
pop.recall12 <- data.frame(
    recall12=names(result.2012),
    Freq=result.2012/sum(result.2012)*sum(result.2016)
)
```

Now we post-stratify the sample design object by the 2012 vote distribution:

```
anes_2016_prevote_desgn_post <- postStratify(
    anes_2016_vprevote_desgn,~recall12,population=pop.recall12)
```

To see the effect of post-stratification, we compare the unmodified and the post-stratified percentages of 2012 votes and their standard errors:

```
100*svymean(~recall12,design=anes_2016_vprevote_desgn)
```

```
                    mean       SE
recall12Obama    39.8844  0.0233
recall12Romney   29.4551  0.0198
recall12Other     1.1429  0.0035
recall12No vote  29.5176  0.0222
```

```
100*svymean(~recall12,design=anes_2016_prevote_desgn_post)
```

```
                    mean SE
recall12Obama    28.01970  0
recall12Romney   25.90182  0
recall12Other     0.95053  0
recall12No vote  45.12795  0
```

As can be seen, post-stratification for the 2012 vote eliminates all sampling variation from the reported 2012 votes. It also eliminates the bias from vote over-reporting.

Of course, the effect on the estimated 2016 vote percentages should be less drastic:

```
100*svymean(~vote16,design=anes_2016_vprevote_desgn)
```

```
                   mean       SE
vote16Clinton   38.3334  0.0291
vote16Trump     32.8720  0.0222
vote16Other      7.5954  0.0104
vote16No vote   21.1992  0.0200
```

```
100*svymean(~vote16,design=anes_2016_prevote_desgn_post)
```

```
                 mean      SE
vote16Clinton 32.6932 0.0222
vote16Trump   32.8370 0.0152
vote16Other    6.9345 0.0101
vote16No vote 27.5352 0.0228
```

The percentages of Hillary Clinton and Donald Trump voters are closer after post-stratification. Here, we seem a bit unlucky because in terms of actual votes cast (the 'popular vote'), Clinton won a plurality, but not according to the post-stratified sample.

Now, we rake the sample design object by the vote distributions of 2012 *and* 2016:

```
anes_2016_prevote_desgn_rake <- rake(
    anes_2016_vprevote_desgn,list(~recall12,~vote16),
    population=list(pop.recall12,pop.vote16),
    control=list(maxit=20))
```

Of course, due to raking, the marginal distributions of the 2012 and the 2016 votes are no longer estimates; this is why the standard errors disappear.

```
100*svymean(~recall12,design=anes_2016_prevote_desgn_rake)
```

```
                   mean SE
recall12Obama   28.01970  0
recall12Romney  25.90182  0
recall12Other    0.95053  0
recall12No vote 45.12795  0
```

```
100*svymean(~vote16,design=anes_2016_prevote_desgn_rake)
```

```
                mean SE
vote16Clinton 26.3355  0
vote16Trump   25.1883  0
vote16Other    3.1324  0
vote16No vote 45.3439  0
```

If we compare this with our earlier results, we come to the conclusion that the actual percentage of non-voters in 2016 is obviously much higher than the sample estimate, be it post-stratified or not.

`calibrate()` expects the names of calibration vectors to be like those of regression coefficients. The function `cal_names()` allows us to determine these:

```
cal_names(~recall12+vote16,anes_2016_vprevote_desgn)
```

```
[1] "(Intercept)"      "recall12Romney"   "recall12Other"
[4] "recall12No vote"  "vote16Trump"      "vote16Other"
[7] "vote16No vote"
```

Since tables of population-level frequencies cannot be used for calibration without modification, we use the following function to obtain the appropriate calibration vectors:

```
calib_counts <- function(formula,frames){
    dframe2coef <- function(data){
        fname <- names(data)[1]
        flevels <- as.character(data[[1]])
        Freq <- data$Freq
        coefs <- c(sum(Freq),Freq[-1])
        names(coefs) <- c("(Intercept)",
                        paste0(fname,flevels[-1]))
        coefs
    }
    vars <- all.vars(formula)
    for(i in seq_along(vars)){
        var_i <- vars[i]
        frame_i <- frames[[var_i]]
        coef_i <- dframe2coef(frame_i)
        if(i==1)
            res <- coef_i
        else
            res <- c(res,coef_i[-1])
    }
    res
}
calib_anes16 <- calib_counts(~recall12+vote16,
                    list(recall12=pop.recall12,
                        vote16=pop.vote16))

calib_anes16
```

(Intercept)	recall12Romney	recall12Other	recall12No vote
250056000	64769045	2376863	112845139
vote16Trump	vote16Other	vote16No vote	
62984828	7832634	113385024	

The names of this calibration vector correspond to the output of the previous call to the `cal_names()` function. This suggests that we can use this vector with `calibrate()`:

```
anes_2016_prevote_desgn_calib <- calibrate(
    anes_2016_vprevote_desgn,~recall12+vote16,
    population=calib_anes16)
```

We now look at the marginal distribution of the recalled votes after calibration:

```
100*svymean(~recall12,design=anes_2016_prevote_desgn_calib)
```

```
                    mean  SE
recall12Obama     28.01970  0
recall12Romney    25.90182  0
recall12Other      0.95053  0
recall12No vote   45.12795  0
```

```
100*svymean(~vote16,design=anes_2016_prevote_desgn_calib)
```

```
                 mean  SE
vote16Clinton  26.3355  0
vote16Trump    25.1883  0
vote16Other     3.1324  0
vote16No vote  45.3439  0
```

Calibration has the same effect on the marginal distribution as raking – the standard errors disappear from the marginal percentages.

The purpose of raking and calibration is an increase in the precision of other statistics – for example, those that describe the relation between variables or factors. We therefore compare the effect of post-stratification and raking on estimates concerning the vote changes between 2012 and 2016.

In the following, we compute the percentages of votes in 2016, conditional on the recalled votes in 2012, based on the unmodified survey design, the post-stratified design, the raked design, and the calibrated design:

```
tab <- svytable(~ vote16 + recall12,
                design = anes_2016_vprevote_desgn)
percentages(vote16 ~ recall12, data=tab)
```

```
            recall12
vote16         Obama      Romney      Other    No vote
  Clinton  76.187161   3.813877   9.241746  22.757762
  Trump     8.644019  74.683608  35.531586  23.783194
  Other     8.228826   7.974947  55.226668   4.516499
  No vote   6.939995  13.527568   0.000000  48.942545
```

Second, we create a table from the post-stratified data:

```
tab_post <- svytable(~ vote16 + recall12,
                design = anes_2016_prevote_desgn_post)
percentages(vote16 ~ recall12, data=tab_post)
```

```
            recall12
vote16         Obama      Romney      Other    No vote
  Clinton  76.187161   3.813877   9.241746  22.757762
  Trump     8.644019  74.683608  35.531586  23.783194
  Other     8.228826   7.974947  55.226668   4.516499
  No vote   6.939995  13.527568   0.000000  48.942545
```

Third, we create a table from the raked data:

```
tab_rak <- svytable(~ vote16 + recall12,
                    design = anes_2016_prevote_desgn_rake)
percentages(vote16 ~ recall12, data=tab_rak)
```

```
          recall12
vote16          Obama    Romney     Other   No vote
  Clinton 70.403656   3.152370 12.125475 12.579417
  Trump    8.177831 63.198219 47.727460 13.458918
  Other    4.213195  3.652234 40.147065  1.383226
  No vote 17.205318 29.997177  0.000000 72.578439
```

Fourth, we create a table from the calibrated data:

```
tab_calib <- svytable(~ vote16 + recall12,
                    design = anes_2016_prevote_desgn_calib)
percentages(vote16 ~ recall12, data=tab_calib)
```

```
          recall12
vote16          Obama    Romney     Other   No vote
  Clinton 69.137748   3.114927 11.193203 13.406539
  Trump    8.016145 62.183500 43.631304 14.227998
  Other    3.637356  3.547990 45.175493  1.694680
  No vote 19.208751 31.153583  0.000000 70.670783
```

We can see that post-stratification for the 2012 vote distribution does not alter the conditional percentages of the 2016 votes, yet raking and calibration do so.

Log-odds ratios are a way to describe the relation between two dichotomous variables. To examine whether raking affects the relations between recalled vote in 2012 and vote in 2016, we compute log-odds ratios of the Obama, Romney, Clinton, and Trump votes.

```
log.odds.ratio <- function(x) log((x[1,1]/x[1,2])/(x[2,1]/x[2,2]))
c(
  unmodified = log.odds.ratio(tab),
  poststratified = log.odds.ratio(tab_post),
  raked = log.odds.ratio(tab_rak),
  calibrated = log.odds.ratio(tab_calib)
)
```

```
   unmodified  poststratified          raked      calibrated
     5.150940        5.150940       5.150940        5.148527
```

We can see that both post-stratification and raking leave log-odds ratios unaffected. Calibration does have an effect, but this appears to be minor (at least in the present case).

7

Dates, Times, and Time Series

In this chapter, we consider temporal data and time-related data. Temporal data are special in so far as they usually do not refer to the properties of things, individuals, organizations, and so on, but refer to the times when events have occurred. Working with temporal data is tricky because the relation between the units of measurement is not uniform (a year may have 365 or 366 days, a month 28, 30, or 31 days) and measures depend on the calendar in use and the time zone. R defines special data types that help deal with these complications.

Another topic discussed in this chapter is time series, both regular and irregular ones. A time series is regular if the time intervals between successive time points are identical in length or if the variation in length is considered irrelevant. In irregular time series, no assumptions about the lengths of the time intervals are made. Thus, while for regular time series it is sufficient that the order of the time points is given in the data, irregular time series require information about dates and times or the length of each time interval. Regular time series are already supported by a standard R package, the *stats* package, while the handling of irregular time series requires additional R packages, which have to be installed separately. In this chapter, we will focus on the extension package *zoo*.

7 1 Dates and times

Managing temporal data – that is, dates and clock times of events – poses a particular set of challenges. First, dates are relative to a particular calendar. The 25th of October refers to different days in the past depending on whether the Gregorian or the Julian calendar is used.[1] Second, times, and by extension also dates, are relative to time zones. The time 12:42 pm in Australia, London, and New York refers to quite different time points. And even though on Howland Island and on the Marshall Islands the clock shows the same time, the dates in both places differ. The existence of several time zones is further complicated by the use of daylight-saving time in many locations. Third, the various units of measurement of time are not convertible in a straightforward way.[2] A minute consists of 60 seconds, an hour consists of 60 minutes, a day consists of 24 hours, a month contains a variety of days, depending on which month of the year is referred to, and a year consists of 12 months, or 365 or 366 days. Finally, there are different conventions for writing down dates and times. The 9th day in November of the year 1990 can be written in short form as '11/09/90' (according to American conventions), '09/11/90' (according to British conventions), or '09.11.'90' (in Germany), while according to the ISO 8601 standard, it would be '1990-11-09'. Forty-two minutes after midnight can be written as '12.42 a.m.', '12:42 am', '0:42', or '00:42'. Having to deal with the variety of calendars, time zones, time units, and time formats could pose considerable challenges if it had to be done 'manually', without support from software. Fortunately, R provides such support by defining object classes for dates, times, and time differences, and functions to convert

---

[1] As is widely known, the so-called October Revolution, which started the Soviet regime in Russia, took place in November according to the Gregorian calendar, which is now used almost everywhere on Earth.

[2] Of course, converting between the various imperial units of measurement of length and volume and between imperial and metric units is also not straightforward; conversions are straightforward at least if one stays in the metric system.

between time zones, to convert between time units, and to format times and dates. These object classes and functions are discussed in the following.[3]

The basic object class intended to contain dates is **"Date"**. Internally, objects of this class are sequences of numbers, where a positive number indicates the number of days since a particular starting date, the so-called 'epoch', and a negative number indicates the number of days before this starting date. When objects of this class are printed, they are shown as Gregorian dates in the ISO 8601 standard. Since dates are internally numbers, it is straightforward to convert numbers into date objects if one specifies a starting date. With such a starting date, a number is interpreted as the number of days since the starting date. Accordingly, a **"Date"** object can be created from a numeric vector by applying the function **as.Date()** with an additional argument **origin=**, which specifies the starting date from which days are counted. For example,

```
as.Date(20,origin="1970-01-01")
```

gives the date as the 21st of January of the year 1970, printed as

```
[1] "1970-01-21"
```

Objects representing dates can be formatted in several ways for the various conventions on the representation of dates. These date formats are specified by strings that contain certain character sequences, such as **"%a"** or **"%W"**, that represent aspects of dates formatted in particular ways. For example, if **d** is a **"Date"** object that represents the 9th of November of the year 1990, then

```
format(d,"%e %B % Y")
```

gives

```
[1] "9 November 1990"
```

while

```
format(d,"%b %d, %y")
```

gives

```
[1] "Nov 09, 90"
```

---

[3]At the time of writing, there does not seem to exist a package on CRAN to convert between dates in the Gregorian calendar and the Julian calendar. It is, however, possible to convert between Gregorian calendar dates and 'Julian dates' - that is, the number of days since the start of the Julian Period, in use by many astronomers.

and

```
format(d,"%Y-%m-%d")
```

gives

```
[1] "1990-11-09"
```

These format strings can also be used the other way round – that is, to translate character strings into `"Date"` objects, using the function `as.Date`. For example, the code

```
as.Date("11/09/90", format="%m/%d/%y")
```

gives

```
[1] "1990-11-09"
```

Since dates are measured in days, it may make sense to expect that if numbers are added or subtracted to `"Date"` objects, the results are from the same class and also represent dates. That is, if, say, 30 is added to a date, the result will refer to the date 30 days later, and if 30 is subtracted from a date, the result will refer to the date 30 days earlier. Indeed, R supports such 'date arithmetic', where adding or subtracting numbers from dates results in valid dates. It should be noted that R is able to keep track of leap years and even takes into account complications such as the fact that the first years of centuries are not leap years but the first years of millennia are. This is demonstrated in the following example.

Since March has 31 days, adding 31 days to the 1st of March gives the 1st of April:

```
d0 <- as.Date("1968-03-01")
d0 + 31
```

```
[1] "1968-04-01"
```

Since 1968 was a leap year, adding 1 day to the 28th of February does not give the 1st of March:

```
d1 <- as.Date("1968-02-28")
d1 + 1
```

```
[1] "1968-02-29"
```

whereas 1900 was an exception to the rule that years with numbers divisible by 4 are leap years:

```
d2 <- as.Date("1900-02-28")
d2 + 1
```

```
[1] "1900-03-01"
```

and 2000 was an exception to the rule that years that start centuries (or end them depending on what is considered as the start of a century) are not leap years:

```
d3 <- as.Date("2000-02-28")
d3 + 1
```

```
[1] "2000-02-29"
```

Therefore, the year 2000 had 366 days:

```
d3 + 366
```

```
[1] "2001-02-28"
```

In order to measure times, R defines the two object classes **"POSIXct"** and **"POSIXlt"**, which are subclasses of the class **"POSIXt"** in the sense that any valid member of any of the first two classes has a class attribute that indicates membership of the third. A **"POSIXct"** object is in fact a numeric vector with the appropriate class attributes (i.e. **"POSIXct"** and **"POSIXt"**). Each number in this vector denotes the number of seconds since midnight on 1st January 1970 where the clock time is Greenwich Mean Time (GMT). Such a vector usually has a **"tzone"** attribute, which affects the time zone used for formatting and printing it.

To create such objects, one can apply the function **as.POSIXct()** to numbers, character vectors, and **"POSIXlt"** objects. In order to successfully apply the function to a numeric vector, one has to specify an **origin=** argument that specifies the starting date from which the seconds are counted. For example,

```
as.POSIXct(7200,origin="1970-01-01")
```

gives 2.00 am GMT on the 1st of January 1970. Unless a time zone is specified, the result is printed in the local time zone. If the local time zone is that of Central European Time, the result looks like this:

```
[1] "1970-01-01 03:00:00 CET"
```

One can change the time zone used for printing the time by using a **tz=** argument in the call to **as.POSIXct()** or by assigning a **"tzone"** attribute to the result of such a call. For example,

```
t0 <- as.POSIXct(7200,origin="1970-01-01",tz="GMT")
```

and

```
t0 <- as.POSIXct(7200,origin="1970-01-01")
attr(t0,"tzone") <- "GMT"
```

are equivalent, and when printed, the resulting object named t0 looks like this:

```
[1] "1970-01-01 02:00:00 GMT"
```

Using format strings, it is also possible to apply `as.POSIXct()` to character strings, as in the following example:

```
as.POSIXct(c("97/11/12 12:45","98/01/23 14:20"),
           format="%y/%m/%d %H:%M", tz="GMT")
```

which gives the result

```
[1] "1997-11-12 12:45:00 GMT" "1998-01-23 14:20:00 GMT"
```

In the same way as days are the basic units of dates, so seconds are the basic units of time. Accordingly, it is possible to add and subtract seconds from times, as in the following example:

```
t0 <- as.POSIXct("2020-02-01 00:00",tz="GMT")
t0
```

```
[1] "2020-02-01 GMT"
```

Adding 3600 seconds means adding 1 hour:

```
t0 + 3600
```

```
[1] "2020-02-01 01:00:00 GMT"
```

Subtracting seconds may also change the date:

```
t0 - 1
```

```
[1] "2020-01-31 23:59:59 GMT"
```

A day is 24 times 3600 seconds:

```
day <- 24*3600
t0 + day
```

```
[1] "2020-02-02 GMT"
```

Recycling also works, so we can create a week:

```
t0 + 1:7*day
```

```
[1] "2020-02-02 GMT" "2020-02-03 GMT" "2020-02-04 GMT"
[4] "2020-02-05 GMT" "2020-02-06 GMT" "2020-02-07 GMT"
[7] "2020-02-08 GMT"
```

A `"POSIXlt"` object has a more complicated structure: it is a list of vectors, all of the same length, which denote years, months, seconds, and so on. That is, a `"POSIXlt"` object that represents 17 dates is actually a list of 17 numbers representing years, 17 numbers representing months, 17 numbers representing days of the months, and so on. For most practical purposes, there is little difference between the two classes for measuring time. It is possible to add and subtract seconds from "POSIXlt" objects in the same way as it is possible with "POSIXct" objects. However, it is more straightforward to extract numeric months (numbers between 1 and 12), days of the year (numbers between 1 and 365 or 366), and so on from "POSIXlt" objects than from "POSIXct" objects. In fact, one can convert "Date" and "POSIXct" into "POSIXlt" objects to extract these components of dates and times. This is demonstrated in the following example. Here, we create a "POSIXlt" object from scratch:

```
t0 <- as.POSIXlt(0,origin="2020-02-01",tz="GMT")
```

and add 1 hour and 30 seconds:

```
(t1 <- as.POSIXlt(t0 + 3630))
```

```
[1] "2020-02-01 01:00:30 GMT"
```

After removing the "class" attribute from t1, we can look into the internal structure of a "POSIXlt" object:

```
str(unclass(t1))
```

```
List of 9
 $ sec  : num 30
 $ min  : int 0
 $ hour : int 1
 $ mday : int 1
 $ mon  : int 1
 $ year : int 120
 $ wday : int 6
 $ yday : int 31
 $ isdst: int 0
 - attr(*, "tzone")= chr "GMT"
```

It is not only possible to extract years, month numbers, days, and hours from "POSIXct" or "POSIXlt" objects but also to construct such objects from numbers that indicate years, month numbers, hours, and so on, with the function ISOdate(). This function takes at least three numeric arguments that correspond to the year, month, and day components of the dates to be generated. The arguments are recycled to the appropriate length if necessary. This is demonstrated in the next example. Here, we create the first days of all months in the year 2000. By default, the time is noon:

```
options(width=66)
ISOdate(2000,1:12,1)
```

```
[1] "2000-01-01 12:00:00 GMT" "2000-02-01 12:00:00 GMT"
[3] "2000-03-01 12:00:00 GMT" "2000-04-01 12:00:00 GMT"
```

```
 [5] "2000-05-01 12:00:00 GMT" "2000-06-01 12:00:00 GMT"
 [7] "2000-07-01 12:00:00 GMT" "2000-08-01 12:00:00 GMT"
 [9] "2000-09-01 12:00:00 GMT" "2000-10-01 12:00:00 GMT"
[11] "2000-11-01 12:00:00 GMT" "2000-12-01 12:00:00 GMT"
```

So to go to the start of the dates, we have to set the hour to midnight:

```
ISOdate(2000,1:12,1,hour=0)
```

```
 [1] "2000-01-01 GMT" "2000-02-01 GMT" "2000-03-01 GMT"
 [4] "2000-04-01 GMT" "2000-05-01 GMT" "2000-06-01 GMT"
 [7] "2000-07-01 GMT" "2000-08-01 GMT" "2000-09-01 GMT"
[10] "2000-10-01 GMT" "2000-11-01 GMT" "2000-12-01 GMT"
```

We can, of course, also create a sequence of days:

```
ISOdate(2000,2,1:29,hour=0)
```

```
 [1] "2000-02-01 GMT" "2000-02-02 GMT" "2000-02-03 GMT"
 [4] "2000-02-04 GMT" "2000-02-05 GMT" "2000-02-06 GMT"
 [7] "2000-02-07 GMT" "2000-02-08 GMT" "2000-02-09 GMT"
[10] "2000-02-10 GMT" "2000-02-11 GMT" "2000-02-12 GMT"
[13] "2000-02-13 GMT" "2000-02-14 GMT" "2000-02-15 GMT"
[16] "2000-02-16 GMT" "2000-02-17 GMT" "2000-02-18 GMT"
[19] "2000-02-19 GMT" "2000-02-20 GMT" "2000-02-21 GMT"
[22] "2000-02-22 GMT" "2000-02-23 GMT" "2000-02-24 GMT"
[25] "2000-02-25 GMT" "2000-02-26 GMT" "2000-02-27 GMT"
[28] "2000-02-28 GMT" "2000-02-29 GMT"
```

'Impossible' dates result in **NA**:

```
ISOdate(2000,2,29:31,hour=0)
```

```
[1] "2000-02-29 GMT" NA                NA
```

While the measures of time points are relative to calendars and time zones, differences in time points or the lengths of time are independent of them. Nevertheless, there are several ways to measure lengths of time: in seconds, hours, days, months, years, and so on. To deal with such lengths of time, R defines the object class **"difftime"**. Objects of this class are usually created by computing the differences between two time points, which may be both **"Date"** and **"POSIXt"** objects. But they can also be created from scratch using the function **difftime()**. Again, such objects are numeric vectors with some additional information attached to them: the unit of time measurement. How one can work with such objects is demonstrated in the following example. To demonstrate that we can always obtain differences between times, no matter whether we have **"POSIXct"** or **"POSIXlt"** objects, we create instances of both:

```
t0 <- as.POSIXlt(0,origin="2020-02-01",tz="GMT")
t1 <- as.POSIXct(0,origin="2020-02-01 3:00",tz="GMT")
```

```
t2 <- as.POSIX1t(0,origin="2020-02-01 3:45",tz="GMT")
t3 <- as.POSIXct(0,origin="2020-02-01 3:45:06",tz="GMT")
```

The unit of measurement for time differences is selected automatically. Usually, it is the largest sensible unit:

```
t1 - t0
```

```
Time difference of 3 hours
```

```
t2 - t1
```

```
Time difference of 45 mins
```

```
t3 - t2
```

```
Time difference of 6 secs
```

```
t3 - t0
```

```
Time difference of 3.751667 hours
```

The last difference is in hours and hour fractions. It might be more sensible to have seconds as units of measurement:

```
diff.t <- t3 - t0
units(diff.t) <- "secs"
diff.t
```

```
Time difference of 13506 secs
```

It is also possible to compute differences between dates:

```
d0 <- as.Date("2020-01-31")
d1 <- as.Date("2020-02-28")
d2 <- as.Date("2020-03-31")
```

Usually, the difference is in days:

```
d1 - d0
```

```
Time difference of 28 days
```

```
d2 - d0
```

```
Time difference of 60 days
```

We may also want to see the difference in hours:

```
diff.d <- d1 - d0
units(diff.d) <- "hours"
diff.d
```

```
Time difference of 672 hours
```

It is also possible to create time durations from scratch from strings

```
as.difftime("0:30:00")
```

```
Time difference of 30 mins
```

and from numbers, where it is necessary to specify the unit of measurement:

```
as.difftime(30, units="mins")
```

```
Time difference of 30 mins
```

The basic data type for times, `"POSIXct"`, is based on numbers with a special interpretation. These numbers are the seconds that have passed from a specific origin date, usually the beginning of 1970 in the UTC (Coordinated Universal Time) time zone. Of course, this origin date can be considered as arbitrary. So it is not surprising that other statistical software packages use other origin times in their internal coding of dates and times. For example, in SPSS, dates are measured by the number of days since 14 October 1582, and times are measured by the number of seconds that have passed since the midnight preceding 14 October 1582. Stata measures dates by the number of days since the start of the year 1960 (i.e. from 1 January) and times by the number of milliseconds since the start of the year 1960 (i.e. 12 midnight of 31 December 1959).

There is already some support for translating dates and times imported from files created by SPSS and Stata, yet this still varies depending on the package one uses for importing the data. If data are imported using the *foreign* package, which usually comes pre-installed with R, then no conversion between the internal representation of times and dates is done (as of version 0.8-80; of course, this may change with future versions of the package). The extension *haven* package converts dates and times into `"POSIXct"` vectors from data files created by SPSS and Stata, while the *memisc* package translates dates and times from data files created by SPSS (as of version 0.99.21; of course, this may change with future versions of the package).

While the translation from dates and times recorded in SPSS and Stata files can be done automatically in the process of importing a data set, it may occasionally be necessary to do such a conversion 'by hand' – that is, explicitly with some lines of R code. Fortunately, such code is easily written once one has understood how dates and times are encoded in data files created by SPSS or Stata. The translation of dates and times encoded according to the conventions of SPSS is illustrated by the following code example, where **dates.spss** is a numeric vector that contains dates in SPSS encoding and `times.spss` is a numeric vector that contains times in this encoding. The corresponding `"POSIXct"` vectors can then be created as follows:

```
dates.R <- as.Date(dates.spss, origin="1582-10-14")
times.R <- as.POSIXct(times.spss, origin="1582-10-14")
```

If times and dates are encoded using the conventions of Stata, the conversion can be a bit more complicated. First, since times in Stata are measured in milliseconds, one has to divide numbers that encode time by 1000 before the call to `as.POSIXct()`. The R help page of `as.POSIXct()` also recommends adding a small number to avoid round-off errors. Thus, conversion code for times in a variable `times.stata` could look like this:

```
times.R <- as.POSIXct((times.stata+.1)/1000, origin="1960-01-01")
```

A further complication is that Stata allows dates to be measured in days, weeks, months, half-years, and years. In case dates are measured in days, the conversion code could look like this:

```
dates.R <- as.Date(days.stata, origin="1960-01-01")
```

If one would like to convert dates measured in weeks and months into a `"POSIXct"` vector, one could use code like this:

```
dates.R <- as.Date(weeks.stata*7, origin="1960-01-01")
```

For monthly dates, the conversion becomes more complicated because all months do not have the same length. One possibility to deal with this could be

```
dates.R <- ISOdate(1960 + months.stata %/% 12,
                   1 + months.stata %% 12, 1)
```

with the conversion of quarterly data using the denominator 4 and of half-yearly data using the denominator 2. Of course, it may be also sensible to express such dates in fractions of years, as in

```
years.R <- 1960 + quarters.stata / 4
```

Occasionally, one can find data sets in which, for the sake of compatibility between software packages, dates are not encoded in a way specific for a software package but in numbers, where years, months, and days are represented by different digits of the number. For example, if time is measured in months, the month April of the year 1979 may be represented by the number 197904. If time is measured in days, the 15th day of that month could be represented by the number 19790415. Vectors that contain such numbers could be translated into `"POSIXct"` vectors with code like this:

```
dates.R <- ISODate(yyyymm %/% 100,
                   yyyymm %% 100, 1)
```

or

```
dates.R <- ISODate(yyyymmdd %/% 10000,
                   (yyyymmdd %% 10000) %/% 100,
                   yyyymmdd %% 100)
```

where `yyyymm` and `yyyymmdd` are variables with the encoded dates.

━━━━━━━━ **Overview Box 7.1** ━━━━━━━━

Date and time classes

`"Date"` objects represent dates in terms of the number of days since a specific starting date, namely 1 January 1970.

`"POSIXct"` objects represent dates and times measured in the number of seconds since a specific starting point, namely midnight of 1 January 1970 at GMT.

`"POSIXlt"` objects are lists that are composed of the year, month, day, hour, minutes, and seconds components of time points.

`"difftime"` objects represent time differences, usually measured in seconds, but it is also possible to measure time differences in hours, days, and so on. Measurement units can be enquired and changed with the function `units()`.

Usually, one has to take into account the starting dates or time zones only if objects of these classes are created from numeric vectors.

If the date and time information is given as a set of numeric vectors that represent years, months, days, hours, minutes, and seconds, a `"POSIXct"` object can be created with the function `ISOdate()`.

───────────────────────────────────────

7█2 Time series

Time series are sequences of measurements ordered by time. One can distinguish between regular time series and irregular time series. In regular time series, measurements occur at regular intervals – for example, every year, every quarter, or every month. In irregular time series, there is no such regularity in the measurement occasions, so the lengths of intervals between measurements may vary.

Regular time series are supported by R from the start by the standard package *stats*. This support is provided by the object class `"ts"`. Objects in this class are vectors or matrices with the appropriate class attribute and a `"tsp"` attribute, which is a three-element vector with the numeric presentation of the starting and end points of the time series (usually measured in years) and the frequency with which measurements occur within the basic time unit (i.e. typically within a year).

A univariate time series object is actually a vector with additional information attached to it, and the order in which values appear in the vector correspond to the time points.

For example, the time series object **presidents** – which comes installed with the R standard package *stats* – contains the quarterly popularity of US presidents from the first quarter of 1945 to the last quarter of 1974. This can be verified by applying the functions **frequency()**, **start()**, and **end()** to this object. The result of

```
frequency (presidents)
```

is

```
[1] 4
```

which means that measures are taken four times within each basic unit of time.

```
start (presidents)
```

gives

```
[1] 1945    1
```

while

```
end (presidents)
```

gives

```
[1] 1974    4
```

The first numbers returned by **start(presidents)** and **end(presidents)** are the time points in terms of the basic unit of time, which in this case seems to be the respective years 1945 and 1974 in the Common Era. Assuming that the basic unit of time used here is 'year', the frequency equals **4** means that individual time points in the time series correspond to quarters. Therefore, the results of **start(presidents)** and **end(presidents)** indicate that the time series starts with the first quarter of 1945 and ends with the last quarter of 1974. (Of course, we can conclude as much from the documentation of that object, which we can obtain using **help(presidents)**.)

Since **presidents** contains quarterly data, it appears like a matrix when printed out. The rows correspond to years, while the columns correspond to quarters:

```
presidents
```

```
     Qtr1 Qtr2 Qtr3 Qtr4
1945   NA   87   82   75
1946   63   50   43   32
1947   35   60   54   55
1948   36   39   NA   NA
1949   69   57   57   51
1950   45   37   46   39
```

1951	36	24	32	23
1952	25	32	NA	32
1953	59	74	75	60
1954	71	61	71	57
1955	71	68	79	73
1956	76	71	67	75
1957	79	62	63	57
1958	60	49	48	52
1959	57	62	61	66
1960	71	62	61	57
1961	72	83	71	78
1962	79	71	62	74
[...]				

Even though the print format of this time series looks like that of a matrix, when plotted, the resulting diagram is a single set of lines:

```
plot(presidents)
```

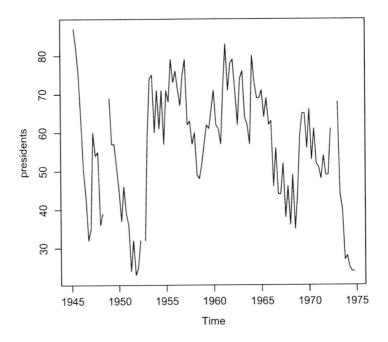

If we want to get a part of a time series that corresponds to the interval between two time points, the best way to achieve this is with the help of the function `window()`, because it allows one to retain the time series information. If instead we apply the bracket operator to the time series object, we only get the 'raw' values of the underlying numeric vector, without any time series information included. For example, if we want to get the data from the **presidents** object for the first three years, applying the bracket operator gives

```
presidents[1:12]
```

```
[1] NA 87 82 75 63 50 43 32 35 60 54 55
```

If we use the `window()` function, the result also contains the relevant time series information:

```
window(presidents,
       start=1945,
       end=c(1947,4))
```

```
     Qtr1 Qtr2 Qtr3 Qtr4
1945  NA   87   82   75
1946  63   50   43   32
1947  35   60   54   55
```

The matrix-like appearance of time series objects is determined by the `"frequency"` part of the time series information attached to them, which is returned by the function `frequency()`. If its value is 4, then R assumes that the data are quarterly, while if its value is 12, it is assumed that the data are monthly. Higher frequencies (e.g. days) are not supported in this way – and there are good reasons for this: different years contain different numbers of days (depending on whether they are leap years or not), as do the various months within a year.

While univariate regular time series objects are vectors with some information about start and end dates and measurement frequency attached, multivariate time series objects are matrices with no such information added. For illustration, we now construct a multivariate time series. First, we import a CSV file with data on unemployment from OECD countries:

```
unemployment <- read.csv("unemployment.csv")
```

The object `unemployment` is a data frame with 30 rows and 30 columns. The first column contains years, and the remaining columns contain yearly unemployment rates for the individual countries. Second, we create a multivariate time series object with the unemployment rates of Germany, France, Italy, and the Netherlands:

```
unemployment.ts <- ts(unemployment[2:5],
                       start = 1970)
```

While using `plot()` with a univariate time series leads to a single line diagram, with a multivariate time series it leads to a combination of line diagrams:

```
plot(unemployment.ts)
```

Obviously, the time series are not stationary but have an upward trend. Therefore, it seems appropriate to look at the differentiated time series – that is, a time series created from the differences between measures obtained from pairs of successful time points. For this, the function `diff()` can be used. It works not only with univariate but also with multivariate time series:

unemployment.ts

```
delta.unemployment.ts <- diff(unemployment.ts)
plot(delta.unemployment.ts)
```

In order to extract the time points from a time series, the function **time()** can be used. The result of a call to this function is a sequence of numbers interpreted as years, days, hours, minutes, seconds, or fractions of these. However, the result is not a **"Date"** or **"POSIXt"** object, and a translation of these numbers into such objects is not straightforward. When **time()** is applied to the **employment.ts** time series, the results are numbers from 1970 through 1999. These numbers clearly refer to years, but it is not straightforward to build valid calendar dates from them.

In a regular time series, all the time intervals between pairs of observations have the same length. This makes construction of the time series simple. All that is needed is a series of observations, a starting point, an end point, and information about the length of time between observations. Irregular time series are more flexible in so far as the length of the time intervals between observations may vary. This makes the construction of such time series more demanding. Instead of just a start point, an end point, and the length of time intervals, the time point of every observation in the time series is required.

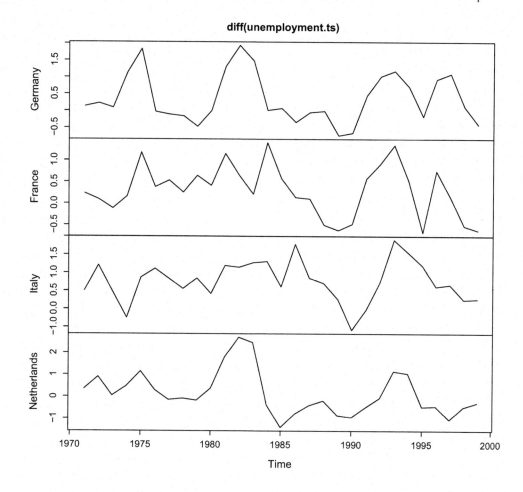

There are several extension packages of R that allow one to work with time series in which the time points are specified in the form of precise dates or even dates and times. The most notable one is the *zoo* package (where 'zoo' stands for 'Z's ordered observations'). Like the *stats* package, the *zoo* package supports both univariate and multivariate time series. A univariate time series object as defined by this package is a combination of a data vector and a vector with the temporal information associated with the elements of the data vector. A multivariate time series object is a matrix with temporal information. The temporal information may be simple numbers, **"Date"** or **"POSIXt"** objects, or a member of any of the other object classes defined in packages such as *chron* or *timeDate*.

The generalized time series objects defined in the *zoo* package can be created using the function **zoo()**, which usually takes two arguments – the data from which the time series is built and a vector that indicates the time points – given by an argument tagged as **order.by=**. The creation of **"zoo"** objects is illustrated in the following with the **presidents** data. We start by extracting the raw numeric data contained in **presidents**:

```
npresidents <- as.numeric(presidents)
```

In the next step, we make sure that the *zoo* package is active and construct an object that represents the time points relevant to the time series. For this, we use the function **yearqtr()** (defined in the *zoo* package)

```
library(zoo)
years <- 1945:1974
quarters <- 1:4
presi.times <- yearqtr(
    rep(years,each=4) +   # each year is repeated 4 times
    rep((quarters-1)/4,30) # the quarters are repeated 30 times
)
```

Now we combine the 'raw' time series data with the information about the time points:

```
zpresidents <- zoo(npresidents,order.by=presi.times)
```

When the time series is printed to the R console, the observations in the time series are shown along with their time points. Unlike the time series objects of the *stats* package, a **"zoo"** object that represents a univariate time series appears as a (named) vector, with the (formatted) time points as element names:

```
zpresidents
```

```
1945 Q1 1945 Q2 1945 Q3 1945 Q4 1946 Q1 1946 Q2 1946 Q3 1946 Q4
    NA      87      82      75      63      50      43      32
1947 Q1 1947 Q2 1947 Q3 1947 Q4 1948 Q1 1948 Q2 1948 Q3 1948 Q4
    35      60      54      55      36      39      NA      NA
1949 Q1 1949 Q2 1949 Q3 1949 Q4 1950 Q1 1950 Q2 1950 Q3 1950 Q4
    69      57      57      51      45      37      46      39
[...]
```

As can be seen by applying the function **str()**, we can take a look at the structure of the univariate time series **"zoo"** object:

```
str(zpresidents)
```

```
'zoo' series from 1945 Q1 to 1974 Q4
  Data: num [1:120] NA 87 82 75 63 50 43 32 35 60 ...
  Index:  'yearqtr' num [1:120] 1945 Q1 1945 Q2 1945 Q3 1945 Q4 ...
```

The output shows that the object has a component that represents the 'raw' data of observations and a component that represents the corresponding time points. These components can be extracted by applying the functions **coredata()** and **index()**:

```
coredata(zpresidents)[1:15] # To save space we only look at the
```

```
[1] NA 87 82 75 63 50 43 32 35 60 54 55 36 39 NA
```

```
index(zpresidents)[1:15]     # first 15 elements.
```

```
 [1] "1945 Q1" "1945 Q2" "1945 Q3" "1945 Q4" "1946 Q1" "1946 Q2"
 [7] "1946 Q3" "1946 Q4" "1947 Q1" "1947 Q2" "1947 Q3" "1947 Q4"
[13] "1948 Q1" "1948 Q2" "1948 Q3"
```

Notably, the function `time()`, which is used to extract the time points from a time series, is synonymous with `index()` when applied to a `"zoo"` object:

```
time(zpresidents)[1:15]
```

```
 [1] "1945 Q1" "1945 Q2" "1945 Q3" "1945 Q4" "1946 Q1" "1946 Q2"
 [7] "1946 Q3" "1946 Q4" "1947 Q1" "1947 Q2" "1947 Q3" "1947 Q4"
[13] "1948 Q1" "1948 Q2" "1948 Q3"
```

In another example, we create a `"zoo"` object that represents a multivariate time series. We again look at the OECD data on unemployment, which we imported from the file `"unemployment.csv"`. We interpret the data as summaries for the respective years, so that the last day of the year appears to be the appropriate date:

```
unemployment <- read.csv("unemployment.csv")
unemployment.z <- zoo(unemployment[,2:7],
                order.by=as.Date(
                    ISOdate(year=unemployment[,1],
                        month=12,
                        day=31)))
```

The resulting object is a matrix with 30 rows and 3 columns, but it is also an object of class `"zoo"`:

```
dim(unemployment.z)
```

```
[1] 30  6
```

```
class(unemployment.z)
```

```
[1] "zoo"
```

This object has proper dates associated with the observations, as we can see when we look at the first few observations:

```
head(unemployment.z)
```

```
           Germany France Italy Netherlands Belgium Luxembourg
1970-12-31   0.557  2.477 4.000       0.868   1.913         NA
1971-12-31   0.689  2.712 4.001       1.213   1.848         NA
1972-12-31   0.912  2.806 4.711       2.114   2.350         NA
1973-12-31   1.000  2.690 4.691       2.151   2.408         NA
```

```
1974-12-31   2.132  2.853 3.942      2.624   2.523      0.067
1975-12-31   3.965  4.028 4.312      3.772   4.522      0.200
```

In fact, both `start()` and `end()` now return a `"Date"` object:

```
start(unemployment.z)
```

```
[1] "1970-12-31"
```

```
end(unemployment.z)
```

```
[1] "1999-12-31"
```

Since the start and the end are dates, we can try to obtain the length of time covered by the time series:

```
end(unemployment.z) - start(unemployment.z)
```

```
Time difference of 10592 days
```

When a subset of a time series is extracted from a `"zoo"` object, the result is again a time series in a `"zoo"` object: Thus,

```
zpresidents[1:8]
```

```
1945 Q1 1945 Q2 1945 Q3 1945 Q4 1946 Q1 1946 Q2 1946 Q3 1946 Q4
    NA      87      82      75      63      50      43      32
```

is another time series of quarterly observations. This is an improvement over the time series as defined in the *stats* packages, where extracting a range of elements results in a numeric vector without time series information.

Any date or time object that has the same class as the time points of a `"zoo"` can be used for subset extraction. For example, since the `zpresidents` time series has observations for quarters of the years from 1945 to 1974, it is possible to extract observations for individual quarters. For example, since the time points of the `zpresidents` time series are quarters of years, an object like

```
as.yearqtr("1945 Q2")
```

```
[1] "1945 Q2"
```

which represents the second quarter of 1945, can be used to obtain the presidential popularity values for the second quarter of 1945:

```
zpresidents[as.yearqtr("1945 Q2")]
```

```
1945 Q2
    87
```

Using **paste()** and the operator to generate number sequences, we can obtain the third quarters of all years of the 1960s and extract the presidential popularity values for them:

```
qtrs3 <- as.yearqtr(paste(1960:1969,"Q3"))
zpresidents[qtrs3]
```

```
1960 Q3 1961 Q3 1962 Q3 1963 Q3 1964 Q3 1965 Q3 1966 Q3 1967 Q3
     61      71      62      62      69      69      56      38
1968 Q3 1969 Q3
     35      65
```

It should be noted that subsetting a *zoo* time series always results in a time series where observations are ordered by increasing dates. This applies even if the index values used for subsetting are out of order. In the following example, the years are in increasing order in the index vector but not the quarters. Nevertheless, dates are in increasing order in the time series subset:

```
qtrs <- paste(rep(1960:1964,each=4),rep(4:1,4),sep="-")
qtrs
```

```
 [1] "1960-4" "1960-3" "1960-2" "1960-1" "1961-4" "1961-3"
 [7] "1961-2" "1961-1" "1962-4" "1962-3" "1962-2" "1962-1"
[13] "1963-4" "1963-3" "1963-2" "1963-1" "1964-4" "1964-3"
[19] "1964-2" "1964-1"
```

```
zpresidents[as.yearqtr(qtrs)]
```

```
1960 Q1 1960 Q2 1960 Q3 1960 Q4 1961 Q1 1961 Q2 1961 Q3 1961 Q4
     71      62      61      57      72      83      71      78
1962 Q1 1962 Q2 1962 Q3 1962 Q4 1963 Q1 1963 Q2 1963 Q3 1963 Q4
     79      71      62      74      76      64      62      57
1964 Q1 1964 Q2 1964 Q3 1964 Q4
     80      73      69      69
```

As with the univariate *zoo* time series, dates and times can be used to extract a subset of a multivariate time series. Thus, we obtain the unemployment rates of four countries for the date 31 December 1997:

```
unemployment.z[as.Date("1997-12-31")]
```

```
           Germany France  Italy Netherlands Belgium Luxembourg
1997-12-31  11.412 12.438 12.251        5.59  12.691      3.616
```

While it is possible to construct an index vector that will extract a subset of a time series for a range of years, this may be quite tedious. A more convenient way of extracting a time series that is related to a range of dates is to use the function `window()`, which works in a similar fashion to how it does for time series objects from the *stats* package. That is, the function is typically called with a starting date or starting time and an end date or end time:

```
window(zpresidents,
       start = as.yearqtr("1969-1"),
       end   = as.yearqtr("1974-2"))
```

```
1969 Q1 1969 Q2 1969 Q3 1969 Q4 1970 Q1 1970 Q2 1970 Q3 1970 Q4
     59      65      65      56      66      53      61      52
1971 Q1 1971 Q2 1971 Q3 1971 Q4 1972 Q1 1972 Q2 1972 Q3 1972 Q4
     51      48      54      49      49      61      NA      NA
1973 Q1 1973 Q2 1973 Q3 1973 Q4 1974 Q1 1974 Q2
     68      44      40      27      28      25
```

Of course, the `window()` function works not only with univariate time series but also with multivariate ones:

```
window(unemployment.z,
       start = as.Date("1980-12-31"),
       end   = as.Date("1989-12-31"))
```

```
           Germany France  Italy Netherlands Belgium Luxembourg
1980-12-31   3.190  6.246  5.574       4.015   8.029      0.721
1981-12-31   4.505  7.396  6.269       5.818  10.279      1.042
1982-12-31   6.441  8.041  6.918       8.519  12.030      1.302
1983-12-31   7.921  8.253  7.694      10.987  13.319      1.630
1984-12-31   7.932  9.660  8.504      10.604  13.363      1.750
1985-12-31   8.002 10.234  8.611       9.191  12.442      1.688
1986-12-31   7.661 10.373  9.896       8.394  11.792      1.478
1987-12-31   7.611 10.479 10.248       7.982  11.461      1.710
1988-12-31   7.598  9.975 10.451       7.785  10.422      1.564
1989-12-31   6.863  9.348 10.214       6.917   9.377      1.420
```

Often, there are observations missing in a time series. The **presidents** time series that we already encountered is an example of this. Such missing values need to be taken care of, in one way or another, to ensure that data summaries result in valid numbers. The function that drops missing values (NAs) from a numeric vector is `na.omit()`. This function is generic and also applicable to objects other than numeric vectors, so it might also work with time series.

Indeed, there is a method of the `na.omit()` function that is applicable to `"ts"` (the time series objects defined in the *stats* package) and `"zoo"` objects. Yet the results may be quite different for these two object classes. The application of `na.omit()` to a `"ts"` object, such as the **presidents** time series, leads to an error condition

```
presidents.o <- na.omit(presidents)
```

and we see the error message

```
Error in na.omit.ts(presidents) : time series contains internal NAs
```

This error message indicates that there are **NAs** between the first and the last valid observation in the time series. Dropping those observations would lead to an irregular time series and is therefore not supported for **"ts"** objects.

This is different for **"zoo"** objects because there can be irregular time series:

```
zpresidents.o <- na.omit(zpresidents)
c("Original length" = length(zpresidents),
  "Length after dropping NAs" = length(zpresidents.o))
```

```
        Original length Length after dropping NAs
                    120                        114
```

Here, no error condition occurs because dropping missing observations just makes some time intervals in the time series longer than others.

The *zoo* package contains a few more functions to handle missing values, most notably the function **na.contiguous()**, which keeps only the longest sequence of valid observations in a time series. This can be illustrated as follows. First, we plot the full time series with dotted lines:

```
plot(zpresidents,lty=3)
```

Then, we add thick lines for the result of **na.contiguous()**

```
lines(na.contiguous(zpresidents),lwd=2)
```

which leads to the following diagram:

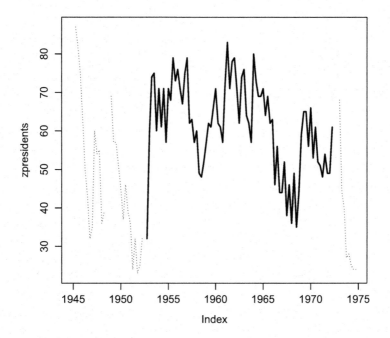

Some other functions even allow the user to fill in the missing values with observed values or values computed from them. These are `na.approx()`, `na.fill()`, `na.locf()`, `na.spline()`, `na.StrucTS()`, and `na.trim()`. It would take too long to describe the working of all these functions, so it has to suffice to illustrate two of them, namely `na.approx()` and `na.spline()`. `na.approx()` fills missing values by a linear interpolation based on the neighbouring observed values, while `na.spline()` uses a spline interpolation.

In this illustration, we use the original time series as 'background' by plotting it first:

```
plot(zpresidents,lwd=2)
```

In the second step, we add lines for the linear and the spline interpolation of missing values provided by `na.approx()` and `na.spline()`, respectively:

```
lines(na.spline(zpresidents),lty=3)
lines(na.approx(zpresidents),lty=2)
```

This results in the following diagram:

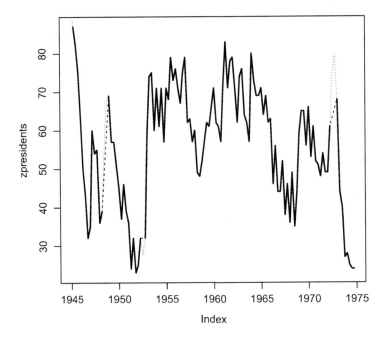

As can be seen, the filled values provided by the linear approximation appear to take the 'shortest way' between adjacent observations, while the spline interpolation captures the 'wiggliness' of the original time series in that some of the filled values appear as 'spikes' in the diagram.

The fact that the values filled in by different techniques can be (even widely) different underlines the uncertainty associated with them. They clearly should not be treated the same as if they were observed, at least not in applications that go beyond mere illustration of a time series.

A common way of creating descriptive summaries of time series is to compute 'running' or 'rolling' statistics, such as running means. A running mean is a mean that is computed not from the whole time series but separately for each applicable observation from a window of neighbouring observations and the relevant observation itself. For example, a running mean computed from a window of size 7 that is centred on each particular observation is computed as

$$\bar{x}_{i,7} = \frac{x_{i-3} + x_{i-2} + x_{i-1} + x_i + x_{i+1} + x_{i+2} + x_{i+3}}{7}$$

that is, it is the average of the three preceding observations, the three succeeding observations, and the actual observation. One could also define a 'left-aligned' variant, where the relevant neighbourhood of an observation consists of the six succeeding observations, and a 'right-aligned' variant, where the relevant neighbourhood contains the six preceding observations.

The *zoo* package supports all three variants of running means or, more generally, three variants of running or rolling statistics. Such running means can be computed with the function `rollmean()`. There are also functions for running medians, running sums, and running maxima, namely `rollmedian()`, `rollsum()`, and `rollmax()`, respectively. It is also possible to compute running or rolling versions of other statistics with the help of `rollapply()`.

It should be noted that the centred, left-aligned, and right-aligned variants of rolling statistics do not really differ in terms of the numbers they result in but in terms of which time points these results are associated with. This is illustrated by the following example of the **presidents** time series after its missing values are dropped using `na.omit()`:

```
zpresidents.o <- na.omit(zpresidents)
```

For illustrative purposes and to keep the amount of output manageable, we focus on a window of the time series that consists of only the first eight observations:

```
zpresidents.o8 <- zpresidents.o[1:8]
```

We call `rollmean()` with the named argument `k=7` to indicate that we require a window width of seven observations:

```
rollmean(zpresidents.o8,k=7)
```

```
 1946 Q1   1946 Q2
61.71429 54.28571
```

Since there are only two complete windows of width 7 that fit into a time series of eight observations, the result is a time series with two observations. Since by default `rollmean()`

computes centred running means, the resulting averages are assigned to the two central time points of the time series from which they are computed.

To get left-aligned rolling means, we call `rollmean()` with the optional argument `align="left"`:

```
rollmean(zpresidents.o8,k=7,align="left")
```

```
  1945 Q2  1945 Q3
61.71429 54.28571
```

The values of the rolling means are the same, but they differ in terms of the associated time points – that is, the first two time points of the time series from which the means are computed.

```
rollmean(zpresidents.o8,k=7,align="right")
```

```
  1946 Q4  1947 Q1
61.71429 54.28571
```

The right-aligned variant associates the resulting values to the last two observations of the time series `zpresidents.o[1:8]`.

When the purpose of rolling statistics is to 'smooth' a time series, then the centred variants of rolling means (or other rolling statistics) seem the most appropriate, as illustrated by the following diagram, which combines the expanded **presidents** time series with centred rolling means with window size 9:

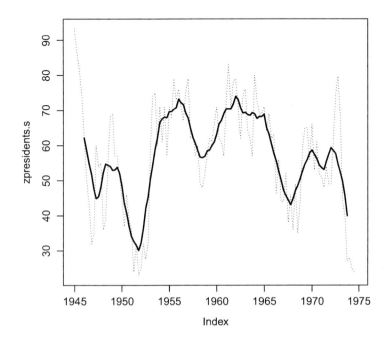

```
zpresidents.s <- na.spline(zpresidents)
plot(zpresidents.s,lty=3)
zpresidents.m <- rollmean(zpresidents.s,k=9)
lines(zpresidents.m,lwd=2)
```

To illustrate the computation of other rolling statistics, we use `rollapply()` to compute rolling standard deviations:

```
zpresidents.sd <- rollapply(zpresidents.s,
                            width=9,
                            FUN=sd)
```

We use these rolling standard deviations to supply approximate 95% confidence intervals to the running means. We base these confidence intervals on the appropriate quantiles of the *t* distribution with 8 degrees of freedom:

```
tv <- qt(.975,df=8)
zpresidents.u <- zpresidents.m+tv*zpresidents.sd/sqrt(8)
zpresidents.l <- zpresidents.m-tv*zpresidents.sd/sqrt(8)
```

Finally, we combine the rolling means with their confidence limits in yet another diagram:

```
plot(zpresidents.m,ylim=c(20,80))
lines(zpresidents.u,lty=2)
lines(zpresidents.l,lty=2)
```

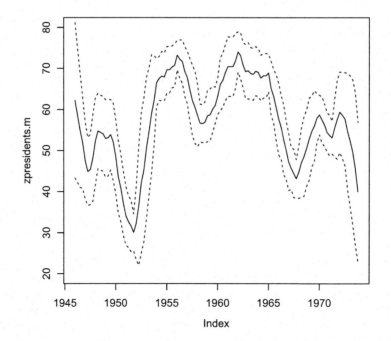

In the previous example, we added **"zoo"** objects together to compute upper and lower confidence limits of running means. This is an instance where an arithmetic operation on such objects results in an object of the same class. In that example, the time series involved had the same length and corresponded to the same time points. But one may very well ask what would have happened if the lengths or the corresponding time points had been different. This is explored in the following example.

For the purpose of the example, we create two partial **"zoo"** time series from the time series **zpresidents** created earlier:

```
zpresidents_1 <- zpresidents[1:4]
zpresidents_2 <- zpresidents[3:6]
```

The two objects named **zpresidents_1** and **zpresidents_2** correspond to different but overlapping time series. We now add these two time series to each other:

```
zpresidents_1 + zpresidents_2
```

```
1945 Q3 1945 Q4
    164     150
```

As can be seen, the **"zoo"** object that results from adding the two **"zoo"** objects **zpresidents_1** and **zpresidents_2** contains only values that are in both time series. As a consequence, the resulting time series is shorter than the time series on which the addition was performed. While this clearly makes sense substantially, it deviates from the usual arithmetic of numeric vectors.

To understand how adding **"zoo"** objects differs from adding ordinary numeric vectors, we create two numeric vectors that correspond to the same observations as the partial time series created above. (We should remember that applying the bracket operator **[]** to a **"ts"** object, like **presidents**, results in a numeric vector.)

```
presidents_1 <- presidents[1:4]
presidents_2 <- presidents[3:6]
```

Because they are numeric vectors of the same length, the result is a numeric vector that contains the result of adding the elements of the two vectors:

```
presidents_1 + presidents_2
```

```
[1]  NA 162 145 125
```

While the result is numerically valid, it is perhaps not sensible substantially, because values corresponding to different points are added together.

The package *zoo* not only defines a variant of arithmetic operations that respect the identity of the time points associated with the elements of time series combined in these operations but also defines a variant of the **merge()** function, which combines several univariate or multivariate time series into a single multivariate time series. This variant differs in three ways from the method of the **merge()** generic function that we encountered in Chapter 3. First, it is not necessary to provide matching variables, because the time point information is used for matching observations. Second, it is possible to merge more than just two time series objects at the same time. Third, by default *all* observations of the time series being merged are kept. (This corresponds to a default setting of **all=TRUE**, while the standard method of **merge()** has the default setting **all=FALSE**.)

For a demonstration of how **merge()** works with **"zoo"** time series objects, we extract three country-specific time series from the multivariate time series object **unemployment.z**, with which we have already worked earlier:

```
Netherlands <- unemployment.z[,4]
length(Netherlands)
```

```
[1] 30
```

```
Belgium <- unemployment.z[,5]
length(Belgium)
```

```
[1] 30
```

```
Luxembourg <- na.omit(unemployment.z[,6])
length(Luxembourg)
```

```
[1] 26
```

By applying **na.omit()** to the **Luxembourg** time series object (which has missing values in the first four observations), we caused this time series to be shorter than the other two time series objects, **Netherlands** and **Belgium**. Nevertheless, we attempt to merge the three time series objects, despite their varying lengths:

```
unemployment.benelux <- merge(Netherlands,
                              Belgium,
                              Luxembourg)
head(unemployment.benelux,n=10)
```

	Netherlands	Belgium	Luxembourg
1970-12-31	0.868	1.913	NA
1971-12-31	1.213	1.848	NA
1972-12-31	2.114	2.350	NA
1973-12-31	2.151	2.408	NA
1974-12-31	2.624	2.523	0.067
1975-12-31	3.772	4.522	0.200
1976-12-31	4.067	5.934	0.332
1977-12-31	3.916	6.745	0.531

```
1978-12-31    3.827   7.321    0.797
1979-12-31    3.648   7.581    0.725
```

Obviously, merging the three time series objects has succeeded. The observations about the years from 1970 to 1973 that are absent in the **Luxembourg** time series are filled with **NAs**.

As already seen, the package *zoo* contains quite a few extensions and adaptations of the features of R to work with regular and irregular time series. The package also provides variants of the functions **read.csv()**, **read.delim()**, **read.csv2()**, **read.delim2()**, **read.table()**, and so on. These variants are named **read.csv.zoo()**, **read.csv2.zoo()**, **read.delim.zoo()**, **read.delim2.zoo()**, and **read.zoo()**. They differ from their 'standard' counterparts (which are defined in the *utils* package) in that they interpret one or more of the columns of the data file (by default the first column) as containing time points instead of substantive observations. These functions can deal with a variety of situations, from situations in which the time points are represented by simple numbers (typically years) to situations in which the time points are represented by several columns containing character strings that indicate parts of dates and times (e.g. years, months, days).

Earlier, we used the function **read.csv()** to read data from the file **"unemployment.csv"** into a data frame and to transfer this data frame (or rather parts of it) into a multivariate **"zoo"** time series object. With **read.csv.zoo()**, the contents of this data file can directly be read into a **"zoo"** object:

```
unemployment_z <- read.csv.zoo("unemployment.csv")
str(unemployment_z)
```

```
'zoo' series from 1970 to 1999
  Data: num [1:30, 1:29] 0.557 0.689 0.912 1 2.132 ...
  - attr(*, "dimnames")=List of 2
  ..$ : NULL
  ..$ : chr [1:29] "Germany" "France" "Italy" "Netherlands" ...
  Index:  int [1:30] 1970 1971 1972 1973 1974 1975 1976 1977 1978 1979 ...
```

Here (as in many similar cases), the first column contains the years, and they are duly transferred into the time index component of the resulting **"zoo"** object.

read.zoo() and the related functions allow one to specify the format in which the time point data are present in the file (they can even figure out the format heuristically). Like **read.table()** and the related functions, they can also read data from a text string. This is illustrated in the following example, where the time format is detected heuristically:

```
Text <- "2012/1/6 20
2012/1/7 30
2012/1/8 40
"
read.zoo(text=Text)
```

```
2012-01-06 2012-01-07 2012-01-08
        20         30         40
```

Alternatively, the format can be given explicitly:

```
read.zoo(text=Text,format="%Y/%m/%d")
```

```
2012-01-06 2012-01-07 2012-01-08
       20          30          40
```

As shown in the next example, dates and times may also be in different columns:

```
Text <- "date,time,x,y
2011-05-08,22:45:21,4,41
2011-05-08,22:45:22,5,42
2011-05-08,22:45:23,5,42
2011-05-08,22:45:24,6,43
"
zobj <- read.csv.zoo(text=Text,
                     index.column=1:2)
zobj
```

```
                    x  y
2011-05-08 22:45:21 4 41
2011-05-08 22:45:22 5 42
2011-05-08 22:45:23 5 42
2011-05-08 22:45:24 6 43
```

The appearance of the multivariate time series object suggests that reading the data was successful even without an explicit format specification, because the first two columns are in standard formats for dates and times.

```
str(zobj)
```

```
'zoo' series from 2011-05-08 22:45:21 to 2011-05-08 22:45:24
  Data: int [1:4, 1:2] 4 5 5 6 41 42 42 43
 - attr(*, "dimnames")=List of 2
  ..$ : NULL
  ..$ : chr [1:2] "x" "y"
  Index:  POSIXct[1:4], format: "2011-05-08 22:45:21" "2011-05-08
        22:45:22" ...
```

The inspection of the object with `str()` corroborates this supposition; the object named `zobj` has a time index component that is a `"POSIXct"` object.

━━━━━ Overview Box 7.2 ━━━━━

Regular and irregular time series

Regular time series are series of observations ordered by time where the time difference between each pair of observations is the same.

(Continued)

Irregular time series are series of observations ordered by time where the time differences between pairs of observations may vary.

━━━━ Overview Box 7.3 ━━━━

Classes to represent time series

"ts" is defined in the standard package *stats*. Objects of this class are intended to represent regular time series.

The time points that correspond to objects of this class are recorded only as numbers, which are interpreted as (fractional) multiples of a basic unit of time, usually years.

"zoo" is defined in the *zoo* package. Objects of this class are intended to represent both regular and irregular time series.

The time points involved here may be recorded in objects from the classes **"Date"**, **"POSIXct"**, **"yearqtr"** (quarters of years, defined in the *zoo* package), and **"yearmon"** (years and months, defined in the *zoo* package), or from a variety of other classes that can be interpreted as dates or times.

━━━━ Overview Box 7.4 ━━━━

Some functions for time series data management

time() returns the time points to which the values in a time series correspond (i.e. the times at which the observations were taken). For **"zoo"** objects, the function **index()** can alternatively be used for this purpose.

coredata() is defined in the *zoo* package. It returns the data contained in a time series - that is, a vector or a matrix without information about time points.

frequency() allows the user to determine how often observations are taken per basic unit of time in a regular time series (**"ts"** objects, as defined by the *stats* package, or **"zooreg"** objects, as defined by the *zoo* package). If the basic unit is years, then, for example, a frequency equal to 4 means that the data are per quarter.

start(), **end()** return the time of the first and the last time point of the time series, respectively.

diff() returns a differenced time series - that is, a time series that contains for each time point the difference of the original time series value and the value at an earlier time point (usually the preceding one).

8

Spatial/Geographical Data

Many social science topics and social phenomena have geographical aspects. Such aspects include the borders of electoral districts, the spatial distribution of settlements or of housing units within municipalities, the trade routes between countries, or the locations where armed conflicts occur. It is not straightforward how such geographical aspects fit into the row-by-column format that social science data sets usually have. This chapter shows how this is possible nevertheless. More importantly, however, the geographical aspects create the possibility of new kinds of relations between observations. For example, housing units may be located closer to or farther away from one another, conflicts may occur only within certain regions, and so on. In this chapter, we explore how one can manage geographical features and the relations between them in order to get some ideas about how to make productive use of them in social science analyses.

The representation of geographical features is nowadays standardized by the Open Geographical Consortium and the International Organization for Standardization (ISO) in the form of the standard ISO 19125 (ISO, 2004). This standard defines certain types of geometrical objects, their textual representation ('well-known text' [WKT] markup), their binary representation ('well-known binary' [WKB] code), as well as their storage and processing in relational databases. Among these geometrical objects, one can distinguish between basic geometrical objects and objects that are composed from them. The most common basic geometrical objects are *points*; collection of points, *line strings*, that is sequences of connected lines; and *polygons*, that is (closed) sequences of lines that enclose an area. The points in turn can be combined into 'multipoints', line strings into 'multilinestrings', and polygons into 'multipolygons'. Finally, arbitrary combinations of these simple and compound objects can form 'geometry collections'. The standard defines other, less often used types of geometrical objects such as 'circular strings' or 'compound curves'. While these geometrical objects are constructed from points in a two-dimensional coordinate system (with '*x* values' and '*y* values'), these geometrical objects become *geographical* objects if these coordinates are interpreted as geographical latitudes and longitudes or have a well-defined relation to latitudes and longitudes (i.e. if a cartographic projection is involved).

R provides data structures designed to collect and represent such geographical features and to enable data management operations that are specific for such geographical shapes. For example, it is possible to check in a straightforward manner whether a set of point locations is situated between a specific area (e.g. of a country) or whether two areas intersect. This chapter describes these data structures, as well as some relevant data management operations, including manipulating cartographical projections and importing data into specific geographical data formats.

8.1 The structure of spatial data in R

There are two major R packages on which most of the other packages that deal with geographical data are built, the *sp* and *sf* packages.

The *sp* package is the older of the two. It defines a variety of spatial object classes, such as `"SpatialPoints"`, `"SpatialLines"`, and `"SpatialPolygons"`, which correspond to geometrical shapes with geographical interpretation (i.e. the coordinates of these shapes are related to geographical latitudes and longitudes). It is possible to join a collection of such shapes with a data frame, where each row of the data frame is matched with a geographical shape or a set of geographical shapes. If a `"SpatialPoints"` object is joined with a data frame, then this results in a `"SpatialPointsDataFrame"` object, and if a `"SpatialPolygons"` object is joined with a data frame, then this results in a `"SpatialPolygonsDataFrame"` object.

An important instance of the use of the object class `"SpatialPolygonsDataFrame"` is the *cshapes* package. This package allows the user to obtain almost all country borders for every year after World War II. In the following example, we obtain such a `"SpatialPolygonsDataFrame"` for the Gambia and assign it to the variable `Gambia`:

```
library(cshapes)
cshape.sp <- cshp()
Gambia <- subset(cshape.sp,CNTRY_NAME=="The Gambia")
```

To get an overview of the object, we obtain a graphical representation with `plot()`:

```
plot(Gambia)
```

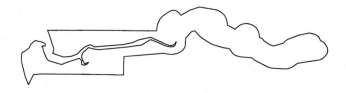

The class of this object is checked as follows:

```
class(Gambia)
```

```
[1] "SpatialPolygonsDataFrame"
attr(,"package")
[1] "sp"
```

The *sp* package is now considered outdated by its original authors and is no longer under active development. It has been superseded by the newer *sf* package, where the package name is an abbreviation of 'simple features'. The name of this package corresponds to the name given to the ISO 19125 standard, 'Simple Feature Access', which indicates that it is the central aim of this package to implement the data model specified by this standard. Therefore, all types of geometrical shapes specified by this standard are represented by object classes implemented in the package. Further, the package offers a variety of useful functions to test and modify relations between geometrical objects and simplifies importing data from files created by common Geographic Information System (GIS) software. For example, it allows the user to import data in the common 'shapefile' format without the need for additional R packages. In contrast, if one used the *sp* package, one would need to use the additional *rgdal* package to import such files.

Apart from its improved compatibility with standards and geographical file formats, a further advantage of *sf* is the simpler and more user-friendly way in which its data structures are constructed. Social scientists and other users of the *sp* and *sf* packages will typically work with 'data-frame-like' structures that combine the properties of geographical units with their geometrical shapes. While with the *sp* package, one would have to deal with 'compound objects' such as `"SpatialPointsDataFrame"` or `"SpatialPolygonsDataFrame"`, with the *sf* package, one will only have to deal with `"sf"` objects, which are just data frames 'enhanced' by geographical information and for which geometrical operations are defined.

We will take a look at the structure of such an 'enhanced data frame', where the data come from the Uppsala Conflict Data Program (UCDP; Sundberg and Melander, 2013). One of the public use data sets provided by the UCDP is the Georeferenced Event Dataset (GED) global version 19.1, which contains data on conflict events, including their start and end dates and their geographical location. This data set is available for download in several formats, including in the native format of R data files. The file in R format is named `"ged191.RData"` and is available as part of a ZIP archive named `"ged191-RData.zip"`. After downloading it, we use the function `unzip()` to extract the file from the ZIP archive and load the contents of the data file into the R workspace:

```
unzip("ged191-RData.zip")
load("ged191.RData")
```

The object contained in the data file is named `ged191`, and it is a member of the classes `"sf"` and `"data.frame"`:

```
class(ged191)
```

```
[1] "sf"          "data.frame"
```

Because it is a data frame, it is easy to check how many variables and how many observations it contains: for the number of observations,

```
nrow(ged191)
```

```
[1] 152616
```

and for the number of variables,

```
ncol(ged191)
```

```
[1] 43
```

The *sf* package includes a `print()` method for `"sf"` objects, which conveniently limits the lines, because the amount of data contained in these objects can be quite large.

```
library(sf)
ged191
```

```
Simple feature collection with 152616 features and 42 fields
geometry type:   POINT
dimension:       XY
```

```
bbox:           xmin: -117.3 ymin: -37.81361 xmax: 155.8967 ymax: 61.25
epsg (SRID):    4326
proj4string:    +proj=longlat +datum=WGS84 +no_defs
First 10 features:
   year                side_b active_year
1  2013                 MUJAO           1
2  2004              Civilians          1
3  2007                PARECO           0
4  2008 Kashmir insurgents             1
5  2008 Kashmir insurgents             1
6  2011                   PKK           1
7  1997              Civilians          0
8  2013                 APCLS           1
9  2010             Al-Shabaab          1
10 2003                  MDJT           1
                           side_a priogrid_gid conflict_new_id
1               Government of Mali       150833           11347
2                              FNI       132182             583
3                             CNDP       127138            4600
4              Government of India       179070             364
5              Government of India       179069             364
6             Government of Turkey       184761             354
7                             ULFA       167587             523
8    Government of DR Congo (Zaire)      127859             283
9             Government of Somalia      132931             337
10              Government of Chad       160235             288
[...]
```

As can be seen, the `print()` method for `"sf"` objects uses a different terminology to refer to the rows and columns of these objects. While the `print()` method for data frames refers to rows as 'observations' and to columns as 'variables', the `print()` method for `"sf"` objects refers to rows as 'features' and to columns as 'fields'. (More precisely, columns that do not contain geographical shapes are referred to as fields.) Further, only the first 10 rows or features are shown, but additionally the `print()` method also shows some geographically relevant information, such as the 'bounding box', which specifies the minima and maxima of the spatial coordinates (in the present case, the latitudes and longitudes) and the type of coordinate system being used (the EPSG [European Petroleum Survey Group] code), as well as whether the coordinates involve a cartographic projection and which projection it is (the 'proj4string'). In the present case, we see that the EPSG code is 4326 – that is, the common coordinate system using latitudes and longitudes (EPSG, 1993).[1] The information by the projection string ('proj4string') says the same; that is, no cartographic projection is used. We will explore how to work with cartographic projections later in this chapter.

We now examine the structure of the object **ged191** using the function `str()`:

```
str(ged191)
```

---

[1] https://en.wikipedia.org/wiki/EPSG_Geodetic_Parameter_Dataset

```
Classes 'sf' and 'data.frame':  152616 obs. of  43 variables:
 $ year            : num   2013 2004 2007 2008 2008 ...
 $ side_b          : chr   "MUJAO" "Civilians" "PARECO" "Kashmir
 $ active_year     : num   1 1 0 1 1 1 0 1 1 1 ...
 [...]
 $ deaths_a        : num   12 0 0 0 1 0 0 0 0 0 ...
 $ deaths_b        : num   16 0 0 2 11 13 0 0 0 2 ...
 $ deaths_unknown  : num   0 0 0 0 0 0 0 80 11 0 ...
 $ low             : num   31 100 4 2 12 13 1 70 11 2 ...
 $ geometry        :sfc_POINT of length 152616; first list elem
 - attr(*, "sf_column")= chr "geometry"
```

As can be seen from the output of this function, the **"sf"** object has mostly the structure of a data frame, but it has an additional attribute, **"sf_column"**, which contains the name of the column with the geographical information, in the present case the column named **"geometry"**.

Knowing the role of the **"sf_column"** attribute, it is possible to extract the geographical shapes associated with the rows or 'features' in an **"sf"** object. There is, however, a more straightforward way by which this information can be obtained – using the function **st_geometry()**:

```
gged191 <- st_geometry(ged191)
gged191
```

```
Geometry set for 152616 features
geometry type:   POINT
dimension:       XY
bbox:            xmin: -117.3 ymin: -37.81361 xmax: 155.8967 ymax: 61.25
epsg (SRID):     4326
proj4string:     +proj=longlat +datum=WGS84 +no_defs
First 5 geometries:
POINT (-3.89474 14.94329)
POINT (30.77583 1.769722)
POINT (28.87694 -1.651944)
POINT (74.72549 34.37893)
POINT (74.16729 34.3726)
```

The object **gged191** is a member of classes **"sfc"** (i.e. some sort of geographical shapes) and **"sfc_POINT"** (i.e. the shapes are points). In fact, the object **gged191** is a list, so that individual shapes can be extracted using the double-bracket operator **[[]]**:

```
gged191[[1]]
```

```
POINT (-3.89474 14.94329)
```

In fact, such an individual shape is a numeric vector with two elements and membership of classes **"XY"**, **"POINT"** (indicating what ISO 19125 object type it corresponds to) and **"sfg"** (indicating that it is an individual geometrical object).

```
class(gged191[[1]])
```

```
[1] "XY"      "POINT" "sfg"
```

Data in the format of the older *sp* package can be translated into the format of the newer *sf* package using the function `as()`. This way it is, for example, possible to translate data obtained from the *cshapes* (Weidmann and Gleditsch, 2016) packages into the new format. We make use of this to extract the countries from South America. To make sure that each country appears only once when we extract data from the *cshapes* database, we set the start of the year 1990 as reference time point:

```
cshapes.1990 <- cshp(as.Date("1990-01-01"))
```

We then convert the result into an object from class `"sf"`:

```
cshapes.1990 <- as(cshapes.1990,"sf")
cshapes.1990
```

```
Simple feature collection with 171 features and 24 fields
geometry type:   MULTIPOLYGON
dimension:       XY
bbox:            xmin: -180 ymin: -55.90223 xmax: 180 ymax: 83.11387
epsg (SRID):     4326
proj4string:     +proj=longlat +ellps=WGS84 +no_defs
First 10 features:
            CNTRY_NAME        AREA        CAPNAME  CAPLONG
0               Guyana  211982.0050     Georgetown    -58.2
1             Suriname  145952.2740     Paramaribo    -55.2
2  Trinidad and Tobago    5041.7290  Port-of-Spain    -61.5
3            Venezuela  916782.2172        Caracas    -66.9
4                Samoa    2955.2124           Apia   -172.0
5                Tonga     464.7473    Nuku'alofa   -175.0
6            Argentina 2787442.0977  Buenos Aires    -58.7
7              Bolivia 1092697.4356        La Paz    -68.2
8               Brazil 8523619.5715       Brasilia    -47.9
9                Chile  745808.4936       Santiago    -70.7
[...]
   ISO1AL3                    geometry
0      GUY MULTIPOLYGON (((-58.17262 6...
1      SUR MULTIPOLYGON (((-55.12796 5...
2      TTO MULTIPOLYGON (((-61.07945 1...
3      VEN MULTIPOLYGON (((-66.31029 1...
4      WSM MULTIPOLYGON (((-172.5965 -...
5      TON MULTIPOLYGON (((-175.1453 -...
6      ARG MULTIPOLYGON (((-71.85916 -...
7      BOL MULTIPOLYGON (((-62.19884 -...
8      BRA MULTIPOLYGON (((-44.69501 -...
9      CHL MULTIPOLYGON (((-73.0421 -4...
```

We can also see that the geographical shapes included in the object are 'multipolygons' – that is, collections of several polygons. This is so because most countries in South America include an area not only on the mainland of the continent but also on several islands off its coast.

Since an **"sf"** object is also a data frame, we can use the function **subset()** to get a subset of the features in the object – that is, a subset of the countries covered by the *cshapes* data:

```
SthAmCntry.names <- c("Argentina",
                      "Bolivia",
                      "Brazil",
                      "Chile",
                      "Colombia",
                      "Ecuador",
                      "Guyana",
                      "Paraguay",
                      "Peru",
                      "Suriname",
                      "Uruguay",
                      "Venezuela")
SthAmCountries <- subset(cshapes.1990,
                         CNTRY_NAME %in% SthAmCntry.names)
```

For good measure, we also create three objects for Brazil, Chile, and Colombia:

```
Brazil <-  subset(cshapes.1990,CNTRY_NAME=="Brazil")
Chile <-   subset(cshapes.1990,CNTRY_NAME=="Chile")
Colombia <-  subset(cshapes.1990,CNTRY_NAME=="Colombia")
```

Since the *cshapes* data also contain the coordinates of the country capitals, we now create an **"sf"** object with the locations of the capitals. In the first step, we collect the coordinates from the variables in the **cshapes.1990** data frame:

```
cap.latlong <- with(cshapes.1990,cbind(CAPLONG,CAPLAT))
```

Next, we create a list of pairs of coordinates contained in numeric vectors:

```
cap.latlong <- lapply(1:nrow(cap.latlong), function(i)cap.latlong[i,])
```

Then, we use the function **st_point()** to create a geometry object from each coordinate pair in the list and put them together into an **"sfc"** object:

```
cap.latlong <- lapply(cap.latlong,st_point)
cap.latlong <- st_sfc(cap.latlong)
```

Now we can create a (modified) copy of the *cshapes* data with the locations of the capitals as 'geometry data' instead of the country border polygons:

```
cshapes.capitals.1990 <- cshapes.1990
st_geometry(cshapes.capitals.1990) <- cap.latlong
```

We also have to copy information about the coordinate system:

```
st_crs(cshapes.capitals.1990) <- st_crs(cshapes.1990)
```

Now we have an "sf" object with all the necessary information:

```
cshapes.capitals.1990
```

```
Simple feature collection with 171 features and 24 fields
geometry type:   POINT
dimension:       XY
bbox:            xmin: -175 ymin: -41.3 xmax: 179 ymax: 64.15
epsg (SRID):     4326
proj4string:     +proj=longlat +ellps=WGS84 +no_defs
First 10 features:
                   CNTRY_NAME          AREA        CAPNAME CAPLONG
0                      Guyana   211982.0050    Georgetown   -58.2
1                    Suriname   145952.2740    Paramaribo   -55.2
2        Trinidad and Tobago     5041.7290 Port-of-Spain   -61.5
3                   Venezuela   916782.2172       Caracas   -66.9
4                       Samoa     2955.2124          Apia  -172.0
5                       Tonga      464.7473   Nuku'alofa  -175.0
6                   Argentina  2787442.0977  Buenos Aires   -58.7
7                     Bolivia  1092697.4356        La Paz   -68.2
8                      Brazil  8523619.5715      Brasilia   -47.9
9                       Chile   745808.4936      Santiago   -70.7
[...]
   ISO1AL3                 geometry
0      GUY       POINT (-58.2 6.8)
1      SUR POINT (-55.2 5.833333)
2      TTO     POINT (-61.5 10.65)
3      VEN      POINT (-66.9 10.5)
4      WSM      POINT (-172 -13.8)
5      TON      POINT (-175 -21.1)
6      ARG     POINT (-58.7 -34.6)
7      BOL     POINT (-68.2 -16.5)
8      BRA     POINT (-47.9 -15.8)
9      CHL     POINT (-70.7 -33.5)
```

Since we will focus on the three countries Brazil, Chile, and Colombia, we extract their capitals:

```
Brasilia <- subset(cshape.capitals.1990,CNTRY_NAME=="Brazil")
Santiago <-  subset(cshape.capitals.1990,CNTRY_NAME=="Chile")
Bogota <-  subset(cshape.capitals.1990,CNTRY_NAME=="Colombia")
```

In the following, we will use the function `plot()` to illustrate some of the things that can be done with spatial data. It should be noted that when `plot()` is applied to an "sf" object, it will not just draw the points and lines from which its geometry is composed but also create a collection of maps where points, lines, polygons, or other geometrical objects are shaded according to the values of the variables in the data frame that belongs to the object:

```
graypal <- function(n)gray.colors(n,start=.2,end=.9,alpha=.5)
plot(SthAmCountries,pal=graypal)
```

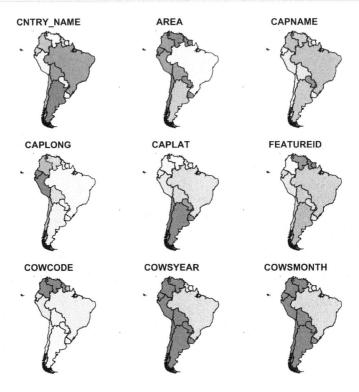

To get just the points, lines, polygons, and so on, we use plot() with the result of st_geometry():

```
plot(st_geometry(SthAmCountries))
```

▬▬▬▬▬▬▬ **Overview Box 8.1** ▬▬▬▬▬▬▬

Main geometrical coordinates

All the geometrical shapes supported by *sf* are constructed from points with at least two coordinates – a horizontal coordinate, denoted by **"X"**, and a vertical coordinate **"Y"**. The points may have up to two more coordinates – a coordinate denoted by **"Z"**, which represents an altitude, and a coordinate **"M"**, which may represent a measure.
The following coordinate systems or 'dimensions' are supported by *sf*:

"XY" coordinates of locations in a two-dimensional space, often representing longitudes and latitudes or transformed longitudes and latitudes

"XYZ" coordinates of locations with altitudes

"XYM" coordinates of locations with additional measures

"XYZM" coordinates of locations with altitudes and additional measures

▬▬▬▬▬▬▬ **Overview Box 8.2** ▬▬▬▬▬▬▬

Common geometrical shapes or geographical features supported by the *sf* package

"POINT" a single point. It usually represents a single geographical location, in which the coordinates are interpreted as (transformed) longitude and latitude. These shapes may also have a third coordinate.

"LINESTRING" a sequence of lines where each line connects two points and each line may be connected at one end with another line. The lines may not intersect one another.

"POLYGON" a collection of closed line strings. Each line string is closed in so far as the end of the last line is connected with the start of the first line, and the lines may not intersect one another. The first closed line string encloses an area (geometrical or geographical), and other line strings (if present) represent holes in this area.

"MULTIPOINTS" a collection of **"POINT"** shapes

"MULTILINESTRING" a collection of **"LINESTRING"** shapes

"MULTIPOLYGON" a collection of **"POLYGON"** shapes

(Continued)

`"GEOMETRYCOLLECTION"` a collection of any of the other shapes

There are 10 other types of geometrical shapes also supported by the *sf* package, but their use is still relatively rare (at the time of writing).

━━━━━━━━━ **Overview Box 8.3** ━━━━━━━━━

Main object classes defined by the *sf* package

`"sfg"` objects contain a single geometrical shape.

`"sfc"` objects are a list of geometrical shapes all of the same type and coordinate system.

`"sf"` objects are data frames with a special column with geometrical shapes. This column is usually a member of the `"sfc"` class and can be identified by the `"sf_column"` attribute of the data frame or `"sf"` object.

8.2 Spatial relations and operations

So far, it may seem that dealing with geographical data is mostly a matter of creating thematic maps. However, besides geographical objects that can be displayed on maps, the *sf* package also defines several spatial operations and ways to obtain data summaries that are based on geographical shapes, which makes it a useful tool for social science data analysis and a topic of a book on social science data management. For example, point locations have distances from one another, while geographical areas or polygons may touch one another or may not and may overlap or may not. This opens up new ways of analysis and poses new challenges for data management, which fortunately can be met using the *sf* package.

The *sf* package defines functions that test for a variety of *spatial relations* among geographical objects. For example, a polygon may contain another polygon if all its edges lie inside the area covered by the polygon, and it may contain a group of points if all of them are inside this area. This relation is checked by the function `st_contains()`. While this is an asymmetric relation, a symmetric relation is that of contiguity; that is, two polygons may 'touch' one another in so far as they have some border lines or some points at their border in common, which is checked by the function `st_touches()`. There are a couple more spatial relations that can be checked with functions from the *sf* package, and the theory behind these spatial relations is developed, for example, in Clementini et al. (1994).

One of the relations that *sf* allows the user to check is whether a shape or feature contains another one, which can be done using the function `st_contains()`. The objects being compared should be members of the class `"sf"` or `"sfc"`, but they do not need to be of the same type. Thus, it can be checked whether a point (e.g. the location of a country's capital) is contained in a polygon (e.g. within the borders of a country). The function `st_contains()` usually returns a *sparse matrix*. A sparse matrix is a matrix stored in computer memory in a way that is very efficient in terms of the space it requires. While this is very efficient when the number of geographical shapes is large, for comparisons with smaller collections of geographical shapes, non-sparse results are more convenient. That is why we call the function `st_contains()` with the argument `sparse=FALSE`:

```
st_contains(Brazil,Brasilia,sparse=FALSE)
```

```
        [,1]
[1,]  TRUE
```

```
st_contains(Brazil,Bogota,sparse=FALSE)
```

```
        [,1]
[1,]  FALSE
```

Obviously, Brasilia is contained by Brazil, but not Bogotá.

The advantage of the result being a matrix is that it allows two geographical features simultaneously. To try this out, we create two `"sf"` objects with three features each and compare them with `st_contains()`:

```
ThreeCountries <- subset(cshape.1990,
                      CNTRY_NAME %in% c("Brazil", "Chile", "Colombia"))
rownames(ThreeCountries) <- ThreeCountries$CNTRY_NAME
ThreeCapitals <- subset(cshape.capitals.1990,
                      CNTRY_NAME %in% c("Brazil", "Chile", "Colombia"))
rownames(ThreeCapitals) <- ThreeCapitals$CAPNAME
st_contains(ThreeCountries,ThreeCapitals,sparse=FALSE)
```

```
        [,1]   [,2]   [,3]
[1,]   TRUE  FALSE  FALSE
[2,]  FALSE   TRUE  FALSE
[3,]  FALSE  FALSE   TRUE
```

A drawback of the current implementation of spatial relations – at least of the *sf* version current at the time of writing – is that the resulting rows and columns are not named, even if the `"sf"` objects have row names. This may or may not change with future updates of *sf*, but for now we have to provide the row and column names ourselves if we want to have a result that is easy to interpret:

```
structure(
    st_contains(ThreeCountries,ThreeCapitals,sparse=FALSE),
    dimnames=list(rownames(ThreeCountries),rownames(ThreeCapitals))
)
```

```
         Brasilia Santiago Bogota
Brazil       TRUE    FALSE  FALSE
Chile       FALSE     TRUE  FALSE
Colombia    FALSE    FALSE   TRUE
```

With `st_touches()`, we can now check whether Chile and Colombia are neighbouring countries of Brazil:

```
st_touches(Brazil,Colombia,sparse=FALSE)
```

```
      [,1]
[1,]  TRUE
```

```
st_touches(Brazil,Chile,sparse=FALSE)
```

```
      [,1]
[1,] FALSE
```

Again, we can also get a matrix of relations of being neighbours. If we call the function with one argument, then all the features in the relevant object are compared:

```
structure(
    st_touches(ThreeCountries,sparse=FALSE),
    dimnames=list(rownames(ThreeCountries),rownames(ThreeCountries))
)
```

```
         Brazil Chile Colombia
Brazil    FALSE FALSE     TRUE
Chile     FALSE FALSE    FALSE
Colombia   TRUE FALSE    FALSE
```

The *sf* package not only allows one to check whether geographical objects touch, contain one another, and so on, but also allows one to compute the area enclosed by a geographical polygon or the distance between geographical points. Again, we use the *cshapes* data on three South American countries to check out these facilities.

To obtain areas, we can use the function `st_area()`. It takes an `"sf"` object or an `"sfc"` and computes the area in square metres:

```
st_area(Brazil)
```

```
8.472314e+12 [m^2]
```

Obviously, square metres are not the right unit of measurement when we deal with entire countries. So we create a way to obtain the area in square kilometres:

```
in_km2 <- function(x) units::set_units(x,"km^2")
in_km2(st_area(Brazil))
```

```
8472314 [km^2]
```

When applied to an object comprising several features, the result is a vector:

```
in_km2(st_area(SthAmCountries))
```

```
Units: [km^2]
 [1]   210585.6   144986.2   910860.6 2780991.8 1086612.6 8472314.3
 [7]   744390.5   255309.8   398803.1 1290857.6   177861.7 1135173.0
```

If we want to have the country names as identifying information, we have to explicitly add them:

```
structure(in_km2(st_area(SthAmCountries)),
          names=as.character(SthAmCountries$CNTRY_NAME))
```

```
Units: [km^2]
   Guyana   Suriname Venezuela Argentina    Bolivia     Brazil
 210585.6   144986.2  910860.6 2780991.8 1086612.6  8472314.3
    Chile    Ecuador  Paraguay      Peru    Uruguay   Colombia
 744390.5   255309.8  398803.1 1290857.6   177861.7  1135173.0
```

The function **st_distance()** can be used to compute the distance between **"sf"** or **"sfc"** objects. Its application is straightforward for computing the distance between country capitals:

```
st_distance(Brasilia,Bogota)
```

```
Units: [m]
         [,1]
[1,] 3663768
```

The function can also be used to compute the distance between a country and a capital

```
st_distance(Chile,Bogota)
```

```
Units: [m]
         [,1]
[1,] 2496612
```

in which case the distance is between the nearest point at the border of the country and the capital. It is also possible to compute the distance between countries, where the distance is between the nearest points at the country borders:

```
st_distance(Chile,Colombia)
```

```
Units: [m]
         [,1]
[1,] 1468577
```

It should be noted that this can be quite time-consuming because all possible pairs of points at the border have to be compared to find the closest ones.

The results are in metres, which is not too sensible when geographical locations are involved. We therefore create a way to obtain the distance in kilometres:

```
in_km <- function(x) units::set_units(x,"km")
in_km(st_distance(Brasilia,Bogota))
```

```
Units: [km]
          [,1]
[1,] 3663.768
```

As with relations, the result of `st_distance()` is a matrix. The function can also be applied to a single `"sf"` or `"sfc"` object, in which case all possible comparisons are made between the shapes contained in the objects:

```
in_km(st_distance(ThreeCapitals))
```

```
Units: [km]
          [,1]      [,2]      [,3]
[1,]     0.000 3014.942 3663.768
[2,] 3014.942     0.000 4232.052
[3,] 3663.768 4232.052     0.000
```

Further, there are functions in the *sf* package that allow one to apply certain geometrical operations on geographical shapes. For example, to form the spatial union of a pair of polygons, one can use the function `st_union()`; to form the spatial intersection of a pair of polygons, one can use the function `st_intersection()`; and to form a spatial difference, one can use the function `st_difference()`. It is even possible to obtain a symmetric difference using `st_sym_difference()`. The following graphic illustrates a spatial union and a spatial intersection.

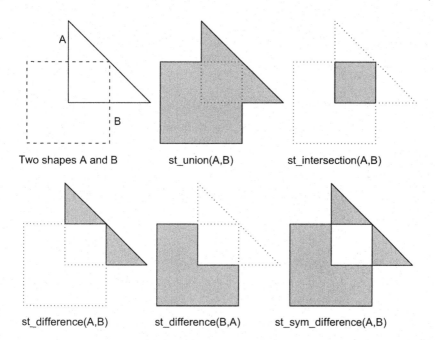

| Two shapes A and B | st_union(A,B) | st_intersection(A,B) |

| st_difference(A,B) | st_difference(B,A) | st_sym_difference(A,B) |

A practical application of `st_union()` is the combination of smaller geographical units into a larger one, for statistical reasons or for reasons of representing results. Here, we combine the shapes of the South American states to obtain the shape of the continent:

```
SouthAmerica <- st_union(SthAmCountries)
```

For illustrative purposes, we plot the borders of the individual countries as well as their union:

```
plot(st_geometry(SthAmCountries))
plot(st_geometry(SouthAmerica))
```

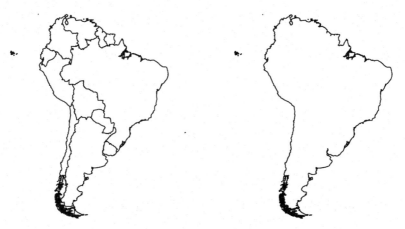

Obviously, there is a piece of South America missing – French Guiana, which is not a sovereign state (and therefore not included in *cshapes* as a South American country) but is (at the time of writing) an overseas department of France.

As already mentioned, `"sf"` objects are data frames. Consequently, it is possible to obtain subsets of observations either by the application of the bracket operator (`[]`) or by the function `subset()`. If the bracket operator is used, rows are selected into the subset based on row indices that are numeric, logical, or character vectors. With `"sf"` objects, it is also possible to use `"sf"` or `"sfc"` objects as row indices. In that case, all rows or features of an `"sf"` object are included in the subset that are contained by the objects used as row indices.

We examine the use of spatial row indices by combining the data of the UCDP with the *cshapes* data. In the following example, we use spatial row indices to select all conflicts in the UCDP data set that have occurred in Colombia.

The object `Colombia` is the border polygon for the country Colombia, while `ged191` contains geolocated conflict event data of the UCDP. In principle, it should be possible to select all those conflicts in `ged191` that occur within the bounds of the `Colombia` polygon simply with

```
Colombia.conflicts <- ged191[Colombia,]
```

```
Error in st_geos_binop("intersects", x, y, sparse = sparse,
    prepared = prepared) :
  st_crs(x) == st_crs(y) is not TRUE
```

However, trying this directly fails, because `Colombia` and `ged191` have different coordinate systems:

```
st_crs(Colombia)
```

```
Coordinate Reference System:
  EPSG: 4326
  proj4string: "+proj=longlat +ellps=WGS84 +no_defs"
```

```
st_crs(ged191)
```

```
Coordinate Reference System:
  EPSG: 4326
  proj4string: "+proj=longlat +datum=WGS84 +no_defs"
```

The coordinate systems differ only in their description strings – the first one contains +ellps=WGS84, while the other contains +datum=WGS84. To make the application of a spatial row index possible, we change the coordinate system of `ged191` to the coordinate system of `Colombia`:

```
ged191_ellips <- st_transform(ged191,st_crs(Colombia))
Colombia.conflicts <- ged191_ellips[Colombia,]
```

Now the creation of a subset of the conflict data is successful. This is illustrated by the following example, where the conflicts that have occurred in Colombia are plotted together with

the outline of the country's borders. In the resulting map, the locations are marked in grey
levels corresponding to the number of civilian deaths:

```
mypal <- function(n)gray.colors(n,start=.2,end=.9,alpha=.5)
plot(st_geometry(Colombia))
plot(Colombia.conflicts["deaths_civilians"],
    add=TRUE,pch=19,cex=.2,
    pal=mypal,
    nbreaks=30
    )
```

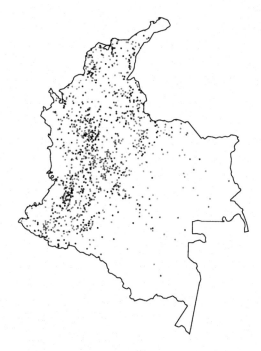

To show that subsets of locations can be created for an arbitrary region, we select all conflicts within a circular area around the country's capital, Bogotá. Such a circular area can be
obtained using the function `st_buffer()`. The function expects the radius to be specified as
an angle and not as a distance. To facilitate the creation of a circular area, we define a helper
function, which translates a kilometre distance into an angle and then calls `st_buffer()`:

```
st_circ <- function(x,dist.km){
    dist.degr <- 360*dist.km/40007.863
    st_buffer(st_geometry(x),dist=dist.degr)
}
```

Using this helper function, we obtain the area around Bogotá

```
Bogota.200km <- st_circ(Bogota,dist.km=200)
```

and the conflicts that have occurred in this area:

```
Bogota.conflicts <- ged191_ellips[Bogota.200km,]
```

The map shows the outline of the borders of Colombia, the locations of conflicts in Colombia as light grey dots, and the conflicts that occur within the 200 kilometre radius around Bogotá as black dots. Also the outline of the 200 kilometre circular area is shown.

```
plot(st_geometry(Colombia))
plot(st_geometry(Colombia.conflicts),
     add=TRUE,pch=1,cex=.3,col="gray80")
plot(st_geometry(Bogota.conflicts),
     add=TRUE,pch=19,cex=.3)
plot(Bogota.200km,lty=3,add=TRUE)
```

In the previous examples, we could see that feature geometries (or geographical shapes) can be used, like indices, as row selectors to create a subset of observations or features from an `"sf"` object. Yet geometrical shapes can also be used as factors according to which aggregates are computed with `aggregate()`. When `aggregate()` is used in the 'usual' way, the levels of one or more factors define groups of observations for which summaries, such as means or sums, are computed. When the function is used with an `"sf"` object, polygons or multipolygons can be used to define such groups of observations. For example, a polygon or multipolygon may be used to define the group of observations of an `"sf"` object that are contained in that polygon or multipolygon by virtue of their associated geographical shapes (which usually are smaller polygons or points). For example, it is possible to compute country summaries of conflicts by countries if the conflicts are georeferenced in terms of their locations and multipolygons referring to country borders are available.

In the following, the computation of aggregates based on geographical shapes is illustrated. We already created in an earlier example the object named `SthAmCountries`, which is a collection of country border multipolygons. We also have a georeferenced conflict event data set available as an `"sf"` object in the R variable `ged191_ellips`. To get the sums of civilian deaths within each of the South American countries, we now apply the function `aggregate()` to `ged191_ellips` with `SthAmCountries` as `by=` argument:

```
aggregate(ged191_ellips["deaths_civilians"],by=SthAmCountries,sum)
```

```
Simple feature collection with 12 features and 1 field
geometry type:   MULTIPOLYGON
dimension:       XY
bbox:            xmin: -109.4461 ymin: -55.90223 xmax: -34.79292
     ymax: 12.59027
epsg (SRID):     4326
proj4string:     +proj=longlat +ellps=WGS84 +no_defs
First 10 features:
    deaths_civilians                          geometry
0                 20 MULTIPOLYGON (((-58.17262 6...
1                 NA MULTIPOLYGON (((-55.12796 5...
3                792 MULTIPOLYGON (((-66.31029 1...
6                  0 MULTIPOLYGON (((-71.85916 -...
7                  0 MULTIPOLYGON (((-62.19884 -...
8                164 MULTIPOLYGON (((-44.69501 -...
9                 NA MULTIPOLYGON (((-73.0421 -4...
10                15 MULTIPOLYGON (((-79.45167 -...
11                 0 MULTIPOLYGON (((-57.67267 -...
12              1021 MULTIPOLYGON (((-69.49973 -...
```

The aggregates are only identified by the geometrical shapes, so in order to combine them with country names, we have to merge them with an `"sf"` object that contains country names:

```
within(
    aggregate(ged191_ellips["deaths_civilians"],by=SthAmCountries,sum),
    country <- SthAmCountries$CNTRY_NAME)
```

```
Simple feature collection with 12 features and 2 fields
geometry type:   MULTIPOLYGON
dimension:       XY
bbox:            xmin: -109.4461 ymin: -55.90223 xmax: -34.79292 ymax: 12.59027
epsg (SRID):     4326
proj4string:     +proj=longlat +ellps=WGS84 +no_defs
First 10 features:
    deaths_civilians                          geometry    country
0                 20 MULTIPOLYGON (((-58.17262 6...    Guyana
1                 NA MULTIPOLYGON (((-55.12796 5...   Suriname
```

3	792	MULTIPOLYGON (((-66.31029 1...	Venezuela
6	0	MULTIPOLYGON (((-71.85916 -...	Argentina
7	0	MULTIPOLYGON (((-62.19884 -...	Bolivia
8	164	MULTIPOLYGON (((-44.69501 -...	Brazil
9	NA	MULTIPOLYGON (((-73.0421 -4...	Chile
10	15	MULTIPOLYGON (((-79.45167 -...	Ecuador
11	0	MULTIPOLYGON (((-57.67267 -...	Paraguay
12	1021	MULTIPOLYGON (((-69.49973 -...	Peru

The previous example may seem redundant if the conflict data already contain the countries where conflicts have occurred, but, of course, it is also possible to obtain aggregates for arbitrary areas. To illustrate the use of arbitrary areas of aggregation, we create two areas within Colombia, a circular region with a radius of 200 kilometres around Bogotá and the rest of the country. To obtain the shape of the area of the rest of Colombia, we use the function st_difference():

```
Bogota.region <- st_circ(Bogota,dist.km=200)
Columbia.rest <- st_difference(st_geometry(Colombia),Bogota.region)
```

The objects Bogota.region and Colombia.outer contain the shapes of the circular Bogotá region and of the rest of the country, respectively. We combine them into an "sfc_GEOMETRY" object:

```
c(Bogota.region,Colombia.rest)
```

```
Geometry set for 2 features
geometry type:    GEOMETRY
dimension:        XY
bbox:             xmin: -81.72015 ymin: -4.236873 xmax: -66.87045
    ymax: 12.59027
epsg (SRID):      4326
proj4string:      +proj=longlat +ellps=WGS84 +no_defs
```

Obviously, it is possible to create heterogeneous geometry objects from geometry objects of different classes. We use such geometry objects to compute the total number of civilian deaths in the circular Bogotá region and in the rest of the country:

```
aggregate(ged191_ellips["deaths_civilians"],
          by=c(Bogota.region,Colombia.rest),
          sum)
```

```
Simple feature collection with 2 features and 1 field
geometry type:    GEOMETRY
dimension:        XY
bbox:             xmin: -81.72015 ymin: -4.236873 xmax: -66.87045
    ymax: 12.59027
epsg (SRID):      4326
```

```
proj4string:    +proj=longlat +ellps=WGS84 +no_defs
   deaths_civilians                        geometry
1             1021 POLYGON ((-72.30035 4.6, -7...
2             4994 MULTIPOLYGON (((-74.86081 1...
```

The result of **aggregate()** shows that a total of 1021 civilian deaths occurred from conflicts in the circular region around Bogotá while 4994 civilian deaths occurred from conflicts in the rest of the country.

▬▬▬ Overview Box 8.4 ▬▬▬

Some spatial relations supported by the *sf* package

st_touches() checks whether each pair of shapes (usually polygons or line strings) have at least a point in common.

st_contains() checks whether a point, line string, polygon, or multipoint lies within the area enclosed by a polygon.

st_crosses() checks whether a line string crosses another one.

st_overlaps() checks whether two polygons cover a common area.

▬▬▬ Overview Box 8.5 ▬▬▬

Some spatial operations supported by the *sf* package

st_distance() returns the distance between two points or, more generally, between two geometrical shapes. The distance is usually measured in metres if the shapes have geographical coordinates. The unit of measurement of the distance can be changed with **set_units()** from the *units* package.

st_area() returns the area enclosed by a polygon. It is usually measured in square metres if the polygon has geographical coordinates. The unit of measurement of the area can be changed with **set_units()** from the *units* package.

st_union() returns a polygon that covers all the area that is covered by two polygons given as arguments.

st_intersection() returns a polygon that covers the area that is covered by *both* of two polygons given as arguments.

st_difference() returns a polygon that covers the area covered by the polygon given as first argument but not by the polygon given as second argument.

st_sym_difference() returns a polygon that covers the area that is covered by at most one of two polygons given as arguments.

Cartographic projections

The coordinates of points, polygons, and other geographical shapes are associated with certain coordinate reference systems. In the previous examples, we encountered two different yet closely related coordinate reference systems, identified with the strings "+proj=longlat +datum = WGS84 +no_defs" and "+proj=longlat +ellps=WGS84 +no_defs", which indicate that latitudes and longitudes are used as coordinates. While latitudes and longitudes are the appropriate type of coordinates for locations on a sphere, they are not well suited for representing geographical shapes on a map, which usually is a flat surface (e.g. the page of a book or a computer screen). The rules according to which latitudes and longitudes are translated into coordinates on a flat surface are called *projections*. There are numerous projections that could be used, ones that keep the angles between lines, ones that keep the ratios between distances of locations, or ones that keep the ratios between areas of polygons. None of these projections is equally useful for all applications, and it is impossible to discuss them exhaustively in the present context. Therefore, yet another illustrative example has to suffice here.

We start the example with the object US_flat in the file "US_flat.RData". It is an "sf" object with data about the mainland US states (i.e. excluding Alaska and Hawaii) and multipolygons that represent the borders of the states:

```
load("US_flat.RData")
US_flat
```

```
Simple feature collection with 49 features and 1 field
geometry type:   MULTIPOLYGON
dimension:       XY
bbox:            xmin: -124.6813 ymin: 25.12993 xmax: -67.00742 ymax: 49.38323
epsg (SRID):     4326
proj4string:     +proj=longlat +datum=WGS84 +no_defs
First 10 features:
                        geometry                    State
1   MULTIPOLYGON (((-87.46201 3...             Alabama
2   MULTIPOLYGON (((-114.6374 3...             Arizona
3   MULTIPOLYGON (((-94.05103 3...             Arkansas
4   MULTIPOLYGON (((-120.006 42...           California
5   MULTIPOLYGON (((-102.0552 4...             Colorado
6   MULTIPOLYGON (((-73.49902 4...          Connecticut
7   MULTIPOLYGON (((-75.80231 3...             Delaware
8   MULTIPOLYGON (((-77.13731 3... District of Columbia
9   MULTIPOLYGON (((-85.01548 3...              Florida
10  MULTIPOLYGON (((-80.89018 3...              Georgia
```

As we can see from the output, the projection string (i.e. the "proj4string" attribute) indicates that the coordinate values of the state borders (the multipolygons') are recorded as latitudes and longitudes, where the zero latitude is defined by the Earth's equator and the zero longitude is the International Reference Median, which runs through Greenwich, London, UK (EPSG, 1993).

When we plot **US_flat**, we notice something is wrong:

```
plot(st_geometry(US_flat),
     graticule=TRUE,axes=TRUE)
```

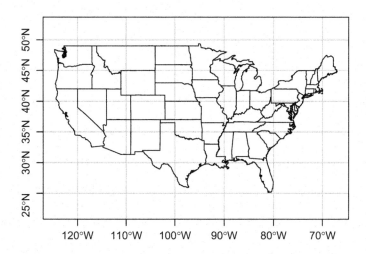

The northern states appear too large and the southern states too small. This is so because in the plot latitudes and longitudes are treated as coordinates in a rectangular coordinate system, as the gridlines (requested by **graticule=TRUE**) indicate. In fact, they are spherical coordinates, so that the relation between the lengths and units of the coordinate system is not constant.

If we want to create a map of the USA in which the apparent sizes of the states are (at least approximately) proportional to their physical area, one option is to apply the 'Lambert azimuthal equal area' projection. For a satisfactory result, we have to centre the projection on the US mainland. For this purpose, we consider the *bounding box* of the geometry of **US_flat**, which contains the minimum and maximum coordinates in latitude and longitude direction:

```
bbox_US <- st_bbox(US_flat)
```

From this, we can compute the midpoint

```
c(xcenter = mean(bbox_US[c("xmin","xmax")]),
  ycenter = mean(bbox_US[c("ymin","ymax")]))
```

```
  xcenter    ycenter
-95.84438   37.25658
```

and use its coordinates to centre the projection:

```
laea <- st_crs("+proj=laea +lon_0=-95.8 +lat_0=37.3")
US_proj <- st_transform(US_flat,laea)
plot(st_geometry(US_proj),
     graticule=TRUE,axes=TRUE)
```

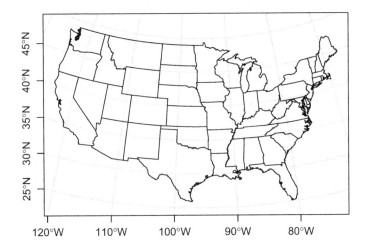

The map now looks better in so far as the relative areas of the US states are correctly rendered. However, this comes at the cost of certain lines not appearing straight on the map, although they are so on the globe (e.g. a major segment of the border between Canada and the USA does not appear straight on the map). Further, the projected coordinates now vastly differ from the original latitudes and longitudes:

```
US_proj
```

```
Simple feature collection with 49 features and 1 field
geometry type:  MULTIPOLYGON
dimension:      XY
bbox:           xmin: -2373444 ymin: -1256820 xmax: 2227765 ymax: 1594607
epsg (SRID):    NA
proj4string:    +proj=laea +lat_0=37.3 +lon_0=-95.8 +x_0=0 +y_0=0 +
    ellps=WGS84 +units=m +no_defs
First 10 features:
                         geometry                 State
1   MULTIPOLYGON (((801328.4 -7...          Alabama
2   MULTIPOLYGON (((-1703665 -8...          Arizona
3   MULTIPOLYGON (((163466.9 -4...          Arkansas
4   MULTIPOLYGON (((-1973845 78...         California
5   MULTIPOLYGON (((-533686.4 3...          Colorado
6   MULTIPOLYGON (((1822015 749...        Connecticut
7   MULTIPOLYGON (((1696046 452...          Delaware
8   MULTIPOLYGON (((1602848 342... District of Columbia
9   MULTIPOLYGON (((1028477 -64...           Florida
10  MULTIPOLYGON (((1401775 -47...           Georgia
```

8●4 Geographical data files

With the variety of geometrical objects on which geographical data can be built, the variety of coordinate systems and cartographic projections, and the diversity of spatial relations and operations possible, the handling of such data is already quite challenging. This is acerbated by the fact that geographical data are recorded in a wide variety of file formats or database systems. Fortunately, many of these formats are already supported by the *sf* package. As part of a fairly complete installation where the system libraries GEOS 3.7.1, GDAL 2.4.0, and PROJ4 5.2.0 are available (the Debian 10 system, on which this volume is being written), *sf* supports about 88 different file formats and types of relational databases. Of course, all these different file formats cannot be discussed here. Therefore, we will look at only two, especially notable file formats.

The first of these two file formats is the ESRI Shapefile format (Environmental Systems Research Institute, 1997). The name of this format is a bit of a misnomer because in this format the data do not come in a single file but as a pair of files, with filename endings '.shx' and '.shp', or as a triplet of files, with an additional file with filename ending '.dbf'. The '.shx' and '.shp' files contain geographical features, while the '.dbf' contains, if present, additional information about each of the geographical features.

As an example, we look at how the UCDP GED Polygons 1.1 data can be imported using st_read(). The data are available for download from http://ucdp.uu.se/downloads/ as part of a ZIP archive file "ucdp-ged-poly-v-1-1-shape.zip".

The contents of the archive file can be viewed and extracted using the function unzip():

```
unzip("ucdp-ged-poly-v-1-1-shape.zip",list=TRUE)
```

```
                                                        Name
1                                          ARCGIS Readme.txt
2    UCDP GED Conflict Polygons Codebook version 1.1-2011.pdf
3                                            UCDPGEDpoly.dbf
4                                            UCDPGEDpoly.prj
5                                            UCDPGEDpoly.sbn
6                                            UCDPGEDpoly.sbx
7                                            UCDPGEDpoly.shp
8                                            UCDPGEDpoly.shx
9                                        UCDPGEDpolyyear.dbf
10                                       UCDPGEDpolyyear.prj
11                                       UCDPGEDpolyyear.sbn
12                                       UCDPGEDpolyyear.sbx
13                                       UCDPGEDpolyyear.shp
[...]
```

We then extract the relevant files with names that start with "UCDPGEDpoly.":

```
unzip("ucdp-ged-poly-v-1-1-shape.zip",
      files=c(
            "UCDPGEDpoly.shx",
            "UCDPGEDpoly.shp",
            "UCDPGEDpoly.dbf"
            ))
```

We can now simply use st_read() to import the shapefile triplet, whereby it does not matter which of the three files is named as an argument to the function:

```
UCDPGEDpoly <- st_read("UCDPGEDpoly.shx")
UCDPGEDpoly <- st_read("UCDPGEDpoly.shp")
UCDPGEDpoly <- st_read("UCDPGEDpoly.dbf")
```

The result is an **"sf"** object:

```
UCDPGEDpoly
```

```
Simple feature collection with 500 features and 20 fields
geometry type:   POLYGON
dimension:       XY
bbox:            xmin: -17.3381 ymin: -34.1831 xmax: 50.8833 ymax: 37.0542
epsg (SRID):     NA
proj4string:     NA
First 10 features:
             pName      lat      lon type_of_vi dyadID_1
1        LNE-1-17-A   4.31667 18.58330          1       17
2      LNE-1-189A-A  -4.30917 15.28470          1        0
3        LNE-1-19-A  12.71670 20.48330          1       19
4       LNE-1-191-A  -5.63333 12.51670          1      191
5        LNE-1-20-A  15.50000 22.91000          1       20
6       LNE-1-210-A   3.80000 45.56670          1      210
7        LNE-1-23-A  14.96670 22.78330          1       23
8        LNE-1-2B-A  33.28330  6.88333          1        0
9      LNE-1-650B-A  14.64370 -6.01970          1        0
10      LNE-1-811-A   9.25944 42.12580          1      811
[...]
    date_last                        geometry
1   2001-12-01 POLYGON ((18.5833 4.31667, ...
2   1997-10-16 POLYGON ((15.315 -4.37972, ...
3   1989-03-03 POLYGON ((20.9052 9.88969, ...
4   1994-11-15 POLYGON ((12.5167 -5.63333,...
5   1990-11-16 POLYGON ((22.7833 14.9667, ...
6   1991-01-28 POLYGON ((45.3667 2.01667, ...
7   1990-11-25 POLYGON ((22.7833 14.9667, ...
8   1991-12-09 POLYGON ((6.88333 33.2833, ...
9   2008-12-20 POLYGON ((-6.0197 14.6437, ...
10  1991-10-10 POLYGON ((42.1258 9.25944, ...
```

We see that the geometrical shapes included in the **"sf"** objects are polygons and not multipolygons as in the case of the *cshapes* data we discussed earlier.

The second of the two file formats we take a closer look at is the format in which data can be obtained from OpenStreetMap (Coast and OpenStreetMap Community, 2004), the crowdsourced map of the world that is freely available under the Open Database License. There are two variants of the OpenStreetMap format: compressed and uncompressed XML. Uncompressed XML files (with filename suffix '.osm') can be obtained by selecting by hand a rectangular area for export from the website www.openstreetmap.org. Alternatively, such data can be obtained programmatically from https://api.openstreetmap.org or from https:// overpass-api.de. Compressed XML files (with filename suffix '.osm.pbf') with geographical data on entire continents can be downloaded, for example, from https://download.geofabrik. de. While data in shapefile format generally contain only one type of geographical features, OpenStreetMap data are organized in layers with different geometries. This is illustrated in the following example.

In the following, we import OpenStreetMap data on a rectangular area around St Paul's Cathedral in the City of London. These data were exported by hand from www.openstreet map.org into a file named "stpauls.osm". To get an overview of the layers in the file, we use the function

```
st_layers("stpauls.osm")
```

```
Driver: OSM
Available layers:
          layer_name        geometry_type features fields
1              points                Point       NA     10
2               lines          Line String       NA      9
3 multilinestrings    Multi Line String       NA      4
4       multipolygons        Multi Polygon       NA     25
5   other_relations Geometry Collection       NA      4
```

To get the 'lines' and 'multipolygons' layers, we have to call **st_read()** with the appropriate **layer=** arguments:

```
stpauls_lines <- st_read("stpauls.osm",layer="lines")
stpauls_polygons <- st_read("stpauls.osm",layer="multipolygons")
```

These layers can be nicely combined to create a map as follows:

```
plot(st_geometry(stpauls_polygons),
     col="gray80",
     xlim=c(-0.1,-0.097),
     ylim=c(51.5135,51.514)
     )
plot(st_geometry(stpauls_lines),add=TRUE)
```

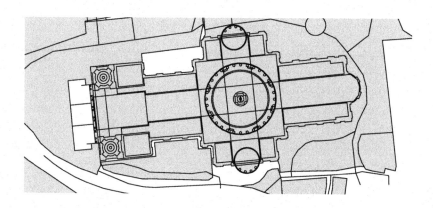

While it is possible to import OpenStreetMap data using the function **st_read()** from the *sf* package, the data thus imported are not easy to use without detailed knowledge about the structure and meaning of the data. A potentially more convenient way is provided by the *osmdata* package, which allows one, for example, to query OpenStreetMap servers for named features within given bounding boxes.

9

Text as Data

1   Manipulation of character strings

The fundamental data type on which most, if not all, facilities for managing and analysing textual data in R are based is the character vector. The name of this data type may be a bit misleading as character vectors are not sequences of single characters (as is the case in the Python programming language, for instance). Instead, character vectors are *character strings*. These character strings are sequences of individual characters, which may vary in length even if they belong to the same character vector.

Basic R already provides quite a few functions that allow one to work with the strings that are the elements of character vectors. First, it is possible to obtain the lengths of these character strings. The function that can be used for this is named `nchar()` and not `length()` because the latter name is already used for the function that returns the number of strings that are the elements of a character vector. For example, given the character vector

```
some_great_rock_bands <- c("Led Zeppelin","Pink Floyd","Queen")
```

the call to the function `length()`

```
length(some_great_rock_bands)
```

gives

```
[1] 3
```

while in order to get the lengths of the character strings, we use `nchar()`, with the result

```
nchar(some_great_rock_bands)
```

```
[1] 12 10   5
```

Second, while the bracket operator, `[]`, when applied to a character vector returns a (sub-)vector with character strings, parts of the character strings can be extracted from a character vector by using the function `substr()`. Thus, to obtain the first two elements of the character vector `some_great_rock_bands`, we can use the code

```
some_great_rock_bands[1:2]
```

```
[1] "Led Zeppelin" "Pink Floyd"
```

while in order to get the first two characters of each string in the character vector, we use

```
substr(some_great_rock_bands,start=1,stop=2)
```

```
[1] "Le" "Pi" "Qu"
```

To see what happens if the position of the required substring extends beyond the end of a character string, we try

```
substr(some_great_rock_bands,start=6,stop=15)
```

```
[1] "eppelin" "Floyd"    ""
```

and see that this does not lead to missing values but to shorter strings or empty strings.

Further, it is possible to check whether certain character sequences or patterns are present in a character vector and substitute such sequences or patterns with other sequences or patterns. Thus, **grep()** returns a numeric index vector that tells which elements in a character string match a certain pattern, whereas **grepl()** returns the corresponding logical index vector. The function **regexpr()** returns a numeric vector that indicates the *first* position of a fixed character sequence or string pattern *in each element* of the character vector (or -1 for the non-matching elements), while **gregexpr()** returns a list of vectors that correspond to *all* positions in each character vector element. It should be noted that these functions take the pattern for which a character string is to be searched as the *first* positional argument. As an illustration of the differences between these functions, we consider again the character vector **some_great_rock_bands**. To obtain the elements of **some_great_rock_bands** that contain **"Zeppelin"**, we use **grep()**:

```
grep("Zeppelin",some_great_rock_bands) # Just the indices
```

```
[1] 1
```

```
grep("Zeppelin",some_great_rock_bands, value=TRUE) # the elements
```

```
[1] "Led Zeppelin"
```

To check whether the substring is present, we use **grepl()**:

```
grepl("Zeppelin",some_great_rock_bands)
```

```
[1]    TRUE FALSE FALSE
```

To demonstrate searching for string *patterns*, we use **grep()** with a *regular expression* as **pattern=** argument. Here, we obtain those band names that end with 'en' or 'in':

```
grep("[ei]n$",some_great_rock_bands,value=TRUE)
```

```
[1] "Led Zeppelin" "Queen"
```

The dollar sign (**$**) represents the end of a character string in regular expressions. The beginning of a character string is represented by a caret symbol (**^**).

In this example, the part **"[ei]"** of the regular expression means that the letters *e* and *i* may be the first characters of the pattern, while the part **"n$"** of the pattern indicates that the pattern matches only strings that end with the letter *n*.

It is not only possible to locate substrings or patterns in character vectors but also possible to replace them with other strings or patterns. Thus, the function `sub()` can be used to replace (or 'substitute') the first occurrence of a string or pattern within each element of a character vector by a given string or pattern, while `gsub()` can be used to replace all occurrences. Again, we look at the vector `some_great_rock_bands` to see the difference between `sub()` and `gsub()`. We first use `sub()` to substitute the first instances of the letter *e* by the letter *i* (not that this makes sense, but we do it anyway)

```
sub("e","i",some_great_rock_bands)
```

```
[1] "Lid Zeppelin" "Pink Floyd"   "Quien"
```

then we use `gsub()` to substitute all instances of the letter *e*

```
gsub("e","i",some_great_rock_bands)
```

```
[1] "Lid Zippilin" "Pink Floyd"   "Quiin"
```

To look at how patterns can be replaced by other patterns, we enclose all single vowels or sequences of vowels in brackets. For this purpose, we make use of the special meaning of parentheses and backslashes in regular expressions and replacement patterns:

```
gsub("([aeiouy]+)","[\\1]",some_great_rock_bands)
```

```
[1] "L[e]d Z[e]pp[e]l[i]n" "P[i]nk Fl[oy]d"
[3] "Q[uee]n"
```

In this example, the parentheses create a pattern group, to which we refer in the replacement by `"\1"`. It is of course possible to have multiple pattern groups, to which one can refer as `"\1"`, `"\2"`, and so on.

Regular expressions are a potentially flexible and powerful tool to manipulate character data. The many possibilities opened up by them cannot be discussed in full detail here. They may be perhaps of more interest to those who want to program packages for the management and analysis of textual data than to the users of such packages. In fact, the construction and usage of regular expressions are topics for entire textbooks (e.g. Friedl, 2006; Goyvaerts and Levithan, 2012). Fortunately, the R help page for the keyword gives an overview of the way regular expressions can be composed. Instead of giving a detailed account of all the possibilities of string manipulation provided by R, an example with actual textual data is discussed in the following in order to give the reader an idea of what the practical management of textual data may look like if the basic facilities of R are used.

In the following, we look at the application of the character string manipulations provided by R for the text of the manifesto of the UK Labour Party on the occasion of the 2017 general election to the House of Commons. The data come from the Manifesto Project (WZB Social Science Research Center Berlin 2009) in the form of a file in CSV format with three columns of data: a column with a character vector containing 'quasi-sentences' – that is, the coding units into which the manifesto text was segmented – and two columns that indicate into which categories the quasi-sentences were categorized.

If the function `read.csv()` encounters columns with character data, usually these data are translated into factors, based on the assumption that the character columns contain categorical data. Since this assumption does not apply in the present case, and we rather want to work with the character data in the file as is, we advise the function not to convert a character string column into factors, by calling it with the optional argument `stringsAsFactors=` `FALSE`. Since the text contains apostrophes in extended UTF-8 (8-bit Unicode Transformation Format) coding, we recode them into their standard 8-bit equivalents.

```
Labour.2017 <- read.csv("UKLabourParty_201706.csv",
                          stringsAsFactors=FALSE)
Labour.2017$content <- gsub("\xE2\x80\x99","'",Labour.2017$content)
str(Labour.2017)
```

```
'data.frame':    1396 obs. of   3 variables:
 $ content : chr  "CREATING AN ECONOMY THAT WORKS FOR ALL" "Labour'
 $ cmp_code: chr  "H" "503" "503" "405" ...
 $ eu_code : logi  NA NA NA NA NA NA ...
```

Since we are only interested in the character data in the resulting data frame, we extract the corresponding column and disregard the other two columns. The results end up in a character vector named `Labour.2017`:

```
Labour.2017 <- Labour.2017$content
```

We take a look at the first five elements of the character vector we thus extracted:

```
Labour.2017[1:5]
```

```
[1] "CREATING AN ECONOMY THAT WORKS FOR ALL"
[2] "Labour's economic strategy is about delivering a fairer, more
[3] "We will measure our economic success not by the number of bill
[4] "Labour understands that the creation of wealth is a collective
[5] "Each contributes and each must share fairly in the rewards."
```

The inspection of the first five elements suggests that the first element is a section headline of the manifesto, because it contains only upper-case letters. Since headlines are apparently indicated by their being all in upper case, we identify them by checking which elements equal their upper-case version. For this, we use the function `toupper()`, which turns all characters in a character vector into their upper-case equivalents if they are not already upper-case letters:

```
Labour.2017.hlno <- which(Labour.2017==toupper(Labour.2017))
```

With the corresponding index numbers, we can select all elements of `Labour.2017` that are headlines

```
Labour.2017.headings <- Labour.2017[Labour.2017.hlno]
Labour.2017.headings[1:4]
```

```
[1] "CREATING AN ECONOMY THAT WORKS FOR ALL"
[2] "A FAIR TAXATION SYSTEM"
[3] "BALANCING THE BOOKS"
[4] "INFRASTRUCTURE INVESTMENT"
```

and, conversely, we can use a negative index to select all elements that are *not* headlines. We turn these elements into lower case:

```
labour.2017 <- tolower(Labour.2017[-Labour.2017.hlno])
labour.2017[1:5]
```

```
[1] "labour's economic strategy is about delivering a fairer, more
[2] "we will measure our economic success not by the number of bill
[3] "labour understands that the creation of wealth is a collective
[4] "each contributes and each must share fairly in the rewards."
[5] "this manifesto sets out labour's plan to upgrade our economy a
```

Next, we select all the quasi-sentences with economic content based on whether they contain the character sequence **"econom"**:

```
ecny.labour.2017 <- grep("econom",labour.2017,value=TRUE)
ecny.labour.2017[1:5]
```

```
[1] "labour's economic strategy is about delivering a fairer, more
[2] "we will measure our economic success not by the number of bill
[3] "this manifesto sets out labour's plan to upgrade our economy a
[4] "britain is the only major developed economy where earnings hav
[5] "we will upgrade our economy, breaking down the barriers that h
```

We find that 68 of the 1335 quasi-sentences distinguished by the manifesto project explicitly deal with the economy or the economic situation.

Many ways to analyse textual data are based on the presence and frequency of various words. Therefore, we split the quasi-sentences into words, relying on the assumption that words are separated from one another by at least one space, comma, period, semicolon, or colon. For this purpose, we make use of the function `strsplit()`:

```
labour.2017.words <- strsplit(labour.2017,"[ ,.;:]+")
str(labour.2017.words[1:5])
```

```
List of 5
 $ : chr [1:18] "labour's" "economic" "strategy" "is" ...
 $ : chr [1:23] "we" "will" "measure" "our" ...
 $ : chr [1:17] "labour" "understands" "that" "the" ...
```

```
$ : chr [1:10] "each" "contributes" "and" "each" ...
$ : chr [1:32] "this" "manifesto" "sets" "out" ...
```

Since we are splitting each of the character strings in the character vector into a character vector with one or more elements, the result of the function `strsplit()` is a *list* of the same length as the character vector. Each element of the list corresponds to one of the character strings that are elements of the character vector.

If we take a 'bag of words' approach – that is, use analytical tools that take into account the frequency with which words occur, without regard of their order or composition – we fuse the elements of the list of character vectors into a single character vector:

```
labour.2017.words <- unlist(labour.2017.words)
labour.2017.words[1:20]
```

```
 [1] "labour's"    "economic"    "strategy"   "is"
 [5] "about"       "delivering"  "a"          "fairer"
 [9] "more"        "prosperous"  "society"    "for"
[13] "the"         "many"        "not"        "just"
[17] "the"         "few"         "we"         "will"
```

By applying the function `table()`, we obtain a simple table of frequencies of the words. We sort this table by the frequency counts, so that the most frequent words come first:

```
labour.2017.nwords <- table(labour.2017.words)
labour.2017.nwords <- sort(labour.2017.nwords,decreasing=TRUE)
labour.2017.nwords[1:20]
```

```
labour.2017.words
  the   and    to  will    of     a    we    in labour
 1202   947   832   664   625   438   418   369   313
  for   our  that    on  with    by    is   are    as
  312   244   232   212   185   161   161   134   112
 have ensure
  108   104
```

We see that the most frequent words do not have very specific meanings; they are 'stop-words', such as *the, and, to, a,* and so on.

━━━━━━━━━━ **Overview Box 9.1** ━━━━━━━━━━

Some important functions specific to character vectors

`nchar()` reports the number of characters in each character string in a character vector.

`substr()` returns a character vector the elements of which are substrings of the element of the character vector given as first argument of the function.

(Continued)

`grep()` returns a numeric vector with the numbers of the elements of a character vector that match a given pattern.

`grepl()` returns a logical vector the elements of which are **TRUE** for each element of a character vector that matches a pattern and **FALSE** for the non-matching elements.

`sub()` returns a character vector in which the first occurrence of a character string pattern in each element is substituted by another pattern.

`gsub()` returns a character vector in which all occurrences of a character string pattern in all elements are substituted by another pattern.

`toupper()` returns a character vector in which all lower-case letters are substituted with upper-case letters.

`towower()` returns a character vector in which all upper-case letters are substituted with lower-case letters.

`trimws()` returns a character vector in which all whitespace characters at the beginning and end (or, depending on the `which` argument, only at the beginning or only at the end) of each character string element are removed.

━━━━━━━━━ Overview Box 9.2 ━━━━━━━━━

Some example patterns in regular expressions

`"[b-e]"` matches any character string that contains the letters `"b"`, `"c"`, `"d"`, `"e"`.

`"^foo"` matches any character string that starts with `"foo"`.

`"bar$"` matches any character string that ends with `"bar"`.

`"<.*>"` matches any character string that contains the character sequence `"<>"` or any sequence with one or more characters between `"<"` and `">"`.

`"[(]\w+[)]"` matches any character string that has at least a single 'word character' between an opening and a closing parenthesis, where a 'word character' may be any letter, any digit, or an underscore. Note that the parentheses need to be put between brackets because of the special meaning that parentheses otherwise have in regular expressions.

The previous example demonstrates that one can get pretty far by using only the standard string manipulation facilities of R. Yet these facilities have the limitation that they treat character strings (and thus texts) as mere sequences of characters. In so far as these character strings are composed of words and sentences of a language, they are more than just character sequences. Also, the way in which written words and sentences are composed of characters varies among languages or language varieties – that is, among what is called 'locales' in the terminology of R and of computing more generally. An extension package that provides for the creation of substrings, for searching and replacing within character strings and character vectors, for splitting up character strings into words and sentences, and for comparing and ordering strings according to country- and application-specific conventions is the *stringi* package. It is possible to replicate the above example using the functions from this package, but this would be repetitive. Also, to deal with larger text corpora, it is better to use functions that are specifically designed for that purpose.

9.2 Working with text corpora with the *tm* package

Doing more serious quantitative text analysis requires more than working just with character strings or character vectors. Instead, one needs to work with potentially very large collections of documents that not only have textual content but also contain additional information about these documents, such as authorship, date of publication, the document headline, the language of the document, and so on. This additional information is usually referred to as *metadata* to distinguish it from the textual data in a document corpus.

One of the first publicly available R packages to support text corpora as a data type is *tm* (Feinerer et al., 2008), where the name of the package stands for 'text mining'. It implements a `"Corpus"` class, where objects in this class are essentially collections of text documents with associated metadata. The `"Corpus"` class has the subclasses `"VCorpus"`, for corpora that reside in the main memory of a computer; `"PCorpus"`, for corpora with text and metadata stored in an external file; and `"SimpleCorpus"`, a simplification of `"VCorpus"` that implements a variety of speed optimizations for the cost of some rigidity in terms of the structure of the data and metadata.

For the sake of flexibility, `"Corpus"` objects are not composed simply of character vectors but of objects that are members of the abstract base class `"TextDocument"`. These objects then can be composed of simple character vectors, in which case they belong to the class `"PlainTextDocument"`, or of parsed XML code, in which case they belong to the class `"XMLTextDocument"`; or they may belong to some other subclass implemented by another R package.

One of the example corpora included in the *tm* package is `acq`, a collection of 50 example news articles from the *Reuters-21578* collection (Lewis, 1997; Luz, 2003). The topic of these articles is acquisitions of companies. In order to access this example corpus, we have to activate it using the `data()` function:

```
data(acq)
```

After activation, we can inspect it. Printing the example corpus to the R console provides us with a summary of its contents:

```
acq
```

```
<<VCorpus>>
Metadata:   corpus specific: 0, document level (indexed): 0
Content:   documents: 50
```

The output tells us that the corpus contains 50 documents but that there are no metadata attached to the corpus itself, neither corpus-specific metadata nor document-specific metadata. As we shall see, this does not mean that there are no metadata available about the individual documents in the corpus.

A simple way of accessing the documents in the corpus is by using the double-bracket opera-tor (`[[]]`), because the corpus `acq` is in fact a list of `"TextDocument"` objects:

```
class(acq[[1]])
```

```
[1] "PlainTextDocument"  "TextDocument"
```

```
acq[[1]]
```

```
<<PlainTextDocument>>
Metadata:   15
Content:    chars: 1287
```

Printing the first document in the corpus shows us that it contains 15 items of metadata and a character vector with 1287 characters in total. If we want to see the text of the document, we need to use the function `inspect()`:

```
inspect(acq[[1]])
```

```
<<PlainTextDocument>>
Metadata:   15
Content:    chars: 1287


Computer Terminal Systems Inc said
it has completed the sale of 200,000 shares of its common
stock, and warrants to acquire an additional one mln shares, to
<Sedio N.V.> of Lugano, Switzerland for 50,000 dlrs.
    The company said the warrants are exercisable for five
years at a purchase price of .125 dlrs per share.
    Computer Terminal said Sedio also has the right to buy
additional shares and increase its total holdings up to 40 pct
of the Computer Terminal's outstanding common stock under
certain circumstances involving change of control at the
company.
    The company said if the conditions occur the warrants would
be exercisable at a price equal to 75 pct of its common stock's
market price at the time, not to exceed 1.50 dlrs per share.
    Computer Terminal also said it sold the technology rights to
[...]
```

Using the function `meta()`, we can obtain the metadata associated with this text document:

```
meta(acq[[1]])
```

```
  author        : character(0)
  datetimestamp: 1987-02-26 15:18:06
  description  :
```

```
heading          : COMPUTER TERMINAL SYSTEMS <CPML> COMPLETES SALE
id               : 10
language         : en
origin           : Reuters-21578 XML
topics           : YES
lewissplit       : TRAIN
cgisplit         : TRAINING-SET
oldid            : 5553
places           : usa
people           : character(0)
orgs             : character(0)
exchanges        : character(0)
```

We see that the document was created in 1987, refers to a place in the USA, is in English, and is headed by the character string "COMPUTER TERMINAL SYSTEMS <CPML> COMPLETES SALE". Using the function DublinCore(), the metadata can be converted into the Dublin Core standard of metadata (Dublin Core Metadata Initiative, 1995):

```
DublinCore(acq[[1]])
```

```
contributor: character(0)
coverage   : character(0)
creator    : character(0)
date       : 1987-02-26 15:18:06
description:
format     : character(0)
identifier : 10
language   : en
publisher  : character(0)
relation   : character(0)
rights     : character(0)
source     : character(0)
subject    : character(0)
title      : COMPUTER TERMINAL SYSTEMS <CPML> COMPLETES SALE
type       : character(0)
```

As we can see, not all of the metadata items attached to the documents in acq can be translated into the Dublin Core standard and can be considered as peculiar to the corpus. On the other hand, all possible Dublin Core metadata items find their counterpart in the metadata of the documents in acq.

Based on the "Corpus" class, *tm* implements ways to access or modify metadata, to assign metadata to documents or to a corpus, to select subsets of documents from a corpus, and to import text documents from external files into a corpus. Beyond the management of documents as parts of a corpus, *tm* also provides ways to transform the document texts, such as dropping 'stopwords' from the documents or reducing words to their word stems. Finally, it allows the user to create term–document matrices, to which quantitative content analysis techniques can be applied that follow the 'bag of words' approach.

We now look at a quite complex example for the management of a text document corpus. The example concerns text documents collected by the Manifesto Project (WZB Social Science Research Center Berlin, 2009). These text documents are the manifestos that parties published on the occasion of elections in democracies after World War II (or in US terminology, their electoral platforms). The Manifesto Project is one of the major resources for the analysis of the ideological or programmatic development of parties in democracies after World War II. Files with text documents can be downloaded free of charge but only after registration at the Manifesto Project website. The text documents come in two variants of files in CSV format. One variant corresponds to manifestos annotated for coding, while the other variant corresponds to the raw manifestos before annotation. In the annotated variant, the CSV file consists of several lines (in addition to a header line with column names). Each line (excluding the header) corresponds to a quasi-sentence, a coding unit that is either a complete sentence or a semantically more or less independent part of one, and two codes are assigned to each quasi-sentence. In the non-annotated variant, the CSV file contains only a header line and a line with a character string and two empty coding fields.

We focus now on the subset of data files that correspond to the manifestos of the Liberal Party and the Liberal Democratic Party of the UK from 1964. Even though they pertain only to a subset, they are located in the file directory `"ManifestoProject"`. We get the names of the files in this directory using the function `dir()`:

```
csv.files <- dir("ManifestoProject",full.names=TRUE,
                 pattern="*.csv")
csv.files
```

```
 [1]  "ManifestoProject/51420_196410.csv"
 [2]  "ManifestoProject/51420_196603.csv"
 [3]  "ManifestoProject/51420_197006.csv"
 [4]  "ManifestoProject/51420_197402.csv"
 [5]  "ManifestoProject/51420_197410.csv"
 [6]  "ManifestoProject/51420_197905.csv"
 [7]  "ManifestoProject/51420_198306.csv"
 [8]  "ManifestoProject/51420_198706.csv"
 [9]  "ManifestoProject/51421_199204.csv"
[10]  "ManifestoProject/51421_199705.csv"
[11]  "ManifestoProject/51421_200106.csv"
[12]  "ManifestoProject/51421_200505.csv"
[13]  "ManifestoProject/51421_201505.csv"
[14]  "ManifestoProject/51421_201706.csv"
```

The names of the CSV files follow a specific pattern: they consist of a code for each party and the publication date of each manifesto (e.g. the date of a manifesto published in October 1964 is represented by `"196410"` as part of the filename).

The CSV files with the text document data are accompanied by a file in XLSX format (which we converted into CSV format) that describes the manifestos collected by the Manifesto Project. This file has one row for each manifesto and six columns for the country code, the name of the country in which the manifesto is published, the party code, the name of the party that published the manifesto, a date shorthand, and the title of the manifesto. The date shorthand is constructed in the same way as in the filenames, so that, for example, October 1964 is represented by the number `196410`.

```
manifesto.metadata <- read.csv("documents_MPDataset_MPDS2019b.csv",
    stringsAsFactors=FALSE)
```

If the files that contain the text documents had been plain text files, the code to read the files into a `"Corpus"` object would have been as simple as

```
manifesto.corpus <- VCorpus(DirSource("ManifestoProject"))
```

but unfortunately the CSV format used by the Manifesto Project is not supported by the *tm* package (at least not 'out of the box'). For this reason, but also in order to make use of the descriptions of the manifestos, we define a function `getMDoc()`, which we use to read each of the downloaded CSV files into a `"TextDocument"` object:

```
getMDoc <- function(file,metadata.file){
    df <- read.csv(file,
                      stringsAsFactors=FALSE)
    content <- paste(df[,1],collapse="\n")

    fn <- basename(file)
    fn <- sub(".csv","",fn, fixed=TRUE)
    fn12 <- unlist(strsplit(fn,"_"))

    partycode <- as.numeric(fn12[1])
    datecode <- as.numeric(fn12[2])
    year <- datecode %/% 100
    month <- datecode %% 100
    datetime <- ISOdate(year=year,month=month,day=1)

    mf.meta <- subset(metadata.file,
                        party==partycode & date == datecode)
    if(!length(mf.meta$language))
        mf.meta$language <- "english"

    PlainTextDocument(
        content,
        id = fn,
        heading = mf.meta$title,
        datetimestamp = as.POSIXlt(datetime),
        language = mf.meta$language,
        partyname = mf.meta$partyname,
        partycode = partycode,
        datecode = datecode
    )
}
```

The first two lines in the function body define a data frame variable `df` that is created by reading the contents of the CSV file using the function `read.csv()`. To make sure that the character strings in the file end up in character vectors instead of being converted into the levels of a factor, the function `read.csv()` is called with the optional argument `stringAsFactors=FALSE`. The character vector in the first column of `df` is then collapsed into a single character string that is assigned to the variable `content`. The next couple of lines, in which the variables `fn`, `fn12`, `partycode`, `datecode`, `year`, `month`, and `datetime` are defined, are used to extract the identifier for the party that published the respective manifesto and the date on which it was published. Then, a list named `mf.meta` is created with metadata collected from the file with the descriptions of the party manifestos. The function then returns a `"PlainTextDocument"` object, constructed from the text string in the variable `content`, with the information about the manifesto title, date, party name, party code, and date code as metadata.

The following code creates a list of `"PlainTextDocument"` objects by applying the function `getMDoc()` to all the CSV files (or, more correctly, their filenames) with the manifesto data. This list then is combined into a `"VCorpus"` object using the function `as.VCorpus()`:

```
UKLib.docs <- lapply(csv.files,getMDoc,
                      metadata.file=manifesto.metadata)
UKLib.Corpus <- as.VCorpus(UKLib.docs)
UKLib.Corpus
```

```
<<VCorpus>>
Metadata:  corpus specific: 0, document level (indexed): 0
Content:   documents: 14
```

```
UKLib.Corpus[[14]]
```

```
<<PlainTextDocument>>
Metadata:  10
Content:   chars: 130585
```

As can be seen, the result of the application of the function `as.VCorpus()` appears to be a valid document corpus object, and its elements seem to be valid `"TextDocument"` objects with several metadata items.

A previous inspection of the documents in the corpus (not shown here) revealed that they contain some Unicode quotation marks that the functions in the *tm* package do not handle well. We therefore change them into ordinary ASCII (American Standard Code for Information Interchange) quotation marks using the function `gsub()`:

```
handleUTF8quotes <- function(x){
    cx <- content(x)
    cx <- gsub("\xe2\x80\x98","'",cx)
    cx <- gsub("\xe2\x80\x99","'",cx)
    cx <- gsub("\xe2\x80\x9a",",",cx)
    cx <- gsub("\xe2\x80\x9b","'",cx)
    cx <- gsub("\xe2\x80\x9c","\"",cx)
    cx <- gsub("\xe2\x80\x9d","\"",cx)
    cx <- gsub("\xe2\x80\x9e","\"",cx)
```

```
    cx <- gsub("\xe2\x80\x9f","\"",cx)
    content(x) <- cx
    x
}
```

We further create a function that changes the content of a text document into lower case:

```
toLower <- function(x) {
    content(x) <- tolower(content(x))
    x
}
```

Using the previously defined functions, we conduct the first step of document preparation. This is done with the help of the function `tm_map()`, which applies a function to each document in a corpus and returns a thus modified one:

```
UKLib.Corpus.processed <- tm_map(UKLib.Corpus,handleUTF8quotes)
UKLib.Corpus.processed <- tm_map(UKLib.Corpus.processed,toLower)
inspect(UKLib.Corpus.processed[[14]])
```

```
<<PlainTextDocument>>
Metadata:   10
Content:    chars: 130585

1 protect britain's place in europe
1.1 giving the people the final say
liberal democrats are open and outward-looking.
we passionately believe that britain's relationship with its neigh
whatever its imperfections, the eu remains the best framework for
it has led directly to greater prosperity,
increased trade,
investment and jobs,
better security
and a greener environment.
britain is better off in the eu.
liberal democrats campaigned for the uk to remain in the eu.
however, we acknowledge the result of the 2016 referendum, which g
the decision britain took, though, was simply whether to remain in
there was no option on the ballot paper to choose the shape of our
[...]
```

After cleaning the documents of Unicode quotation marks and changing them to lower case, we apply the functions `removeNumbers()` and `removePunctuation()`, which are provided by the *tm* package, to the documents in the corpus:

```
UKLib.Corpus.processed  <-  tm_map(UKLib.Corpus.processed, removeNumbers)
UKLib.Corpus.processed  <-  tm_map(UKLib.Corpus.processed, removePunctuation)
inspect(UKLib.Corpus.processed[[14]])
```

```
<<PlainTextDocument>>
Metadata:   10
Content:    chars: 127677

 protect britains place in europe
 giving the people the final say
liberal democrats are open and outwardlooking
we passionately believe that britains relationship with its neighb
whatever its imperfections the eu remains the best framework for w
it has led directly to greater prosperity
increased trade
investment and jobs
better security
and a greener environment
britain is better off in the eu
liberal democrats campaigned for the uk to remain in the eu
however we acknowledge the result of the  referendum which gave th
the decision britain took though was simply whether to remain in o
there was no option on the ballot paper to choose the shape of our
[...]
```

The next step of document preparation is the removal of the so-called stopwords, which are words that are so common in a language that they should be dropped from a quantitative content analysis. After removing the stopwords, excess whitespace is also removed:

```
UKLib.Corpus.processed  <-  tm_map(UKLib.Corpus.processed,removeWords,
                                               stopwords("english"))
UKLib.Corpus.processed  <-  tm_map(UKLib.Corpus.processed,
                                               stripWhitespace)
inspect(UKLib.Corpus.processed[[14]])
```

```
UKLib.Corpus.processed  <-  tm_map(UKLib.Corpus.processed,removeWords,
                                               stopwords("english"))
UKLib.Corpus.processed  <-  tm_map(UKLib.Corpus.processed,
                                               stripWhitespace)
partial_out(inspect(UKLib.Corpus.processed[[14]]),.trim=TRUE,
                                               .width=66)
```

```
<<PlainTextDocument>>
Metadata:   10
Content:    chars: 98034

 protect britains place europe giving people final say liberal dem
```

The last step of text preparation is *stemming*; that is, inflected words are reduced to their word stems – for example, 'giving' is reduced to 'give':

```
UKLib.Corpus.processed <- tm_map(UKLib.Corpus.processed, stemDocument)
inspect(UKLib.Corpus.processed[[14]])
```

```
UKLib.Corpus.processed <- tm_map(UKLib.Corpus.processed, stemDocument)
partial_out(inspect(UKLib.Corpus.processed[[14]]),.trim=TRUE, .width=66)
```

```
<<PlainTextDocument>>
Metadata:   10
Content:    chars: 82851

protect britain place europ give peopl final say liber democrat op
```

Finally, we create a term–document matrix for the corpus – that is, a matrix that has a column for each text document and a row for each term or word that occurs at least once in the corpus:

```
UKLib.dtm <- DocumentTermMatrix(UKLib.Corpus.processed)
UKLib.dtm
```

```
<<DocumentTermMatrix (documents: 14, terms: 5858)>>
Non-/sparse entries: 23507/58505
Sparsity          : 71%
Maximal term length: 27
Weighting         : term frequency (tf)
```

It should be noted that apart from the handling of UTF-8 quotes, all the transformations that we applied explicitly can be done as part of the creation of the document–term matrix:

```
UKLib.dtm <- DocumentTermMatrix(
    tm_map(UKLib.Corpus,handleUTF8quotes),
    control=list(
        tolower=TRUE,
        removePunctuation=TRUE,
        removeNumber=TRUE,
        stopwords=TRUE,
        language="en",
        stemming=TRUE
    ))
```

While this may seem more efficient, the stepwise approach followed in this example has the advantage of a finer control over the individual transformations applied to the corpus.

The *tm* package can be considered as the 'classical' approach to the management of corpora of text documents for the preparation of quantitative text analysis, since it supports a metadata standard such as Dublin Core and allows one to load documents in a considerably wide range of formats, such as plain text, XML, and JSON. It is also flexible and extensible in so far as it allows one to handle corpora that are too large to fit into the main memory of a computer and therefore have to be kept in files on the disks of the computer and in so far as it allows one to define new subclasses of the **"Corpus"** class and new document sources. Unfortunately, all this flexibility comes at the price of complexity, which does not make it easy to benefit from this flexibility. An alternative that is growing in popularity, in particular in political science, is the *quanteda* package, which simplifies some aspects of the user interface and provides some features that are not yet (at the time of writing) included in *tm*, such as the possibility to tokenize documents not only by words but also by *n*-grams (sequences of words of a given length) or whole sentences or even paragraphs.

=========== Overview Box 9.3 ===========

Some basic concepts of data management relevant for the preparation of quantitative text analysis

Corpus: a collection of text documents.

Document: part of a corpus, the unit of analysis in quantitative text analysis, represented in R by a character vector or a single character string.

Metadata: information about a text document, such as who is the author, when the document was created, and so on.

Token: an occurrence of a piece of language that can be subsumed under a type or a term - usually the occurrence of a word.

Dictionary: a set of terms that are indicative of an aspect of the meaning of a document.

Stopword: a word that is too frequent in a given language to be relevant for the information or content one wants to extract from a document.

Stemming: reducing the words in a document to their grammatical roots by removing prefixes and suffixes and other markers of inflection.

Document-term matrix: a matrix with one row for each document in a corpus and one column for each term, where each matrix contains the number of tokens in the document that can be subsumed under the relevant term or another statistic about the tokens.

Term-document matrix: a transposition of a document-term matrix; that is, rows correspond to terms, while columns correspond to documents.

***n*-gram:** a sequence of *n* (two or more) tokens viewed as a unit that carries meaning or information.

=========== Overview Box 9.4 ===========

Some data management functions in the *tm* package

`VCorpus()` creates a corpus from a document source, where the document source may be a character vector, a directory of text files, or some other storage of text documents.

`as.VCorpus()` creates a corpus from a character vector or some other appropriate object in the R workspace.

MetaData() returns a list with metadata associated with either a corpus or a text document.

inspect() shows the text of a document.

tm_map() applies a function to each document in a corpus.

removeWords() removes words from the text of a document.

stemDocument() stems the words in a document.

DocumentTermMatrix() creates a document-term matrix from a document corpus.

TermDocumentMatrix() creates a term-document matrix from a document corpus.

Improvements provided by the *quanteda* package

Like *tm*, the concept of the text corpus lies at the heart of the *quanteda* package (Benoit et al., 2018); however, its implementation is simpler. There is only a single class named **"corpus"**, which is designed to contain documents in the form of simple character strings. That is, it does not allow the documents of which a corpus is composed to reside outside the computer's main memory. Instead, it is based on the assumption that texts are imported from files in various formats using the accompanying *readtext* package. In fact, a **"corpus"** object as defined by the *quanteda* package is just a character vector with some additional information attached to it. Here, the character strings of which the character vector is composed represent the document, and additional information and metadata about the document are contained in a data frame attached to the character string as one of its attributes. This makes it possible to apply the character string manipulation functions discussed at the beginning of the chapter. Also, the bracket operator is adapted in such a way that if a subset of the corpus is created with it, then the appropriate information about the documents thus selected is retained. Further, the package provides a variant of **subset()** that allows one to create a subset of a corpus based on conditions satisfied by the values of document-level variables or 'docvars', which are discussed below. This variant is not yet (at the time of writing) a method of the generic function **subset()**, which we encountered in Chapter 5, but it is a function with a different name, **corpus_subset()**.[1] Another potentially very useful function for corpus manipulation is **corpus_reshape()**, which allows one to change a corpus of complete documents into a corpus of sentences or paragraphs. Finally, it is possible to convert **"VCorpus"** objects as defined by the *tm* class into *quanteda*'s **"corpus"** class. That way, one can further process with *quanteda* data that have been already prepared with *tm*.

These facilities for the manipulation of text corpora are demonstrated in the following example. In this example, we make use of the example data object **data_corpus_inaugural**, which is included in the *quanteda* package and contains the inaugural speeches of US presidents from George Washington to Donald Trump.

---

[1]This is the state of affairs at the time of writing. Given that *quanteda* is under continued development, it would be no surprise if a **subset()** method function is included in the package in the near future.

```
library(quanteda)
quanteda_options(print_corpus_max_ndoc=3)
```

We put a limit on the number of documents shown when the `print()` function is applied to a `"corpus"` object. The results can be seen here:

```
data_corpus_inaugural
```

```
Corpus consisting of 58 documents and 4 docvars.
1789-Washington :
"Fellow-Citizens of the Senate and of the House of Representa..."

1793-Washington :
"Fellow citizens, I am again called upon by the voice of my c..."

1797-Adams :
"When it was first perceived, in early times, that no middle ..."

[ reached max_ndoc ... 55 more documents ]
```

As can be seen, *quanteda* defines a `print()` method for `"corpus"` objects that allows one to display the beginning of a corpus without flooding the console output.

As can be easily verified, despite all the special functions defined for `"corpus"` objects, `data_corpus_inaugural` is a character vector

```
mode(data_corpus_inaugural)
```

```
[1] "character"
```

yet it has a `"class"` attribute named `"corpus"`:

```
class(data_corpus_inaugural)
```

```
[1] "corpus"     "character"
```

Using the bracket operator, we can get the first three documents in the corpus:

```
data_corpus_inaugural[1:3]
```

```
Corpus consisting of 3 documents and 4 docvars.
1789-Washington :
"Fellow-Citizens of the Senate and of the House of Representa..."

1793-Washington :
"Fellow citizens, I am again called upon by the voice of my c..."

1797-Adams :
"When it was first perceived, in early times, that no middle ..."
```

The output refers to 'docvars'. These are variables in a data frame that are an attribute named "docvars" of the corpus. This data frame can be obtained using the function docvars():

```
str(docvars(data_corpus_inaugural))
```

```
'data.frame':    58 obs. of  4 variables:
 $ Year      : int  1789 1793 1797 1801 1805 1809 1813 1817 1821 1825 ...
 $ President: chr  "Washington" "Washington" "Adams" "Jefferson" ...
 $ FirstName: chr  "George" "George" "John" "Thomas" ...
 $ Party     : Factor w/ 6 levels "Democratic", "Democratic-
     Republican",..: 4 4 3 2 2 2 2 2 2 2 ...
```

Individual document variables can be explicitly accessed using the function docvars() if it is called with the name of a document variable as an additional argument:

```
docvars(data_corpus_inaugural,"Year")
```

```
 [1] 1789 1793 1797 1801 1805 1809 1813 1817 1821 1825 1829 1833
[13] 1837 1841 1845 1849 1853 1857 1861 1865 1869 1873 1877 1881
[25] 1885 1889 1893 1897 1901 1905 1909 1913 1917 1921 1925 1929
[37] 1933 1937 1941 1945 1949 1953 1957 1961 1965 1969 1973 1977
[49] 1981 1985 1989 1993 1997 2001 2005 2009 2013 2017
```

For convenience, it is possible to use the dollar operator ($) to access these variables:

```
data_corpus_inaugural$Year
```

```
 [1] 1789 1793 1797 1801 1805 1809 1813 1817 1821 1825 1829 1833
[13] 1837 1841 1845 1849 1853 1857 1861 1865 1869 1873 1877 1881
[25] 1885 1889 1893 1897 1901 1905 1909 1913 1917 1921 1925 1929
[37] 1933 1937 1941 1945 1949 1953 1957 1961 1965 1969 1973 1977
[49] 1981 1985 1989 1993 1997 2001 2005 2009 2013 2017
```

Based on the conditions applied to the variables in the "docvars" attribute, it is possible to obtain a subset of the corpus with all inaugural speeches after the year 1945:

```
corpus_subset(data_corpus_inaugural, Year > 1945)
```

It is fairly easy to define an appropriate method of the subset() generic function

```
subset.corpus <- function(x,...) corpus_subset(x,...)
```

so that it is possible to use the function subset() with the intended result:

```
subset(data_corpus_inaugural, Year > 1945)
```

```
Corpus consisting of 18 documents and 4 docvars.
1949-Truman :
```

```
"Mr. Vice President, Mr. Chief Justice, and fellow citizens, ..."

1953-Eisenhower :
"My friends, before I begin the expression of those thoughts ..."

1957-Eisenhower :
"The Price of Peace Mr. Chairman, Mr. Vice President, Mr. Chi..."

[ reached max_ndoc ... 15 more documents ]
```

Since a "corpus" object is a character vector, it is relatively straightforward to obtain those documents that contain certain words or regular expressions using the function grep(). Here, we define a function that uses grep() to select all documents that contain a word or a regular expression:

```
docs_containing <- function(x,pattern,...) x[grep(pattern,x,...)]
```

The application of this function shows that so far Donald Trump has been the only president to use the word *carnage* in his inaugural speech:

```
c_sub <- docs_containing(data_corpus_inaugural,"[Cc]arnage")
c_sub$President
```

```
[1] "Trump"
```

We now use the function corpus_reshape() to obtain a corpus of sentences within speeches:

```
inaugural_sntc <- corpus_reshape(data_corpus_inaugural,
                      to="sentences")
inaugural_sntc
```

```
Corpus consisting of 5,015 documents and 4 docvars.
1789-Washington.1 :
"Fellow-Citizens of the Senate and of the House of Representa..."

1789-Washington.2 :
"On the one hand, I was summoned by my Country, whose voice I..."

1789-Washington.3 :
"On the other hand, the magnitude and difficulty of the trust..."

[ reached max_ndoc ... 5,012 more documents ]
```

We now create a data frame that contains the length of each sentence in each speech:

```
sntcl <- cbind(docvars(inaugural_sntc),
              len=nchar(inaugural_sntc))
head(sntcl)
```

```
                  Year   President FirstName Party len
1789-Washington.1 1789 Washington    George   none 278
1789-Washington.2 1789 Washington    George   none 478
1789-Washington.3 1789 Washington    George   none 436
1789-Washington.4 1789 Washington    George   none 179
1789-Washington.5 1789 Washington    George   none 515
1789-Washington.6 1789 Washington    George   none 654
```

Using **aggregate()**, we compute the average sentence lengths for each speech, which means assuming that there is no year when two US presidents were sworn in. We then plot average sentence lengths against year, enhanced with a scatter plot smoother (Cleveland, 1979):

```
sntcl.year <- aggregate(len~Year,data=sntcl,mean)
with(sntcl.year,
     scatter.smooth(Year,len,ylab="Average length of sentences in characters"))
```

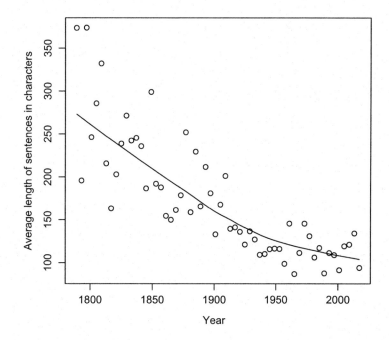

The diagram suggests that sentences in inaugural speeches grew shorter over time, at least if the number of characters per sentence is concerned.

The function **corpus_reshape()** allows an optional argument **to="documents"**. This suggests that the document corpus on which **corpus_reshape()** is applied can be recovered by applying the function a second time. The following code demonstrates that this is indeed the case:

```
inaugural_ <- corpus_reshape(data_corpus_inaugural,
                             to="documents")
all(inaugural_$Year == data_corpus_inaugural$Year)
```

```
[1] TRUE
```

We compare the year document variable of the original document corpus with the corresponding document variable of the recovered corpus and confirm that the number of documents in both corpora is the same and the documents are in the same order.

Besides `"corpus"`, *quanteda* also defines a class `"tokens"`, which is intended to contain the tokens of the documents in a corpus, obtained using the function `tokens()`. An object of `"tokens"` contains a character vector of tokens for each document from which the tokens are extracted and has a `"docvars"` attribute that contains the document-level variables. With the help of `tokens()`, it is possible to gain instructive insights into the structure of documents, as illustrated by the following example.

We continue with the corpus of inaugural speeches of US presidents. But first, we limit the amount of output created by printing `"token"` objects:

```
quanteda_options(print_tokens_max_ndoc=3,
                 print_tokens_max_ntoken=6)
```

In the following, we look at how the average number of words per inaugural speech has changed over time. For this, we first use `tokens()` to obtain the number of tokens in the documents:

```
inaugural_toks <- tokens(data_corpus_inaugural)
inaugural_toks
```

```
Tokens consisting of 58 documents and 4 docvars.
1789-Washington :
[1] "Fellow-Citizens" "of"              "the"
[4] "Senate"          "and"            "of"
[ ... and 1,531 more ]

1793-Washington :
[1] "Fellow"   "citizens" ","        "I"        "am"
[6] "again"
[ ... and 141 more ]

1797-Adams :
[1] "When"     "it"       "was"      "first"    "perceived"
[6] ","
[ ... and 2,571 more ]

[ reached max_ndoc ... 55 more documents ]
```

We then obtain the number of tokens using the standard R function `length()` and match the lengths with the document variables:

```
inaugural_ntoks <- sapply(inaugural_toks, length)
inaugural_ntoks <- cbind(docvars(inaugural_toks),
                         ntokens = inaugural_ntoks)
```

We finally create a scatter plot with a smoothing curve:

```
with(inaugural_ntoks,
     scatter.smooth(Year,ntokens,
                    ylab="Number of tokens per speech"))
```

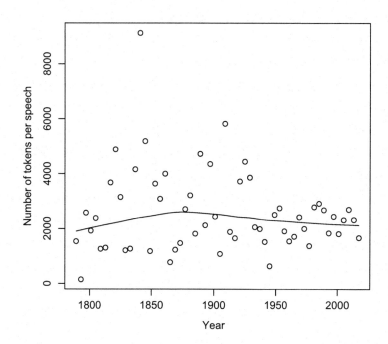

Apparently, there is no clear trend in the average length of the speeches in terms of the number of tokens, where the tokens are words and punctuation. However, the variation in speech lengths seems to decline; that is, a 'standard length' of speeches seems to emerge.

Previously, we used **corpus_reshape()** to get a corpus of sentences in the US presidents' speeches. We use this to obtain the number of tokens within sentences.

```
inaugural_sntc_toks <- tokens(inaugural_sntc)
inaugural_sntc_ntoks <- sapply(inaugural_sntc_toks, length)
inaugural_sntc_ntoks <- cbind(docvars(inaugural_sntc_toks),
                              ntokens = inaugural_sntc_ntoks)
```

We aggregate the number of tokens per year:

```
inaugural_sntc_ntoks <- aggregate(ntokens~Year,mean,
                                  data=inaugural_sntc_ntoks)
```

Finally, we create a smoothed scatter plot:

```
with(inaugural_sntc_ntoks,
     scatter.smooth(Year,ntokens,
                    ylab="Number of tokens per sentence"))
```

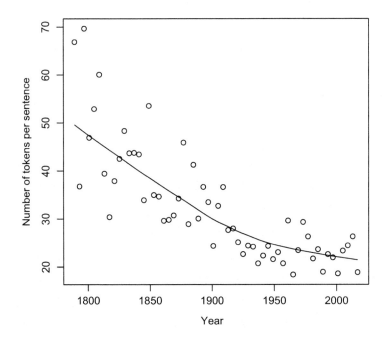

The result parallels our previous ones: the complexity of inaugural speeches declines, not only in terms of the number of characters per sentence but also in terms of the number of tokens (words) per sentence.

The *quanteda* package allows one to create the so-called document–feature matrices. They are a generalization of the document–term matrices that we previously encountered, in so far as they can refer to frequencies not only of words or stemmed words (i.e. 'terms') but also of combinations of words, such as *n*-grams, sentences, or even paragraphs, and they can also refer to frequencies in which categories of terms occur, where the categories are defined by *dictionaries*. That way, *quanteda* supports content analysis procedures that go beyond the 'bag of words' approach. An important improvement in *quanteda*'s document–feature matrices is that they retain the information about the documents in the `"docvars"` attribute of the corpora from which they are created. This allows the inclusion of covariates to analyses based on document–feature matrices, such as in structural topic modelling (Roberts et al., 2016).

We now apply the facilities of the *quanteda* package to a section of the Manifesto Project corpus. This section comprises the manifestos of the Liberal Party and Liberal Democratic Party of the UK.

We start by creating, using the function `dir()`, a list of CSV files (or, more correctly, a character vector of filenames) that are located in the directory 'ManifestoProject':

```
csv.files <- dir("ManifestoProject",
                 full.names=TRUE,
                 pattern="*.csv")
length(csv.files)
```

```
[1] 14
```

The length of the character vector indicates that there are 14 CSV files in the directory.

We now use the function `readtext()` from the *readtext* package (which is a companion package of *quanteda*) to read in the CSV files:

```
library(readtext)
UKLib.rt <- readtext("ManifestoProject/*.csv",
                     text_field=1,
                     docvarsfrom="filenames",
                     docvarnames=c("party","date"))
nrow(UKLib.rt)
```

```
[1] 4228
```

In the present case, where the function `readtext()` is applied to a group of CSV files, the result is a data frame that contains the contents of all the CSV files. The `readtext()` function has a variety of features that are useful when importing text data. For example, it allows one to reconstruct document variables from filenames. Since the manifesto filenames follow a specific pattern, in which the first part of the filename corresponds to the party code and the second part refers to the publication date and both parts are connected by an underscore (the character '_'), we can construct the document variables `"party"` and `"date"` from the filenames.

The directory contains both CSV files in which the entire manifesto text is contained in a single line and CSV files in which the manifesto text is segmented into several lines (where each line corresponds to a quasi-sentence), so that the total number of rows reflects neither the total number of documents in the corpus nor the total number of quasi-sentences in the document.

In order to build up a corpus, we need a data frame in which each line corresponds to a single document. Fortunately, the data frame that results from `readtext()` contains information that allows one to identify the individual documents, the variables `party` and `date` that we reconstructed from the filenames. Therefore, we can use the function `aggregate()` to combine the rows of the data frame that correspond to the same manifestos. While a typical use of `aggregate()` involves the creation of group means, it is also possible to use other aggregating functions. In the present case, we adapt the function `paste()`, which can be used to combine the character strings in a character vector into a single character string:

```
UKLib.rta <- aggregate(text~party+date,
                       FUN=function(x)paste(x,collapse=" "),
                       data=UKLib.rt)
nrow(UKLib.rta)
```

```
[1] 14
```

We now have a data frame with one row for each document. We then need a variable that can be used as document identifier. We construct this variable from the variables `party` and `date`:

```
UKLib.rta <- within(UKLib.rta,
                doc_id <- paste(party,date,sep="_"))
```

Now that there is a document identifier in the data frame, we can successfully use the function `corpus()` to create a `"corpus"` object from the data frame:

```
UKLib.corpus <- corpus(UKLib.rta)
UKLib.corpus
```

```
Corpus consisting of 14 documents and 2 docvars.
51420_196410 :
"""THINK FOR YOURSELF"""  The Liberal Party offers the elector..."

51420_196603 :
"For All the People: the Liberal Plan of 1966  BRITAIN DEMAND..."

51420_197006 :
"What a Life!  There must surely be a better way to run a cou..."

[ reached max_ndoc ... 11 more documents ]
```

The individual files with manifesto texts are accompanied by a file that describes the documents, which is named `"documents_MPDataset_MPDS2019b.csv"`.[2] Since the `"docvars"` attribute of the object `UKLib.corpus` is a data frame, the additional information in the file can be merged with this attribute:

```
manifesto.metadata <- read.csv("documents_MPDataset_MPDS2019b.csv",
                                        stringsAsFactors=FALSE)
docvars(UKLib.corpus) <- merge(docvars(UKLib.corpus),
                            manifesto.metadata,
                            by=c("party","date"))
str(docvars(UKLib.corpus))
```

```
'data.frame':    14 obs. of   6 variables:
 $ party      : int   51420 51420 51420 51420 51420 51420
    51420 51420 51421 51421 ...
 $ date       : int   196410 196603 197006 197402 197410 197905
    198306 198706 199204 199705 ...
 $ country    : int   51 51 51 51 51 51 51 51 51 51 ...
```

---

[2]This file is originally a file in XLSX format and is available at the time of writing from the webpage with the coded Manifesto Project data under the link. For the purposes of this example, the XLSX file has been translated into CSV format.

```
$ countryname: chr   "United Kingdom" "United Kingdom" "United
    Kingdom" "United Kingdom" ...
$ partyname   : chr   "Liberal Party" "Liberal Party" "Liberal Party"
"Liberal Party" ...
$ title       : chr   "Think for Yourself - Vote Liberal" "For all
    the People: The Liberal Plan of 1966" "What a Life!" "Change
    the Face of Britain" ...
```

Now the `UKLib.corpus` object comprises the manifesto texts along with information about the parties that published the manifestos, the country in which these parties exist or existed, when the manifestos were published, and what their titles are.

We can now use the function `dfm()` to create a document–feature matrix. We require that punctuation, numbers, and other symbols are removed by using the optional arguments `remove_punct=TRUE`, `remove_number=TRUE`, and `remove_symbols=TRUE`, respectively. Further, with the option `remove=stopwords("english")`, stopwords are removed, and with the option `stem=TRUE`, the terms in the document–feature matrix are stemmed – that is, reduced to their grammatical roots.

```
UKLib.dfm <- dfm(UKLib.corpus,
                remove_punct=TRUE,
                remove_numbers=TRUE,
                remove_symbols=TRUE,
                remove=stopwords("english"),
                stem=TRUE)
```

Notably, we can still access the information contained in the document-level variables, which allows us, for example, to analyse the corpus using structural topic modelling (Roberts et al., 2016):

```
str(docvars(UKLib.dfm))
```

```
'data.frame':    14 obs. of  6 variables:
$ party      : int   51420 51420 51420 51420 51420 51420 51420
    51420 51421 51421 ...
$ date       : int   196410 196603 197006 197402 197410 197905
    198306 198706 199204 199705 ...
$ country    : int   51 51 51 51 51 51 51 51 51 51 ...
$ countryname: chr   "United Kingdom" "United Kingdom" "United
    Kingdom" "United Kingdom" ...
$ partyname  : chr   "Liberal Party" "Liberal Party" "Liberal Party"
    "Liberal Party" ...
$ title      : chr   "Think for Yourself - Vote Liberal" "For all
    the People: The Liberal Plan of 1966" "What a Life!" "Change
    the Face of Britain" ...
```

As with the *tm* package, it is possible to take more fine-grained control over the preprocessing of the documents in the corpus. For this, preprocessing can also be separated into several steps. However, in accordance with the ideas behind the *quanteda* package, these steps are not taken with the `"corpus"` object itself but with objects derived from it. The first of these steps is creating a `"tokens"` object using the eponymous function `tokens()`:

```
UKLib.toks <- tokens(UKLib.corpus,
                     remove_punct=TRUE,
                     remove_numbers=TRUE)
UKLib.toks
```

```
Tokens consisting of 14 documents and 6 docvars.
51420_196410 :
[1] "THINK"     "FOR"        "YOURSELF" "The"        "Liberal"
[6] "Party"
[ ... and 8,859 more ]

51420_196603 :
[1] "For"       "All"        "the"       "People"   "the"        "Liberal"
[ ... and 31,792 more ]

51420_197006 :
[1] "What"      "a"          "Life"      "There"    "must"      "surely"
[ ... and 23,968 more ]

[ reached max_ndoc ... 11 more documents ]
```

We could now use the functions `tokens_select()`, `tokens_remove()`, or `tokens_keep()` to filter out tokens that are not desired in the later analysis, but we defer this kind of filtering to a later phase, when we have created the document–feature matrix.

Without loss of the information on document-level variables, the function `dfm()` can now be applied to the `"tokens"` object. This is possible because `dfm()` is a generic function with method functions not only for `"corpus"` objects but also for `"tokens"` objects. In fact, the method for `"corpus"` objects internally makes use of the function `tokens()`. This is why arguments such as `remove_punct=` can be applied to both the `dfm()` and the `tokens()` function, because the former passes these arguments on to the latter.

```
UKLib.dfm <- dfm(UKLib.toks)
```

We now have a document–feature matrix where the features are tokens (excluding punctuation and numbers).

We remove the stopwords of the English language from the document–feature matrix:

```
UKLib.dfm <- dfm_remove(UKLib.dfm,
                        pattern=stopwords("english"))
```

Alternatively, we can also remove the stopwords from the `"tokens"` object with the help of the function `tokens_remove()`.

Finally, we use the function `dfm_wordstem` to reduce the tokens in the document–feature matrix to their grammatical roots:

```
UKLib.dfm <- dfm_wordstem(UKLib.dfm,language="english")
```

As already mentioned, an important addition to the toolbox for the processing of text corpora provided by the *quanteda* package is the ability to define and use `"dictionary"` objects. A `"dictionary"` object is created using the function `dictionary()` from a list structured in such a way that each list element is a character vector of words that belong to a particular category and the names associated with the list elements are labels for these categories. Here, we create a very simple dictionary for the term categories 'Military' and 'Economy':[3]

```
milecondict <- dictionary(list(
                Military=c("military","forces","war","defence",
                   "victory","victorious","glory"),
                Economy=c("economy","growth","business","enterprise",
                   "market")
))
```

Such a `dictionary` object can be passed to the function `dfm()` as a `dictionary=` argument. The result is now a document–feature matrix with counts of the occurrences of these word categories rather than the occurrences of (stemmed) words:

```
UKLib.milecon.dfm <- dfm(UKLib.corpus,
                    dictionary=milecondict)
UKLib.milecon.dfm
```

```
Document-feature matrix of: 14 documents, 2 features (0.0% sparse)
      and 6 docvars .
                features
docs            Military Economy
   51420_196410       11      29
   51420_196603       40      83
   51420_197006       31      77
   51420_197402       14      50
   51420_197410        5      31
   51420_197905       23      34
[ reached max_ndoc ... 8 more documents ]
```

We can now plot the relative frequency of occurrence of these categories against time. First, we collect the time points:

```
time <- with(docvars(UKLib.milecon.dfm),
          ISOdate(year=date%/%100,
                  month=date%%100,
                  day=1))
```

Next, we obtain the total number of counts:

```
UKLib.ntok <- ntoken(UKLib.corpus)
```

---

[3]This dictionary may seem very unsophisticated in that the number of terms included is rather small. It is constructed here only for the sake of illustration, of course.

We then extract the frequency counts of the categories 'Military' and 'Economy' and divide them by the total number of tokens to get the relative frequencies:

```
milit.freq <- as.vector(UKLib.milecon.dfm[,"Military"])
econ.freq <- as.vector(UKLib.milecon.dfm[,"Economy"])
milit.prop <- milit.freq/UKLib.ntok
econ.prop <- econ.freq/UKLib.ntok
```

Finally, we create line diagrams that show the development of the relative frequencies:

```
op <- par(mfrow=c(2,1),mar=c(3,4,0,0))
plot(time,milit.prop,type="p",ylab="Military")
lines(time,lowess(time,milit.prop)$y)
plot(time,econ.prop,type="p",ylab="Economy")
lines(time,lowess(time,econ.prop)$y)
par(op)
```

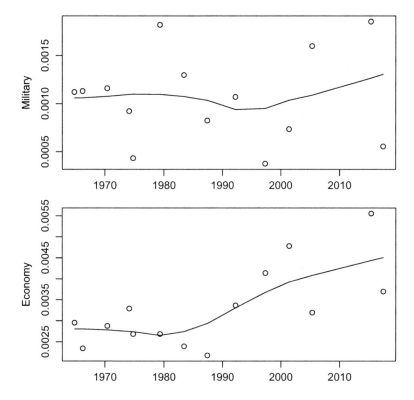

=== Overview Box 9.5 ===

Important functions in the *readtext* and *quanteda* packages

`readtext()` reads text data into an object that can be easily converted into a `"corpus"` object.

`corpus()` creates a `"corpus"` object from a character vector or from text data read in by `readtext()`.

docvars() returns a data frame with document-specific information. Each row of this data frame corresponds to a document in the corpus.

corpus_subset() allows one to create a subset of the corpus where documents are selected based on conditions on the document-level variables (which are accessible with **docvars()**).

corpus_reshape() returns a rearranged copy of a corpus where documents are split into sentences or paragraphs or where sentences and paragraphs are aggregated back into documents.

tokens() splits each document into tokens and returns a **"tokens"** object with the same **docvars()** information as the corpus from which it is created.

tokens_select(), tokens_remove(), tokens_keep() return a **"tokens"** object with a subset of the tokens kept or removed based on the given criteria.

dictionary() creates a **"dictionary"** object that assigns sets of terms to categories and thus allows one to count the number of their occurrences.

dfm() creates a document-feature matrix (a generalization of a document-term matrix) where the features may be terms, n-grams of terms, or categories defined by a **"dictionary"** object.

dfm_remove() removes features from a document–feature matrix based on the given criteria.

dfm_wordstem() transforms a document-feature matrix where the features are words into a document-feature matrix in which the features are stemmed words.

BIBLIOGRAPHY

ANES (2015). *The American National Election Studies 2008 time series study*. Ann Arbor, MI: Inter-university Consortium for Political and Social Research [distributor], 2015-11-10. https://doi.org/10.3886/ICPSR25383

ANES (2019). *The American National Election Studies 2016 time series study*. Ann Arbor, MI: Inter-university Consortium for Political and Social Research [distributor], 2019-09-05. https://electionstudies.org/data-center/2016-time-series-study/

Bache, S.M., and H. Wickham (2014). *magrittr: A forward-pipe operator for R* (R package version 1.5). https://CRAN.R-project.org/package=magrittr

Benoit, K., K. Watanabe, H. Wang, P. Nulty, A. Obeng, S. Muller, and A. Matsuo (2018). quanteda: An R package for the quantitative analysis of textual data. *Journal of Open Source Software, 3*(30), 774. https://doi.org/10.21105/joss.00774

California Health Interview Survey (2007). *CHIS 2005 Adult Public Use File, Release 1* [Computer file]. Los Angeles, CA: Center for Health Policy Research. https://healthpolicy.ucla.edu/chis/data/Pages/GetCHISData.aspx

Campbell, A., and R.L. Kahn (2015). *ANES 1948 time series study*. Ann Arbor, MI: Inter-university Consortium for Political and Social Research [distributor], 2015-11-10. https://doi.org/10.3886/ICPSR07218.v4

Chambers, J. (2008). *Software for data analysis: Programming with R*. New York, NY: Springer. https://doi.org/10.1007/978-0-387-75936-4

Chambers, J. (2016). *Extending R*. Boca Raton, FL: Chapman & Hall/CRC Press.

Clementini, E., J. Sharma, and M.J. Egenhofer (1994). Modelling topological spatial relations: Strategies for query processing. *Computers & Graphics, 18*(6), 815–22. https://doi.org/10.1016/0097-8493(94)90007-8

Cleveland, W.S. (1979). Robust locally weighted regression and smoothing scatterplots. *Journal of the American Statistical Association, 74*(368), 829–36. https://doi.org/10.1080/01621459.1979.10481038

Coast, S., and OpenStreetMap Community (2004). *OpenStreetMap Project*. www.openstreetmap.org

Dowle, M., and A. Srinivasan (2019). *data.table: Extension of 'data.frame'* (R package version 1.12.8). https://CRAN.R-project.org/package=data.table

Dublin Core Metadata Initiative (1995). DCMI: Home. https://dublincore.org/

Efron, B., and R.J. Tibshirani (1994). *An introduction to the bootstrap.* Boca Raton, FL: CRC Press. https://doi.org/10.1201/9780429246593

Elff, M. (2019). *memisc: Management of survey data and presentation of analysis results* (R package version 0.99.17). https://CRAN.R-project.org/package=memisc

Environmental Systems Research Institute (1997). *ESRI shapefile technical description* (White paper). Redlands, CA. www.esri.com/library/whitepapers/pdfs/shapefile.pdf

EPSG (1993). *European Petroleum Survey Group geodetic parameter dataset.* www.epsg-registry.org/

Feinerer, I., K. Hornik, and D. Meyer (2008, March). Text mining infrastructure in R. *Journal of Statistical Software, 25*(5), 1–54. https://doi.org/10.18637/jss.v025.i05

Fox, J., and S. Weisberg (2011). *An R companion to applied regression* (2nd edn). Thousand Oaks, CA: Sage.

Friedl, J. (2006). *Mastering regular expressions.* Sebastopol, CA: O'Reilly Media.

Garbuszus, J.M., and S. Jeworutzki (2018). *readstata13: Import 'Stata' data files* (R package version 0.9.2). https://CRAN.R-project.org/package=readstata13

GESIS (2017). *Allgemeine Bevölkerungsumfrage der Sozialwissenschaften* (German general social survey). Mannheim and Cologne, Germany.

Goyvaerts, J., and S. Levithan (2012). *Regular expressions cookbook.* Sebastopol, CA: O'Reilly Media. https://doi.org/10.1016/S1353-4858(12)70100-9

Heath, A.F., R.M. Jowell, and J.K. Curtice (1983). *British General Election Study, 1983; Cross-section survey* [Computer file]. Colchester, England: UK Data Archive [distributor]. www.britishelectionstudy.com

IBM (2017). *IBM SPSS statistics for Windows* (version 25.0). Armonk, NY.

ISO (2004). *Geographic information: Simple feature access.* Geneva, Switzerland. www.iso.org/standard/40114.html

Kusnierczyk, W. (2012). *rbenchmark: Benchmarking routine for R* (R package version 1.0.0). https://CRAN.R-project.org/package=rbenchmark

Larmarange, J. (2020). *labelled: Manipulating labelled data* (R package version 2.5.0). https://CRAN.R-project.org/package=labelled

Levy, P.S., and S. Lemeshow (2013). *Sampling of populations: Methods and applications.* Hoboken, NJ: Wiley.

Lewis, D. (1997). *Reuters-21578 text categorization collection distribution 1.0.* https://kdd.ics.uci.edu/databases/reuters21578/reuters21578.html

Lumley, T. (2004). Analysis of complex survey samples. *Journal of Statistical Software, 9*(1), 1–19. https://doi.org/10.18637/jss.v009.i08

Lumley, T. (2010). *Complex surveys: A guide to analysis using R.* Hoboken, NJ: Wiley. https://doi.org/10.1002/9780470580066

Lumley, T. (2019). *survey: Analysis of complex survey samples* (R package version 3.35-1). https://CRAN.R-project.org/package=survey

Luz, S. (2003). *XML-encoded version of Reuters-21578.* https://rdrr.io/rforge/tm/man/readReut21578XML.html

Müller, K., and H. Wickham (2019). *tibble: Simple data frames* (R package version 2.1.1). https://CRAN.R-project.org/package=tibble

National Center for Health Statistics (2011). *NHANES 2009-2010 laboratory data.* Atlanta, GA. https://wwwn.cdc.gov/nchs/nhanes/search/datapage.aspx?Component=laboratory&CycleBeginYear=2009

Organisation for Economic Co-operation and Development (2018). *OECD data.* Paris, France. https://data.oecd.org/

Pfaff, B. (2018). *PSPP version 1.8.0.* Boston, MA.

R Core Team (2018). *foreign: Read data stored by 'Minitab', 'S', 'SAS', 'SPSS', 'Stata', 'Systat', 'Weka', 'dBase', . . .* (R package version 0.8-70). https://CRAN.R-project.org/package=foreign

R Core Team (2020). *R: A language and environment for statistical computing.* Vienna, Austria: R Foundation for Statistical Computing.

Roberts, M.E., B.M. Stewart, and E.M. Airoldi (2016). A model of text for experimentation in the social sciences. *Journal of the American Statistical Association, 111*(515), 988–1003. https://doi.org/10.1080/01621459.2016.1141684

Roßteutscher, S., R. Schmitt-Beck, H. Schoen, B. Weßels, C. Wolf, I. Bieber, L.-C. Stovsand, M. Dietz, P. Scherer, A. Wagner, R. Melcher, and H. Giebler (2018). *Pre-and post-election cross section (cumulation) (GLES 2017)* (ZA6802 Data file version 3.0.0). GESIS Data Archive, Cologne, Germany. www.gesis.org/wahlen/gles/daten/

RStudio, Inc (2020). *RStudio version 1.2.5019.* https://rstudio.com

SAS Institute (2013). *SAS version 9.4.* Cary, NC.

StataCorp (2019). *Stata version 16.* College Station, TX.

Sundberg, R., and E. Melander (2013). Introducing the UCDP georeferenced event dataset. *Journal of Peace Research, 50*(4), 523–32. https://doi.org/10.1177/0022343313484347

Thompson, M. (1997). *Theory of sample surveys.* Boca Raton, FL: Chapman & Hall/CRC Press. https://doi.org/10.1007/978-1-4899-2885-6

Warnes, G.R., B. Bolker, G. Gorjanc, G. Grothendieck, A. Korosec, T. Lumley, D. MacQueen, A. Magnusson, J. Rogers, et al. (2017). *gdata: Various R programming tools for data manipulation* (R package version 2.18.0). https://CRAN.R-project.org/package=gdata

Weidmann, N.B., and K.S. Gleditsch (2016). *cshapes: The CShapes dataset and utilities* (R package version 0.6). https://CRAN.R-project.org/package=cshapes

Wickham, H. (2011). The split-apply-combine strategy for data analysis. *Journal of Statistical Software, 40*(1), 1–29. https://doi.org/10.18637/jss.v040.i01

Wickham, H. (2016). *ggplot2: Elegant graphics for data analysis.* New York, NY: Springer. https://doi.org/10.1007/978-3-319-24277-4

Wickham, H. (2017). *tidyverse: Easily install and load the 'Tidyverse'* (R package version 1.2.1). https://CRAN.R-project.org/package=tidyverse

Wickham, H., R. Francois, L. Henry, and K. Muller (2018). *dplyr: A grammar of data manipulation* (R package version 0.7.5). https://CRAN.R-project.org/package=dplyr

Wickham, H., and G. Grolemund (2016). *R for data science: Import, tidy, transform, visualize, and model data.* Sebastopol, CA: O'Reilly Media.

Wickham, H., and L. Henry (2019). *tidyr: Tidy messy data* (R package version 1.0.0). https://CRAN.R-project.org/package=tidyr

Wickham, H., J. Hester, and R. Francois (2018). *readr: Read rectangular text data* (R package version 1.3.1). https://CRAN.R-project.org/package=readr

Wickham, H., and E. Miller (2018). *haven: Import and export 'SPSS', 'Stata' and 'SAS' files* (R package version 1.1.1). https://CRAN.R-project.org/package=haven

WZB Social Science Research Center Berlin (2009). *The Manifesto Project.* https://manifesto-project.wzb.eu

INDEX